Jews & Blacks

A DIALOGUE ON RACE, RELIGION, AND CULTURE IN AMERICA

Michael Lerner

&

Cornel West

With a Post-O.J.,
Post–Million Man March Epilogue

A PLUME BOOK

PLUME
Published by the Penguin Group
Penguin Books USA Inc., 375 Hudson Street,
New York, New York 10014, U.S.A.
Penguin Books Ltd, 27 Wrights Lane,
London W8 5TZ, England
Penguin Books Australia Ltd, Ringwood,
Victoria, Australia
Penguin Books Canada Ltd, 10 Alcorn Avenue,
Toronto, Ontario, Canada M4V 3B2
Penguin Books (N.Z.) Ltd, 182–190 Wairau Road,
Auckland 10, New Zealand

Penguin Books Ltd, Registered Offices:
Harmondsworth, Middlesex, England

Published by Plume, an imprint of Dutton Signet,
a division of Penguin Books USA Inc.
This is an authorized reprint of a hardcover edition published by G. P. Putnam's
Sons. For information address G. P. Putnam's Sons, 200 Madison Avenue,
New York, New York 10016.

First Plume Printing, February, 1996
10 9 8 7 6 5 4 3 2 1

 REGISTERED TRADEMARK—MARCA REGISTRADA

CIP data available.

Printed in the United States of America

BOOKS ARE AVAILABLE AT QUANTITY DISCOUNTS WHEN USED TO PROMOTE
PRODUCTS OR SERVICES. FOR INFORMATION PLEASE WRITE TO PREMIUM
MARKETING DIVISION, PENGUIN BOOKS USA INC., 375 HUDSON STREET,
NEW YORK, NEW YORK 10014.

BLACK NATIONALISM * ZIONISM * ANTI-SEMITISM *
RACISM * QUOTAS AND AFFIRMATIVE ACTION *
ECONOMIC DIFFERENCES * SUBURBS AND INNER CITIES *
LOUIS FARRAKHAN * PALESTINIANS *
CONSERVATIVES * LIBERALS

Two groups that have been at the center of American cultural and
intellectual creativity—and at the heart of progressive social change—
now find themselves at great odds. Healing this rift requires a move
beyond their two communities, to a new understanding of the tremendous conflicts shaping American culture and politics at the end of the
20th century. Using the seminal relationship of Black and Jews as ful-
crum, two of America's most respected intellectuals explore the many
difficult issues that will challenge our nation in coming decades. In
doing so, Cornel West and Michael Lerner present a powerful—and
essential—approach to facing the realities of America today.

"Cornel West (is) the preeminent African-American intellectual of our
generation . . . one of the few cultural critics in this country equally
concerned with matters spiritual and material."

—Henry Louis Gates, Jr.

"Michael Lerner is America's preeminent liberal Jewish intellectual—
and one of America's deepest political and social theorists."

—Rabbi Michael Paley,
Wexner Heritage Foundation

MICHAEL LERNER is the author of *Jewish Renewal: A Path to Healing and Transformation*, and editor of *Tikkun*, a bimonthly Jewish critique of politics, culture, and society.

CORNEL WEST, the author of the best-selling *Race Matters* and nine
other books, is a professor of Afro-American studies and the philosophy of religion at Harvard University.

Contents

Acknowledgments

We wish to thank Vivienne Cato for her very fine work in helping to edit what was, in fact, five years of tapes and discussions. We also wish to thank Jane Isay for her tireless work in refining, editing, and focusing the material, which was originally twice the length. Her patience, wisdom, and publishing smarts were deeply appreciated.

This book is dedicated to the legacies of
Martin Luther King, Jr.,
and Abraham Joshua Heschel,
and to our sons,
Clifton West and Akiba Lerner.

Introduction—CW

Why are Blacks and Jews in the United States the most unique and fascinating people in modern times? Why have both groups contributed so disproportionately to the richness and vitality in American life? Can we honestly imagine what twentieth-century American democracy would be like without the past and present doings and sufferings of Blacks and Jews? What forms will progressive politics take, if any, with escalating tensions between these two historically liberal groups?

When historians look back on the emergence, development, and decline of American civilization, they obviously will note its distinctive features—constitutional democracy and precious liberties (with its class, gender, and especially racial constraints), material prosperity, technological ingenuity, ethnic and regional diversity, market-driven yet romantic popular culture, relative lack of historical consciousness, and an obsession with progress in the future. Yet these historians would miss much if they failed to acknowledge and examine the two most extraordinary peoples in U.S. history—people of African descent and people of Jewish origins and persuasion. Needless to say, all people are, in some significant sense, extraordinary. But Blacks and Jews stand out in a glaring manner.

Both Jews and Blacks are a pariah people—a people who had to make and remake themselves as outsiders on the margins of American society and culture. Both groups assumed that the status quo was unjust and therefore found strategies to survive and thrive against the odds. Both groups defined themselves as a people deeply shaped by America but never *fully* a part of America. Both groups appealed to biblical texts and relied on communal bonds to sustain themselves—texts that put a premium on justice, mercy, and solidarity with the downtrodden, and bonds shot through with a deep distrust, suspicion, even paranoia, toward the powerful and privileged. Both groups have been hated and despised peoples who find it difficult, if not impossible, to fully overcome group insecurity and anxiety as well as truly be and love themselves as individuals and as a people. Wearing the masks, enduring petty put-downs, and coping with subtle insults remains an everyday challenge for most Blacks and some Jews in America.

Both groups are the most modern of modern people in that they have created new and novel ways of life, innovative and improvisational modes of being in the world. Their entree into modernity as degraded Others—dishonored slaves (Blacks) and devalued non-Christians (Jews)—forced them to hammer out the most un-American yet modern of products—tragicomic dispositions toward reality that put sadness, sorrow, and suffering at the center of their plights and predicaments. This tragicomic character of the Black and Jewish experiences in modernity—coupled with a nagging moral conscience owing to undeniable histories of underdog status and unusual slavery-to-freedom narratives in authoritative texts—haunts both groups.

And what Blacks and Jews have done with their intelligence, imagination, and ingenuity is astounding. Twentieth-century America—a century that begins only a generation after the emancipation of penniless, illiterate, enslaved Africans and the massive influx of poor Eastern European Jewish immigrants—is unimaginable without the creative breakthroughs and monumental contributions of Blacks and Jews. At the very highest levels of achievement, we have Louis Armstrong and Aaron Copland, Duke Ellington and Leonard Bernstein, John Coltrane and George Gershwin, Sarah Vaughan and Irving Berlin, Toni Morrison and Saul Bellow, W. E. B. Du Bois and Hannah Arendt, Romare Bearden and Jackson Pollock, August Wilson and

Arthur Miller, Paul Robeson and Pete Seeger, Ralph Ellison and Irving Howe, Kathleen Battle and Beverly Sills, Richard Pryor and Lenny Bruce, Willie Mays and Sandy Koufax, Andre Watts and Itzhak Perlman, Jacob Lawrence and Mark Rothko, Babyface (Kenneth Edmonds) and Carole King, Thurgood Marshall and Louis Brandeis, Marvin Gaye and Bob Dylan, James Baldwin and Norman Mailer, Lorraine Hansberry and Neil Simon, Aretha Franklin and Barbra Streisand, Billy Strayhorn and Stephen Sondheim. This short and incomplete list of towering Black and Jewish figures is neither an act of providence nor a mere accident. Rather it is the result of tremendous talent, discipline, and energy of two ostracized groups who disproportionately shape the cultural life of this country.

Furthermore, Jewish power and influence—though rarely wielded in a monolithic manner—in the garment industry, show business, medical and legal professions, journalism, and the academy—has had a major impact on the shaping of American life. We are reminded of the fundamental centrality of learning in Jewish life when we realize that as of 1989, of fifty American Nobel Laureates in the medical sciences—such as biochemistry and physiology—seventeen were Jews.

This latter point—the matter of relative Jewish zeal in business and education—is a delicate one. It does not mean that Jews are innately smarter than others or that they are involved in some secret conspiracy to control the banks and newspapers, as implied by the anti-Semitic remarks of General George Brown, Chairman of the Joint Chiefs of Staff, in a lecture at Duke University in 1974. Instead these realities reflect the dominant Jewish ways of gaining access to resources, status, and power against anti-Semitic exclusions in other spheres and over three thousand years of autonomous institution-building based on self-help and self-development around literary and mathematical skills.

African-Americans also have a rich history of business enterprise and scientific achievements—yet the entrepreneurial ethic has been set back by racist attacks (nearly two-thirds of those lynched at the turn of the century were businessmen), and exclusion from significant access to capital and credit, weak communal bonds to sustain business efforts, underfunded Black schools and colleges that downplay independent business efforts, and vicious stereotypes that undercut motivation to study math and natural sciences.

In fact, the fundamental differences between Blacks and Jews in America have been the vast impact of slavery and Jim Crow on limiting the Black quest for self-confidence in literary and scientific matters, and the containment of most Black folk in rural and agrarian areas until World War II, where access to literacy was difficult. In stark contrast, American Jews have always been primarily an urban people trying to find safe niches in industrial (and anti-Semitic) America, who fall back on strong and long traditions of independent institution-building. In this regard, the experiences of Blacks and Jews have been qualitatively different in a deeply racist and more mildly anti-Semitic America.

Yet, ironically, Jews and Blacks have been linked in a kind of symbiotic relation with each other. Whether they are allies or antagonists, they are locked into an inescapable embrace principally owing to their dominant status of degraded Others, given the racist and Christian character of the American past and present. First, because anti-Black and anti-Jewish waves are an omnipresent threat in this country. Second, because their support of progressive politics cast them as potential threats to the status quo in their critical and dissenting roles. And third, because both groups not only have a profound fascination with each other but also because they have much at stake in their own collective identities as a pariah and "chosen" people—be it in covenant with a God that "chooses" to side with the underdog or against a nation that "chooses" to treat them unequally or unkindly.

When Michael Lerner—from whom I've learned so much and come to love so dearly—and I began our dialogue, we knew we had to build upon the rich legacies of Martin Luther King, Jr., and Abraham Joshua Heschel. We had to cast our exchange in such a way that we highlighted moral ideals and existential realities bigger and better than both Black and Jewish interests. We had to examine what it means to be human as Jews and Blacks and how this relates to keeping alive the best of a precious yet precarious experiment in democracy. We also had to examine the ways in which we could revitalize progressive politics in the light of prophetic traditions in the Black and Jewish heritages. This is why our Black-Jewish dialogue—much like relevant, Black-Brown, Jewish-Asian or Black-Red dialogue—is but an instance of the human struggle for freedom and democracy. And any such struggle is predicated on the democratic faith that we everyday people can critically examine our individual and collective pasts, honestly confront our difficult present, and imaginatively project an all-embracing moral vision for the future. Our courageous foremothers and forefathers as well as our innocent children and grandchildren deserve nothing less.

Introduction—ML

One of the greatest pleasures of my life in the past six years have been the numerous occasions in which Cornel West and I have holed ourselves away from our respective worlds and spent full days, and on one occasion a full week, talking and recording our conversations. The dialogue contained in this book represents only a fraction of the wide range of philosophical, political, religious, and personal issues that we touched on. We got to know each other's lives, sources of joy and fear, emotional realities, and range of intellectual interests. We read each other's books and articles, we hung out with each other's families, and we grew increasingly excited about the other. In the process, I not only came to deeply respect Cornel's incredible intellect but to love him.

Something deep and profound happened to both of us in the course of our dialogue. Though we started with many common assumptions, we had many areas of tension and disagreements. Often these took the form of disagreements about specific interpretations of a current reality—e.g., interpreting Israel's role in the world, or the role that Jews were playing in a particular election, or what Jesse Jackson's most recent statements meant. Over the years, as this dialogue grew, we reflected on contemporary events as they were happening. The transcript of that whole dialogue would have been five times as long as what we are actually presenting in this book, and would have represented views that we no longer hold, because we kept changing what we were thinking as the dialogue continued.

Once we were able to fully express and explore the tension points and differences in perceptions between us, we often found common ground, and each of us changed our perceptions and the public statements we were making—in part because of these dialogues. That we had not reached total convergence was highlighted by a photograph printed in the *New York Times* on June 13, 1994, showing Cornel and I in heated argument outside the NAACP-sponsored National Black Summit which I was picketing (in protest of the inclusion in that meeting of the Minister Farrakhan) and Cornel was attending. But the CNN footage was equally significant—filming the warm embrace that we gave each other before we started to argue.

Many Jews have the perception that it is not so easy to involve Blacks in a dialogue aimed at healing the rifts between Blacks and Jews. Apart from the ministers and community relations personnel, Jews report that they often find it hard to attract Blacks to particpate in on-going dialogues on this topic. They sometimes report feeling that there's more interest in healing the relationship among Jews than among Blacks.

To the extent that this is true, the following explanations are sometimes proffered: that many Blacks face immediate economic oppression and are more concerned to change those circumstances than to reconcile with a group that they see as being economically advantaged (though this won't quite explain the difficulties Jews have in attracting middle-class Blacks); that many Blacks see Jews as whites (and hence don't see any need to work on some special relationship with them); and that in the post-Holocaust years Blacks have seen Jews trying to rob from them their identity as "the most oppressed group" and may find it more difficult to reconcile with a group to whom they are in most respects so close, a kind of sibling rivalry.

I do not profess to know whether this Jewish perception is true. But to the extent that it is true, we are hoping that the appearance of this dialogue might encourage others in both communities to renew their efforts to create local dialogues of their own. This dialogue is not meant to be a solution or final "answer" to the problems we explore, but an invitation to others to join us in the dialogue, to expand it broadly, to add points that we may have missed, and to help us in the process of reconciliation and repair. Let the healing begin! That is not just our title; it is our fervent appeal to both communities.

Yet I do think it important to state why this issue resonates so deeply for Jews. It is not merely a survival issue. Though at one point in this dialogue I play with various paranoid fantasies of what might happen to Jews in America should Black anti-Semitism become a deeper and more pervasive reality, and though I genuinely worry about the way that America's crisis of meaning may lead to a dramatic resurgence of xenophobic nationalism and anti-Semitism, I don't believe that this quite explains why the Black-Jewish issue is so central for many liberal and progressive Jews.

For Jews in the modern world, the central question is the nature of Jewish identity. We do not have a distinctive skin color, and in the multicultural bouquet of modern America it's quite possible for many Jews to leave their Jewishness behind, fully assimilate into the American secular mainstream, and risk very little. For those who choose to remain identified as Jews, the questions of "Why remain Jewish?" and "What constitutes our identity as Jews—what does it mean to be a Jew?" become central, even burning issues on the individual and psychological level.

In *Jewish Renewal* (Putnam, 1994) I describe the growing number of Jews who are turning back to the Jewish tradition and finding within it a radical understanding of the nature of Jewish identity and Jewish destiny. Jewish identity as constituted by the Torah tradition consists of being a witness to God as the force in the universe that makes possible the transformation of that which is to that which ought to be.

Though the "natural attitude" toward existence is that everything is fixed and set, that the world is as it must be and little can be changed, the Jewish attitude is that the world is not a timeless and fixed entity but a created being that is sustained every day by the intention of its Creator. Moreover, human beings are created in the image of God, and charged to be partners with God in the process of changing the world from that which is to that which ought to be. Jewish destiny is to be part of the vanguard that brings this understanding to the world, that becomes a light to the nations precisely because it proclaims this possibility, and to be involved in the healing and transformation process.

The goal of this transformation is to rectify the oppression of the powerless. *We* were slaves. So now that we are free, our task is to spread that freedom, and to identify with the powerless. The most frequently repeated injuctions of Torah are variations on the following theme: "When you come into your land, do not oppress the stranger. Remember that you were strangers in the land of Egypt."

The very fact of needing such an injunction is a realistic recognition on the part of Torah that there will be a tendency to oppress the stranger. As Freud was to point out thousands of years later, there is in most human beings a "repetition compulsion," a tendency to act out on others that which was done to us.

Yet the exciting proclamation of Torah is that we *don't* have to do this, that the chain of violence and cruelty can be broken, that we can identify with the oppressed and recognize that they, too, are created in the image of God and deserve the same dignity that we deserve.

God is the force in the universe that makes possible that transcendence of the repetition compulsion and that ability to recognize the Other as the potential embodiment of a self-constituting, free, conscious, creative, and loving being. Moreover, the Torah tells us that if we are to stay in touch with the God energy within ourselves, we need to be able to recognize the Other's needs as our own needs. Hence, the Torah commandment: "ve-ahavta la-ger" ("Thou shalt *love* the stranger").

This was a revolutionary message, not only for the ancient world, but for the medieval and modern world as well. Most systems of oppression thrive on convincing both the oppressed and those who benefit from the oppression that the way things are is natural, fixed, inevitable, and unchangeable.

No wonder, then, that ruling elites have always hated the Jews, worried about their passion for social justice, and done their best to portray them as "weird" and "untrustworthy" and "manipulators" whom everyone else would do best to avoid or distrust. No wonder, too, if Jews, faced with the resulting hostility and oppression, have often tried to play down the revolutionary message of their tradition, temper it from within, and, ever since the Hellenist oppression following Alexander's conquest of Judea in the fourth century before the common era, to make Judaism more a "religion" like other religions, less a revolutionary and transformative way of life.

No wonder, also, if it became hard to see "the Other" in the humane terms mandated by Torah when the others with whom you were likely to come into contact had more social power than the Jews (who, after the destruction of the Temple, were always the strangers in someone else's land) and treated Jews with disrespect if not outright murderous hatred. Goyim-bashing became part of the defensive armoring of the Jewish people, and Blacks were just another of the many groups of non-Jews that might potentially turn on us at any moment.

Yet as the trauma of our suffering and past oppression began to recede, many Jews were able to recognize that their new safety, particularly in the United States, conferred on us a new responsibility. Not only were we beneficiaries of American abundance (bought by Americans at the cost of genociding American Indians and then enslaving millions of Africans and killing millions more in the process), we were also less likely to become the primary victimized Other in the U.S. precisely because that role was already filled by African-Americans. That might have made Jews enthusiastically embrace mainstream American racism, to justify to ourselves our own fortune. But given the legacy of Torah and the way it has helped us interpret our own history, we instead began to identify with the struggles of American Blacks.

If that identification has withered somewhat in the past decades, the fault lies not only with the attractions and allures of the dominant ethos of selfishness, but also with the way Jews have perceived that some Blacks seemed to be repudiating our interest, seeing us as indistinguishable from whites, forgetting the commitments and sacrifices Jews had made to the Black struggle, and in other ways pushing us away.

Yet liberal Jews cannot deny either the upsurge of a political and cultural conservatism in some sectors of the Jewish world, often disproportionately represented among those who are affiliated with Jewish establishment organizations.

This conservative turn has not been followed by most Jews. Jews remain more likely to vote for liberal candidates and to support liberal and progressive social change programs than most other sectors of the population. But the intellectual foundation of this attachment to caring for others is being severely eroded, not only by the attractions of "fitting in" to contemporary American materialism and its culture of narcissism but also by tendencies within the more religious sectors of the population to interpret Jewish ethical obligations as applying primarily to fellow Jews, and hence to conveniently find a way of retaining all the ritual trappings of Judaism while abandoning its most challenging obligations to recognize God in the Other. Even injunctions about caring for "the stranger" get reinterpreted to mean "those who have converted to Judaism" or "the resident alien who agrees to live by Jewish laws." The God of transformation, the Possibility of Possibility, becomes a contained entity that one worships on Shabbat and at home, but that does not interfere with the fervent and morally unrestricted pursuit of power and wealth in the economic marketplace.

Such a Judaism, however, stripped of its revolutionary message, no longer a witness to the possibility of transcendence, and has lost its attraction to many younger Jews. Not ready to abandon their Jewishness, suspecting that there are deep treasures built into the cultural and religious and philosophical heritage of the Jewish people, these younger Jews are deeply troubled by the way Judaism is defined by the Jewish establishment.

If Jewishness is about something more than lox and bagels and gefilte fish, it has to be about bringing a message to the world. And turning back to Torah, we find that message in the task of the Jewish people to become testifiers to the possibility of breaking the chain of violence and cruelty and establishing a world based on justice, love, caring, and recognition of the God within each other.

Yet all these flowery words seem empty if Jews ignore that we live in a society where African-Americans are being systematically demeaned, where racism continues to flourish, and where economic oppression yields degradation and daily suffering. It becomes immediately obvious that this reality poses an immediate demand on the Jewish people: to challenge those who believe that the suffering cannot or should not be alleviated, to join in the struggles to change all those societal institutions that perpetuate poverty and racism, and to connect with the oppressed in a way that recognizes their fundamental humanity and fundamental similarity with us, our sisterhood and brotherhood with them. To do this in a way that is not condescending, that does not assume that we are "morally higher" or "better," but rather out of a deep recognition of God's presence in each human being, is our challenge.

If Judaism cannot recognize the God within those who have previously been treated as "demeaned Other," it has no future. This is a moment when we are celebrating the steps taken by the State of Israel to recognize that the Palestinian people have the same right to national self-determination and dignity as the Jews. In the American Jewish community that same struggle has taken place in the efforts to overthrow patriarchal aspects of Jewish life and Jewish religious practice. Both of these are central struggles, and both are connected to the equally pressing task of overcoming the racism and economic oppression that is the dirty little not-so-secret reality of American life.

To put this simply: if Jews can turn their backs on the suffering of Blacks, they become like the American majority. They would be no worse than anyone else. But in so doing, they would be embracing a worldview that is indistinguishable from the rest of American life—so in that case, why bother to stay Jewish, with all the attendant hassles, risks, and separations from others? It is only if Jews can stay connected to our task as witnesses to God's presence and hence as witnesses to the possibility of transformation of the ethos of selfishness to the ethos of caring (what I call "a Politics of Meaning") that retaining one's Jewishness has a substantive point.

So for Jews, the relationship with Blacks is not a "nice feel good" kind of thing—it speaks to our fundamental identity as a people. If we turn away, as some Jews want to do, and say, "It's no longer in our interests to be so involved and to make financial sacrifices through supporting candidates who want to redistribute our tax monies to the poor," we are not just sacrificing the best interests of African-Americans, we are simultaneously undermining the center of our being as Jews. The very way of thinking that leads some Jews to turn their backs on Black suffering is a way of thinking which creates a Jewish world which will be abandoned by future generations of Jews. So healing our relationship to Blacks is part of overcoming the distortions in the Jewish world and reclaiming a Judaism that is most deeply authentic with Jewish roots and Jewish destiny and hence most deeply connected to God.

No wonder, then, that this relationship has special importance to Jews. The centrality of this issue, and our desire to let the healing begin, is a sign of Jewish spiritual health. But healing the relationship is only a part of the task, a first step in the process of healing American society itself so that racism and poverty may, with God's help and with our willingness to make the necessary economic and political changes, be quickly eliminated.

The electoral victory of the Right in 1994 gave even greater urgency to the task of healing the rifts between Blacks and Jews. Seventy-eight percent of Jews voted Democratic in 1994, a higher percentage than any other ethnic group except African-Americans. Jews and Blacks are the backbone of the liberal and progressive forces in the U.S. If we cannot heal the tensions between us, there is little hope of stemming the national flow of energy toward despair, cynicism, and selfishness that produces the climate in which the Right replaces our legitimate hunger for community with a xenophobic nationalism and fear of immigrants and those with different lifestyles, diverts our desire for mutual recognition into anger at others who supposedly are getting the recognition we have been denied, and channels our fears about our ability to sustain loving relationships into anger at gays, feminists, and liberals who are blamed for undermining families. Anyone who does not wish to live in a society dominated by the values of the Christian Right, the Rush Limbaughs, and the Newt Gingriches has a stake in helping us repair and heal the tensions between Blacks and Jews. So the issues raised here should be of urgent concern to many who are not part of either community. I welcome their involvement with us and their support. What happens between Blacks and Jews will have consequences for all of us.

CHAPTER 1

Personal Dimensions

It's easy for two male intellectuals to get lost in abstract ideas and avoid the way that our thinking emerged from our own personal life experience. So we decided we would begin our dialogue by talking about each other's lives.

M.L. It's difficult for me to know whether blackness plays the same role in a Black person's life that Jewishness plays in a Jewish person's life. Are they parallel concepts? I'd like to hear about the discovery of your blackness, and how that's connected to your skin color.

C.W. Blackness is thoroughly inescapable, so you have to confront it very early on. This is not just because of the white supremacist patterns of thought and action in this society: in your own tradition your blackness is highlighted. Growing up in the Black community, different shades and hues of blackness are always highlighted in the lingo, in the streets, in the barbershops and beauty salons.

M.L. What do you mean, shades and hues? Actual physical color?

C.W. Shades of black. Actual color. Even though we are all equally objects of white supremacist abuse outside the Black community, a lot of this has to do with the "huism" inside it. The blacker the skin, the more one is talked about and made aware of that blackness. I can't speak on behalf of the brothers and sisters of a darker hue, but I'm sure they experience blackness in a very different way than I do, because of my brownness. You see this in Black history when you look at those first Blacks who were able to gain entry into mainstream white society. Education, jobs: those with a lighter hue usually were the first to get in.

M.L. Does this mean that those people came from a cultural background which had had a heavy white influence?

C.W. No, not at all. Culturally they were just as Black as brothers and sisters of a darker hue, but they were looked upon more favorably.

M.L. In other words, lighter skin only represents more rape, not more family contact or contact with white society.

C.W. It represents more than that. But, in part, the cultural exposure to whiteness in the larger society would come only because of those institutions that let in the light-skinned persons, not from within the Black community itself.

M.L. One might imagine that Black people would relate to lighter-skinned Blacks by seeing them as heavier victims since their families had been more exposed to rape by white men. But that's not how it's operated, has it? Instead, they're more denigrated. Is the reason for this that white acceptance of lighter-skinned Blacks put them under suspicion of alliance with the enemy?

C.W. No, dark-skinned Blacks are more denigrated. I think part of it was just because whites looked favorably upon these light-skinned persons. The ideals of beauty and skin appearance were primarily those that came from the larger white society. When Blacks talk about what is beautiful or handsome, what is good hair or so-called bad hair, European white ideals of attractiveness are disproportionately influential. What's interesting is that the issue of rape, as real as it has been historically, doesn't surface in everyday consciousness of skin differences. When I think of who were considered the pretty girls, very rarely were they the darker girls—unfortunately!

M.L. So how did your blackness enter your consciousness and shape what you were as a child?

C.W. Blackness was fundamental. You have to understand blackness on two levels: as hue color and as cultural. Growing up under segregated conditions in Sacramento, California, blackness was fundamental because it was all I knew. Black kids, Black schools, Black sports. All the Blacks were new to that community. They had come from Kansas and Oklahoma, from Alabama, Mississippi, and Texas. When we arrived in 1958, I was five years old.

M.L. Where had your family come from?

C.W. My parents were both born in Jim Crow Louisiana, but Dad grew up in Tulsa, Oklahoma, and Mom in Orange, Texas. They met in Nashville, Tennessee, at Fisk University and moved to Tulsa, then Topeka, Kansas, then Sacramento all during the next three years, so all of us were transplants. Given the segregated conditions in Sacramento at the time, all Black folks ended up together. Although most of us were working class, it was cross-class, and we had a wonderful, wonderful time together. I lived in a Black world that was completely saturated with the song, the music, the rhetoric, the language of Black love, Black joy, Black community. I don't want it to sound idyllic, but in terms of my own childhood it nearly was. Dad and Mom, along with Cliff, Cynthia and Cheryl, were amazing!

M.L. That's a long way from most people's view of the poor Black.

C.W. Exactly. Though we weren't so much poor as stable working class. For us, blackness was not a contested thing, it wasn't something you discovered that changed your life. That was one of the things that struck me when I went to college: a lot of the young Black people there had been in a world of whiteness and were finding for the first time Black role models, and it was changing their life. That was alien to me. I had already been nestling in my blackness, in terms of my origins, in terms of who I dreamed about and fell in love with and looked up to and admired.

M.L. What about your education before going to college?

C.W. I graduated from elementary school in 1964. I got kicked out of the Black school when I was in third grade for beating up the teacher, and some other bad stuff.

M.L. You were beating up the teacher when you were nine years old?

C.W. I beat up a pregnant teacher—thank God she was not hurt —and they kicked me out of school. For six months I couldn't get into any school, and then they put me in this "enrichment" school. That was my first interaction with a significant number of white students.

M.L. What was going on with you at nine years old that caused you to be so full of anger and upset?

C.W. I don't really know. It didn't have anything to do with the family, the family was wonderful. I was just full of energy, I had a lot of rage, I behaved badly. Everyone in my neighborhood knew I was headed for jail, I was getting into fights every day. I was hanging out with some tough kids, trying to be the best, which meant machismo, posturing, kicking more behinds than anyone else. But when I got into the enrichment program things took off. There were a couple of marvelous teachers, Cecilia Angell and Nona Sall, who were influential. Plus I had been converted. I became a Christian when I was seven or eight, about the time I got into trouble. I was really able to turn around from being a bully, violent and abusive—people saw a fundamental change in my life. I used to have kids lined up with their lunch money every morning. I almost killed a guy when I was eight, from sheer rage. After the conversion the only residue of those years was a temper. A real spiritual change was going on.

M.L. How did you get converted?

C.W. It just happened right there in the church. It was a classic conversion. You look at your life, you look at your past cruelties in the face, and you look at the model of Jesus, at the issue of love, caring and kindness, and you say you'll never stoop so low again. You dedicate your life to a certain way of behavior and you really try to take it seriously. There's no doubt that the change people saw in me allowed me to rechannel a lot of that anger and rage much more positively and constructively.

M.L. Was this conversion about Jesus? Tell me about it.

C.W. I was so young, you know, and I accepted the theology of the Black Baptist church of which I was a part. It was fundamentally about Jesus, somebody who had loved and cared deeply enough to offer you the possibility of going another way, living in a different manner. It was the love, I think, that was the most attractive thing about Jesus. It seemed to me the most attractive way of being in the world, and as real to me as this table.

M.L. What was your relationship with Jesus? Was he a role model?

C.W. He was a model but also a source of power, because at this young age we're talking about a personal relationship, which had to do with providing the strength and the power to live a life of love.

M.L. You imagined Jesus talking to you and you talking back to Jesus?

C.W. Oh very much so, a daily dialogue. Also there was a sense of being "called" to be someone who spoke with and for a larger group. Even when I was a bully, people in the church knew I had some talent: it was just not being channeled the right way. With the conversion it became clear I was changing the channels. In my church you were designated a leader early on, owing to your ability to speak, to interact with people, your social skills; so that by the age of ten or eleven people were already saying that I was going to be the next preacher. Although I always shunned that, because I respect the calling too much. In that calling there were, of course, certain models that were fundamental, of which my grandfather, C.L. West, and Willie P. Cooke and King were central. I went to hear King speak when I was a teen in Sacramento.

M.L. What year was that?

C.W. Nineteen sixty-three. There was no doubt that there was something about the brother that was really quite moving. I got the impression that on the spiritual level he was on the same wavelength as I in terms of his talk about Jesus, love, care, and so forth. He was part of the same tradition, even though I'm not at all sure that King was ever such a gangster as I was at an early age.

Jesus as both person and image, and ideal and model was fundamental, and we can't talk about that without talking about the larger community. It meant that from early on I was intent on looking at people as people, not as abstract universals, people who have been drenched by their history and culture but whose humanity is still trying to pierce through. Interestingly enough, this insight wasn't available to me at the level of gender or sexual orientation. You looked at women and gays in certain ways, you tried to keep some human contact: but my political consciousness at that time was much more race-oriented, toward equally treating persons of all different colors.

M.L. When you were growing up, in junior high and high school, how did race shape who you were as a person?

C.W. When I was very small, whiteness was something that appeared only on television. There was very little interaction with white persons, and no consciousness at all of Jewishness at an experiential level. In our religious discourse in church, Jews were very important, as precursors for the Savior's coming. In both junior and high school, even though I was making straight A's and was president of both schools, most of my world was preoccupied with athletics. The first time we ever interacted with white young people was in sports contests, and we nearly invariably won. As kids our talent had been cultivated in such a way that we were better than young white folks, across the board, in any sport we competed in. At the same time, I was being put on the track to college. In my classes I was one of only a few Black persons, but where I was living was a Black neighborhood. So I'm walking to school with all Black folk, coming home with them, playing sports with Black folk dominating, but I'm sitting in class on the college preparatory track with me and maybe one other Black person.

M.L. What was that like for you?

C.W. That's a good question. I started living in two worlds, very compartmentalized. And I began raising questions. Such as, why was it that so many of my partners, who to me seemed as sharp as I was, were not excelling in school? Although I became friends with some of the whites and Asians in these college-track courses, my closest relationships were still within sports, with mainly, though not exclusively, Black friends.

To be Black at that time was a question of style, of being able to revel in a cultural way of life. We knew we had our own world, with its lingo, its way of walking and talking. It was also a highly sexualized state because we also felt a certain superiority over a lot of the white boys in relation to women. We had a certain suave style, a cool style: we believed it, a lot of other people believed it, and it was one way in which our blackness was set apart from whiteness.

M.L. You were someone who was doing well: everybody loved you, you were going to be elected school president, you were big in sports. When did the moment come when, instead of seeing your blackness as an obstacle you could overcome, you decided to identify seriously with your people as a people?

C.W. I think it was always there since my conversion in church, which was linked to the plight of Black folk. It was reinforced by King and especially by the rise of the Panther party, by reading Malcolm X's autobiography. Just going to James Brown concerts every year was one small example of what it meant to be in a context where Black joy and Black love and Black community were taking place. Since it was always there, I never ever felt any specific need to identify, and I certainly never felt a need to distance myself in any degrading way. That was something I encountered later on, in college, when I saw some people having trouble relating to their blackness, feeling they had to either wash it with whiteness or uncritically celebrate it with a superficial blackness. To me both these options were fake and I never took them seriously.

M.L. Tell me a little bit about what it was like at college.

C.W. Harvard was a different world. I met East Coast brothers and sisters, very sophisticated and refined, who'd been exposed to a world of ideas I didn't know anything about.

M.L. When did you start?

C.W. It was 1970 when I arrived. I was seventeen years old, so I had to learn quickly and find my footing. I found it immediately among Black folk. In high school I'd had white friends, and in fact my best friend was Chicano, Rick Delgado, but at Harvard my closest friends were Black. They hadn't necessarily grown up in the neighborhoods I did and many of them had gone to prep schools. I hadn't even heard of prep schools when I got to college. And, of course, my political consciousness escalated. I was already a Democratic Socialist; I had already been very influenced by the Panther party and by people like Michael Harrington, just reading on my own.

M.L. How did they affect your thinking?

C.W. King and Malcolm X were the crucial figures for me. The Panthers talked about Marxism and socialism, but I was always looking at it through Christian lenses. Always. For me there was always a vital spiritual dimension to politics. Issues of death, disease, and despair have always been the fundamental issues of being human, and you didn't get too much talk about these issues in political circles. When I talked about music or religion with the Panthers, or about what kept them going after their mother died, they hadn't even conceived of these issues as being important. Yet it was clear that Aretha Franklin, James Brown, John Coltrane, and other artists helped keep them sane. That's why my work with Black liberation theologian James Cone was very important. Here was somebody who was trying to hold onto some spiritual issues whilst making the link to radical political struggles. Cone provided a space for radical Black Christians to be affirmed. Although, since the Panthers and myself had already had our fights between porkchop nationalists and serious socialist internationalists, at the time Cone wrote his book I thought it was a work of petit-bourgeois nationalism. It didn't talk about class or socialism at all, only about Black-White issues.

M.L. Are you saying that in high school you were already considering yourself part of the Panthers?

C.W. Very much so. If not part of, then influenced by. I could never join them because they never appreciated religion the way I did, but I was deeply influenced by them. I read their paper, I dialogued with them all the time. They were right down the street from the church, and I considered myself a socialist internationalist like them. I deeply admired the courage of Huey Newton, of Bobby Seale, of Bobby Hutton. What Cone's book did was to create a whole new space for people like myself to occupy, even though I disagreed with his Black Nationalism at the time. I certainly did agree with his attempt to merge radical politics and Christianity.

M.L. Describe for me what he actually said.

C.W. Cone's idea was that Black Power was the major way in which God was working in the world. His claim was that Christianity was fundamentally an affirmation of humanity, and that Black Power was an affirmation of Black humanity. In a racist society, then, Black Power was not in any way contradictory to the Gospel. The major anti-Christ in our society were the racist institutions, including the religious ones. Which was a rather extravagant and provocative claim, but I resonated deeply with the book and when I got to college I immediately went to work for the Panthers.

M.L. In Cambridge?

C.W. In Boston. I worked for the Black Panthers' breakfast program for three years, feeding children every morning. Mainly I appreciated the Panthers' more universal and internationalist perspective at a time when Black Nationalism of various varieties was growing. Of course, I always considered myself at home with certain elements of Black Nationalism because Black humanity was something I took for granted. I believed the resurgence of Black pride and Black love was fundamental. So I resonated with a lot of what Black nationalists talked about. It was their separatist twist that was too narrow, and their avoidance of class that wasn't analytically sharp enough. Even the talk about Black cultural distinctiveness, which I could get behind, usually collapsed into Black nationhood, which for me was a call for Black unity without any serious critical engagement about what constitutes a nation. And it was just too authoritarian, not democratic enough. Black peoplehood and Black nationhood are not synonymous.

M.L.   You were co-president of the Black Student Union at Harvard, so clearly blackness was a major part of your consciousness.

C.W.   Only as major as it had been when I was nine, in that it was something taken for granted as fundamental. Even in Union debates and our dialogue with progressives, it was never anything to make a lot of brouhaha about.

M.L.   So when you say that in college blackness took on a new dimension, what was that about?

C.W.   I think it was intellectual as much as anything else. Through interacting with Martin Kilson and Preston Williams I was exposed to a whole Black intellectual tradition, of towering figures like Du Bois and St. Claire Drake and a host of others whom we read voraciously. But all that went hand in hand with discovering the intellectual world of Weber, Marx, and Nietzsche, amongst others. I knew the blackness I was discovering was part of the world. You couldn't understand Du Bois without understanding Weber and Marx; they were always intertwined. I didn't use the Black intellectual tradition as a crutch on which to hang my sense of who I was: it broadened and deepened me rather than enclosed me.

M.L.   My own experience was of an asymmetry between Blacks and whites at the level of progressive political action. White leftists wanted Blacks, but Blacks didn't necessarily want white leftists so much.

C.W.   That's true. By my time at Harvard, the early 1970s, the alliance between the Black and white Left had broken down completely. The Black Power movement and the subsequent Black nationalist movement had severed most of those links, although I can remember a number of Progressive Labor people who would beg Black folk to be part of their dialogue. Most of them would shun it, though I didn't—I actually enjoyed the interaction.

M.L. How do you explain that difference between yourself and the others?

C.W. I think it reflected a deep disagreement about the role of the Black-white alliance in progressive politics.

M.L. That was an intellectual difference. Maybe there was something about the experience you had growing up that made it easier for you to be with whites.

C.W. I don't know. It was probably more in the interpretation of that experience. I could have been through the same set of childhood events and come out as a Black nationalist. It would have been feasible given the heavy racism I witnessed in junior high and high school.

M.L. You haven't said a thing about that!

C.W. I just take it for granted, you know. I'll give you an example. My brother wrote an essay one time for a contest, which he would have won, except that the teacher vowed he didn't write it. They accused my mother of writing it, which was crazy. You could see they found it impossible to believe that a young Black brother could write such a brilliant essay. I witnessed this, and I said, OK, this is the kind of school I'm going to. For me personally, racist encounters were there but were negligible. It was always on the edges: people questioning whether the talent you had was really there.

Here's another incident. When I ran for president of the student body the first time, it was a very close race. Everybody felt that there had been some messing with the ballot since this would have been the first time there was a Black president, and they asked me for a recount. I was too vain. I said, "I'll run next time and win, bottoms up." It almost caused a riot in the school, because they played with the ballot in such a way that the white guy ended up winning over me.

M.L. And you thought that—

C.W. That it had something to do with race. But I never allowed it to surface, I just said I'd run the next time. I ran the next time and got 80 percent of the vote which vindicated me in that sense, but it could have been a nasty situation because some very ugly race riots took place in that school.

M.L. While you were there?

C.W. Yes, we had some big ones. Our school was in a white neighborhood where they bussed in a lot of Black folk, and many just didn't get along. People were crying; there were many meetings with the student council about how to improve race relations. One of the problems was just a matter of language: Black folk were saying, "Right on!" and white folk thought they were saying, "RIOT on!" So it just escalated. These white cats in Sacramento believed in fighting, they weren't the no-backbone, milquetoast kind of white cats who just buckled under—this was some serious kind of swinging, no guns yet but knives and everything else. This was not 1994 when people are afraid of Black folk; the white folk tried to kick Black behind, we tried to kick white behind. But I wasn't part of the violence at that time; I was trying to reconcile them.

M.L. You were caught right in the middle of it.

C.W. To the degree that the racism of the institution was rightly being called into question, I identified with Black folk. At the same time I felt that a lot of them were engaged in attacks on innocent white folks that were just wrong on moral grounds and I would say so. That upset some Black folks sometimes. They'd ask, "Which side are you on?" and I'd say, "I'm on the right side." "Is that our side? How right are you?"

M.L. What was that interaction like?

C.W. It could be tense at times. I think in some interesting way the Black folk knew I identified with them just because I was with them all the time. Even though they saw me in these white classes. They just knew, that's Corn, that's his thing, he's one of those smart Negroes who goes to the college prep classes; but he's a track star also, he's fundamentally into sports, he comes to our parties. He's still one of us.

But, Michael, tell me about *your* family background.

M.L. I grew up in a Zionist family. My father was one of the leaders of the Zionist movement in New Jersey and had a strong consciousness of the Holocaust. Many members of my family were murdered during the Nazi genocide of Jews. Both of my parents had gotten active in the Zionist movement in the late thirties, and this was a real movement experience. It defined their lives, it shaped all that they did: there was a sense that Jewishness was going to define your fate, literally—you might get wiped out—so the most important question was to provide some degree of security.

C.W. Did they ever think seriously of going to Israel themselves? Or were they committed to being in America?

M.L. Like many American Jews, they faced a crisis once the State was founded in 1948. A year later my father visited Israel but came back deciding not to move.

C.W. On what grounds, do you think?

M.L. They thought they could do more to help Israel here than they could by emigrating there. They could gain influence in the American political arena to help get Israel support from the United States.

C.W. Were they big shots in New Jersey politics?

M.L. They weren't in 1949, but they saw it as a future possibility. Which did happen: my father became a judge, my mother became the campaign manager for several New Jersey governors—Meyner, Hughes, and Byrne—and for nineteen years administrative aide and political advisor to U.S. Senator Williams. My father eventually became the director of the Alcohol and Beverage Control Commission for New Jersey, so he was on the cabinet of the governor. So they did achieve a degree of power, though what that power was is very questionable. By the time I was eleven or twelve I was seeing that it was actually their ability to sell themselves to one WASP after another who would offer them some reward in return for help in getting elected and achieving power themselves. My parents' own power was completely derivative and dependent on their fawning over these various

WASP politicians, who in turn served a ruling elite of wealthy WASPS.

C.W. There were no highly visible Jewish politicians they could make links with?

M.L. They were the most highly visible Jewish politicians in the state themselves. There never had been a Jewish governor in New Jersey at that time—although there is a Jewish Senator now. My parents were traveling in Democratic party circles. You would more likely run into Harry Truman at my house than some big shot in the Jewish establishment. Through my parents I met J.F.K., Lyndon Johnson, Jimmy Carter, and a host of others.

From the time I first became conscious of being Jewish I was aware of a real split in Jewish consciousness. Was the goal to become Jewish, or to hide your Jewishness and try to pass? That kind of a choice is certainly a different one from that facing any Black person, for whom fitting in and assimilating is never an issue. But again, the question of whether or not it was a real choice for Jews was—

C.W. Itself part of the discussion.

M.L. Right. Part of the discussion was over whether that choice was real or a self-delusion. As Zionists, they were to some extent committed ideologically to saying that Jewishness would always marginalize us in the Diaspora and that's why we need a Jewish State; on the other hand, they were acting as though, somehow, they could make it in America. This was the more surprising because they were Zionists, as opposed to the conformists in the organized Jewish community. In the twenties, thirties and forties, many of the big institutions were focused on playing down their Jewishness. You didn't see in the '40s any kind of disruptive demonstrations by American Jews demanding that the government bomb the train tracks to Auschwitz, even though it was known what was going on there. The organized Jewish community, particularly its top leadership, behaved obsequiously to Roosevelt. They would raise the issue and sort of whisper in his ear, but they were not willing to confront him in an out-and-out way: they felt obligated and grateful that America was fighting in the war at all.

Growing up in the fifties, sixties and seventies was a generation of

Jews learning a Judaism that had been watered down to fit America. All that was controversial or politically confrontational had been effectively marginalized. Judaism had become a "religion" to be pursued in private life and synagogue, but its revolutionary challenge to injustice and oppression in economic and political life had been reinterpreted to be merely symbolic and inspirational rather than an actual imperative to challenge and transform the world. This left a neutered Judaism that had lost its authentic, deep quality. The Hebrew schools' aim was to show these kids how "American" their Jewish heritage was, so that there would be no conflict and so we could feel good about being Jewish. Meanwhile we were implicitly thinking, "If Judaism is the same as being American, what do we have to be in Hebrew school for?" I don't blame the children for rebelling against this, but as a result classes were a melee of people throwing spitballs at each other and acting out their frustrations. I had a more positive attitude, but it was pretty hard to learn anything there.

C.W.   Was it your sense of being Jewish that gave you this positive attitude?

M.L.   I was trying to understand what had led my parents to be Zionists. I also had some sense of the mysterious nature of what my grandfather was into.

C.W.   Your grandfather the Orthodox rabbi?

M.L.   Yes. After forty years here he spoke only Yiddish, no English. The way I understood him by the time I was twelve and he died, was that he was saying in the biggest capital letters to America, "No." Meaning, "I am here physically, but I am not here emotionally. This is just another stop in *galut,* in exile, and I refuse to emotionally invest in a society that is so materialistic and divorced from God." He was glad to have escaped the atrocities in Europe, but his level of rejection was intense. He decided to spend his days studying Talmud, barely eking out a living; which to my parents' sensibilities was pure craziness. "How can you not try to make it in America? This is what one does here!"

C.W.   In Marcuse's language, it was his "grand refusal."

M.L.   A very grand refusal! The Talmud is basically a compilation of laws and discussions that have this grand refusal quality to them because it was put together starting 120 years after the Romans destroyed the Temple, but it focuses on how we're running our lives as though we're still back in the Land of Israel. On the one hand, Talmud discourse was sustaining and kept Jews connected to the possibility of a different reality. On the other, it's a wild denial of reality. But through this denial of reality Jews have created a masterful theology for sustaining revolutionary consciousness, something I explain in my book *Jewish Renewal*.

C.W.   So there you are as an eight-year-old attending Hebrew school three times a week: how did it fit with your experience at your other school?

M.L.   I was sent to a very sensitive and progressive private school, Far Brook Country Day in Short Hills, New Jersey. Although not affiliated with any particular branch of Christianity, it was really very Christian. They were mainline Protestants. I was an oddball at that school for being just about the only Jewish kid. Even when there were other Jews in the class, I didn't know it because they weren't coming out as Jews. There were little incidents, often to do with Christmas. One year everyone had to paint little windows with decorations, so I did mine with a menorah, which a teacher encouraged me to do. Then some kid comes up me and slugs me and says, "You killed Christ!" This wasn't the majority sentiment, but nobody dealt with it seriously, sat this guy down and said, "Hey, Michael didn't kill Christ."
Here's another one. You know how in the public schools the Christmas play is a mishmash of American culture—Christmas as Jingle Bells and Santa Claus? Well, at my private school we did a Nativity play about the birth of Jesus. It was a sensitive and beautiful rendition of the Christmas story, but they really took it seriously. Which put me in an awkward position, coming from this Zionist family.

C.W.   You were actually in the play?

M.L.   I was in the play as one of the shepherds hearing the angels announce the birth of Jesus. Meanwhile I'm going to Hebrew school in the afternoons, where there are about 120 kids at my grade level.

All the kids at Hebrew school spent all day together at the local public school which had a population that was 80 percent Jewish, and the last thing they wanted is to be going to another school to learn yet more stuff. They want out. Their assimilating parents were sending them there to please their own parents, not from any commitment of their own, so these kids were feeling like the innocent sacrifices. Why should they be sent to Hebrew school to learn stuff their own parents didn't even believe in?

C.W. So you were the oddball there, too, because you actually wanted to be there!

M.L. Exactly. For me it was a total delight finally to be with other Jews and not be in the minority. After I went at age eleven to Camp Ramah—a Hebrew-speaking summer camp which was more religious than my parents were—I refused to go back to my Protestant private school. The year before, I'd already been complaining to my parents about having to sing Christian songs at assembly each day. I refused to sing them: I was thinking, "This is not mine; I don't feel comfortable here." My parents had been happy with the school, but after I raised this my father accepted my feelings. My mother was upset, and became more so the more I got into Judaism.

C.W. She saw you going back!

M.L. She even saw me going down the economic ladder, because for her, traditional Judaism was lower middle-class. It was the economic marginality she had been struggling to get out of. The more people made it economically, the less they were into Judaism, and the way they "made it" was by violating a lot of Jewish laws.

C.W. What would be an example?

M.L. Keeping the Sabbath by not working. If you were a small businessperson you were going to work on Saturdays because everyone else did, and if you were selling to non-Jews, how could you close on Saturday and expect to make a living? Except for the kosher food stores, all the stores in our neighborhood were open on Shabbat. My experience, then, was of finding Jewishness more and more counterposed to "making it" in America. This kind of conflict exists for aspiring professionals today as well. Try doing medical school and residency, or try to get a partnership in a law firm, or try to get the special training seminars as a social worker, marriage counselor, or psychotherapist, or any of a wide variety of other scientific or human sciences careers, particularly if you don't live in New York City where there are so many religious Jews that they can sometimes alter the dynamics slightly, and you come right up against the fact that a lot of the professional training seminars and conferences require you to violate Shabbat. So many people feel forced to choose how important making it is versus other values. And if making it is so important, then where do the traditional Jewish ethical concerns wind up? This came to a head around Blacks. You couldn't be growing up in fifties America and not notice that Blacks were being screwed over. Even in your own home, where housekeepers were always Black.

C.W.   You had housekeepers? In a middle-class home?

M.L.   Maybe by this point we were upper middle class!

C.W.   Did you form relationships with them?

M.L.   I'd try, but they would be cut off fairly quickly. It was a weird situation. On one hand, they had so much power over little children, but on the other they were powerless. I was often very angry at my parents for bringing in these Black people to have power over me, and their presence was a visible symbol of the way my parents were absent when I needed them to be present. Who were they to have this power, particularly when my parents didn't even respect them? I could have gone in the direction of anger toward Black people for exercising this power and being substitute parents in some way, but I didn't. Instead I became very angry at my parents for participating in the racism of the larger society. It seemed to me we were treating Black people the way we were upset that Jews had been treated throughout history. How could we have just gone through the Holocaust and not be more sensitive to the need to struggle against other forms of racism?

C.W.   Where do you think your anti-racist sentiments come from?

M.L. Well, of course, they came from the Holocaust experience, and from trying to understand over and over again how people could have let this happen.

C.W. Were there other kids who were struggling with you over this?

M.L. I think there must have been, but we didn't talk about it. There was no context in which to talk about it, because Hebrew school didn't deal with the Holocaust. There, it was all about how great Israel was doing; and meanwhile none of us knew a thing about Israel, none of us had been there. But the Holocaust was a deep dark secret that was known but not talked about, even though many of us had lost family in it. It drew energy: a lot of kids read about it, and it was incomprehensible to me how it could have happened. It was that consciousness that made it impossible for me to understand how anybody could go along with racism toward Blacks.

C.W. Were there any Black folk in your neighborhood that you got to know?

M.L. More and more Blacks were moving into Newark, and moving closer to the Weequahic section where most Jews were living. In my ninth grade the school was located on the border of the Black and Jewish neighborhoods. My first encounters were absolutely horrendous. Black students made up probably 20 percent of my school, and some of the older ones, who were clearly waiting to drop out of school, were really scary types to me. A number of them were coming to school with alcohol on their breath. There were two in particular, who were in my English class, who were demanding money every day from kids.

C.W. You had to give it up or get beat up!

M.L. Exactly. "Got a nickel?" When I didn't have a nickel they slugged me, really hit me in a way that hurt, and made me upset and scared not to have a nickel for them.

C.W. I used to do the same thing in school.

M.L. You were asking other kids for a nickel?

C.W.   Remember, they lined up and gave me their lunch money.

M.L.   OK, maybe you were that guy! Maybe you were the man! But no matter how tough you were at eight, I believe that these six-teen-year-olds were still more threatening.

The whole school was pervaded by a real threat of physical intimi-dation. You felt scared to walk through the hallways. I remember trying to decide, where am I least likely to encounter these guys? If I go out for lunch, will they be outside? Each day was a scary experi-ence, and I remember an incredible sense of relief when these guys one day went on a real spree of violence, stabbed two kids and were themselves—

C.W.   Suspended?

M.L.   Sent to prison. In that situation I wouldn't say it would have been irrational or racist of me to want to get away. It wasn't because I hated Blacks. I didn't care who they were. If the same group of people had been white Italians, white Irish, or a bunch of crazy Jews, I would still want to be away from that situation. It wasn't a matter of racism.

C.W.   My hunch is that some of the Black kids in that school who were as threatening as lambs would still be perceived as scary in the same way as those folks who are actually harassing you. What about the other Black folks at your school: the mainstream quiet ones who got on with their work. Did you have any relationships with them?

C.W.   Not really, at least not that first year in ninth grade.

C.W.   Why was that? Was there no mixing going on?

M.L.   The ones who were scary set the tone. You didn't want to find out whether the next Black you met would be someone like the ones who were shaking you down, or a nice guy. In tenth grade, though, the school was in another building, back in the heart of the Jewish ghetto. It was a whole different feeling. Students were tracked into college prep classes, and there I met Blacks and got friendly with them. On the other hand, there were Blacks who were not on that track, but who were really hot in basketball. With them there was some tension because sports was what they were excelling in, plus the sexuality you mentioned—

C.W.   They were getting all the pretty girls!

M.L.   All the pretty girls, the cheerleaders, are rooting for them.

C.W.   Are the cheerleaders Black or white?

M.L.   White. White cheerleaders for Black basketball stars. Which created a level of tension. Of course, in sports there were white kids I would have had nothing to say to, so I had no more to say to them as Blacks either, except to say, "You're Black and I identify with you because we've both experienced racism." I therefore experienced an internal split between the Black movement, with which I identified, and concrete, real, live Black people, with whom I didn't necessarily identify! Yet despite my encounters being mainly with the scary kind, we did elect a Black person for class president.

C.W.   Wasn't this still the fifties?

M.L.   Absolutely! But this was a liberal Jewish community, in which a kind of "We-love-you-because-you're-Black" dynamic was going on. It was purely symbolic. There was no power connected to this office. We wanted to make a symbolic statement that amongst the various candidates, all of whom were relatively smart and inoffensive, we wanted the Black guy because to us he symbolized the oppressed group that we didn't want to distance ourselves from. I wish that consciousness was as present in the Jewish masses today as it was in 1956 or 1960, when I was in high school. You then went out of your way to be nice to the Blacks in your college prep classes.

C.W.   What was behind that, though? Was it a need to be liked by Blacks, or a need to feel pity for them since they're catching so much hell, or a desire to not be part of that hell-catching?

M.L.   For me and most of my friends it was a sense that they were like us, victims. They were still being screwed over, even if they weren't going to any concentration camps and getting murdered.

C.W. The Holocaust was still imprinted on your mind, then. Even though I'm told that it wasn't really talked about then.

M.L. It wasn't widely talked about publicly until 1967, but it was definitely in the mind of every liberal Jewish kid and contributed eventually to Jewish involvement in the Civil Rights movement.

C.W. It's interesting that even as young Jewish people of that generation were running from their Jewish identity, the weight of the Holocaust was quite heavy on them.

M.L. That's because the identity they were running away from was the *official* Jewish identity, which, as I said, did not have much focus on the Holocaust. The official Jewish identity, as experienced by most kids in Hebrew schools, had little spiritual focus, and was associated in kids' minds either with a set of restrictive practices that kept them different from others (and it sometimes seemed, different for the sake of difference), with a mechanical identification with Israel (which couldn't mean much to children who had never been there), and with a set of ethical teachings which were so general and flowery that they never seemed to have much concrete application to any controversial reality. The ethical teachings would lead us to support Blacks in the South, but certainly not to question their poverty in the North; to support social justice, but certainly not to question the ethos of the competitive market or the corrupt business practices and ruthless competition for grades in high school or for entrance to professional schools in college or for clients or customers once one started a career. In short, it was a sanitized Judaism, far from the revolutionary tradition that is built into Torah and which had inspired Jews through much of Jewish history. We were offered a Judaism that made it easy for Jews to "fit in" to the economic and political system in America, even as it restricted us to a particular ethnicity. It wasn't till college that I found that we'd all had similar experiences.

C.W. What was it that prevented these Holocaust memories from being articulated in public Jewish spaces?

M.L. Shame, for one thing. In 1950s America, the goals were money, success and power. Jews wanted to be powerful, not victims.

The more American you are, the less you want to identify with the shame of powerlessness. Were we supposed to come forward and say, "Look at us, we're the victims of the Holocaust"? Plus, once the Black movement started, there was shame amongst the American Jewish leadership about their failure to do what the Blacks were doing: shame, first of all, that they hadn't done enough to protect their brethren during the Nazi period; and second, that they had survived. There were a fair number around who had come from the camps, so there was a lot of survivor guilt. "Why did we make it when the others didn't?" I myself remember crying over this issue by the age of eleven or twelve.

C.W. Why you were alive and the others weren't?

M.L. How I had a right to be alive when my extended family in Europe had been wiped out. After all, it was just by chance that I hadn't been there too. Compounding that was another level of guilt many Jews felt, not directly related to the Holocaust, but connected with not having moved to Israel and chosen a Jewish life.

Most American Jews were interested in normalizing their life in America, and in the past fifty years that has often meant becoming like the mainstream culture, focused on making it and accumulating wealth and power. But a Judaism based on fear of non-Jews and a desire to "make it" in America wasn't very compelling to a post-Holocaust generation who had much less fear of non-Jews and didn't need the connections they could make among Jews to assist them in advancing in the much larger non-Jewish world that had opened up to them. Most of my contemporaries were never exposed to a Judaism that was ethically sensitive or spiritually alive, so they had no way of knowing that the Judaism they were leaving behind when they left the Jewish world after their Bar or Bat Mitzvahs had much more to offer besides conservatism, conformism, and spiritual deadness. Compared to that, I was remarkably blessed to have become close with Abraham Joshua Heschel and his extraordinarily deep spiritual vision of Judaism, a vision that I had never encountered in Hebrew School or synagogue.

C.W. Had you encountered Abraham Joshua Heschel by the time you were in high school?

M.L. I first met him when I was twelve, when he was the guest speaker at the synagogue. Meeting him was my key formative experience. After that I started reading his book *God in Search of Man:* I used to read a chapter every Shabbat. That next summer I encountered him at Camp Ramah. He saw I was reading his book and he invited me to come speak to him regularly at the Jewish Theological Seminary, because there weren't that many thirteen-year-olds reading his work!

Getting to know Heschel in my teenage years, and being in contact with Ramah, I realized that the Judaism my contemporaries were rejecting wasn't the real Judaism. If I hadn't known any better, I would have rejected that watered-down version too.

C.W. How did your understanding of Judaism become linked to race issues?

M.L. Race issues are never very far away, because Judaism is built around the story of the Jews moving from slavery to freedom. Now in America we were in a land in which another group of people had gone from slavery to freedom, except that the freedom wasn't yet complete. You didn't have to be a genius to make those parallels.

C.W. Yet a number of Jewish brothers and sisters who were deeply steeped in their tradition were not making that connection.

M.L. If you look at the organized Jewish community in the fifties, a lot of them were actually seeing the link. The American Jewish Congress, even the American Jewish Committee, for example: they hadn't yet made their right-wing turn. The rabbi of my own synagogue, Joachim Prinz, was president of the American Jewish Congress and eventually he became one of the ten convenors of the March on Washington in 1963.

Toward the end of high school in the late fifties Blacks suddenly became an issue in the North like they had been before in the South. All of a sudden they started moving into the neighborhood. From being twenty percent it became more like 30, then 35 percent, and they were coming closer . . . They ceased to be an abstraction down South that you were "for"; not just the basketball stars or the goody-two-shoes Blacks you were electing as class president. They were suddenly also the people who were going to lower the price of your house and bring crime to your neighborhood. Before 1959, crime in that area of Newark, the Weequahic section, was unheard of. The real estate agents really played on people's fears. They used to take ads in the Jewish papers, boasting about having sold yet another house, but implicitly saying, "The Black people are coming so you'd better sell quick, before your property value plummets!" So starting around 1959 there was an exodus. And even though my parents were outraged at what the estate agents were doing, they too moved out in 1960.

C.W. Where did they go?

M.L. South Orange. Not very far in a literal sense, but psychologically a long way away. There weren't any Blacks in South Orange. Moving there was making it into the *goyishe* world.

C.W. What happened to the area where you grew up?

M.L. From the early sixties on there was a mass exodus of the Jews, and it's now all Black. And all burnt out. Our house is still standing, though.

C.W. Does a Black family live there now?

M.L. Yes, but the whole area is totally unrecognizable—the deterioration is unbelievable. The riots of 1967 played a part in this. It used to be a middle middle-class neighborhood and now it looks like a burnt-out war area.

C.W. Let's move on to your college experience. You went to New York, didn't you?

M.L. Yes. I went to Columbia because the Jewish Theological Seminary was there.

C.W. And Heschel! That's the connection!

M.L. I wanted to continue my studying with him—so he and I met to discuss Jewish theology and general issues in philosophy. At Columbia it was the first year they had eliminated quotas. Of course, they didn't call them Jewish quotas—they were just geographical distribution quotas. That year for the first time they admitted people on the basis of their grades, their College Boards, their extracurricular activities, and their recommendations—and the class was 60 percent Jewish.

C.W. What impact did the Jewish Bohemian intellectual crowd have on you? The Mailers and the Bellows and the Malamuds?

M.L. None. That is, I loved their writing, but they didn't shape my consciousness, because by the time I was in college my consciousness had been shaped by Judaism. I thought Bellow, for example, had such a sense of cynicism about the world that I just couldn't see what his relationship was to Judaism. Ethnicity, maybe. These were writers who'd made a previous generation of Americans feel Jewish because they'd made it in the literary world. They made them feel validated. But for people like me who grew up after the Holocaust, America was more home than host. If I'd been five years older these guys would have been my absolute gods. But Bellow reflected the conservative consciousness that was being celebrated in the Jewish establishment— which is why they and their friends in the media lionized him. Many of the writers most acclaimed were those who had given up on social transformation, were as deeply cynical about social movements as they were about religious or spiritual consciousness, and instead reflected the extreme individualism and isolated consciousness of the lonely intellectual entrepreneur. Their cynicism—deepened not only by the Holocaust and the distortions of communism as manifested in Stalinist Eastern Europe but also by an inability to understand what it was about Judaism that remained valid and capable of addressing the contemporary world—led them to a kind of lonely "see through everything, believe in nothing" worldview that they thought was revolutionary but actually fit very well into the needs of the dominant society.

For the next generation, those of us who became sixties activists, these writers were part of the problem. For most of my generation, they were part of the problem because they were so accommodationist to American society's individualism and materialism; to me, another way of stating that same problem was to say that they were too assimilated—not because they didn't maintain their ethnicity, but because they didn't maintain the revolutionary perspective built into Judaism.

C.W.   So when you saw Lionel Trilling standing up at the front of the class, it didn't mean that much to you?

M.L.   Any of us who were moved by the spirit of the early sixties were unwilling to buy these elitists, who were Jews pretending to be more American and more *goyish* than the *goyim* and who were waving Matthew Arnold to show us how completely they were identified with the high culture. For many of these Jews, literature had replaced God and the various "gods that failed" (most importantly, communism) as the central way to place meaning in life, and they saw themselves defending the high literary tradition against the philistinism of contemporary American life. Just as they and their parents' generation might have railed against betrayers of the working class and a few generations before other Jews might have railed against idolatry. Trilling and his whole generation of Jewish literati were worshipping at the altar of English and American writers, finding there the secular salvation that had eluded them elsewhere—and finding, too, the respectability that comes by fitting in to the dominant ethos of the society and showing how you really are not *too* Jewish. That dynamic—that I later encountered among liberal and Left Jews in the Movement—was first most apparent among those who considered themselves the New York Intellectuals and who were determined that Matthew Arnold, not Abraham Heschel or J. B. Soloveitchik or Franz Rosenzweig or Martin Buber, would be their guide.

Those of us who attended Ivy League schools were confronted with Jewish teachers who never thought to include Jewish texts like Talmud or Maimonides or Midrash or anything from the rich cultural heritage of the Jews into the Western canon. Instead, they became the cheerleaders for the Western literary and philosophical tradition, and hence they felt as threatened by Jews committed to Judaism as twenty years later they would feel threatened by feminist, gay, and Third World multiculturalists. These literary lights, the darlings of the *Commentary* and the *New Republic* crowd, were the vanguard of assimilation. But by the mid-sixties, we Jews were getting another model. That model was the Blacks, who were asserting their identity as a minority, not claiming to be like everyone else and clamoring to be let in.

C.W.   Had you read Richard Wright and Ellison?

M.L.   They were on my high school curriculum, as was Baldwin.

C.W.   Yet you weren't a radical at Columbia. Where would you have placed yourself, on the ideological spectrum?

M.L.   I was in a place comparable to where someone from the *New Republic* would be now: namely, seeing through a lot of crap, but being skeptical about the possibility of change and not seeing it as my struggle. Yet, because of Heschel, I was much more hopeful and optimistic that things could change with regard to issues of Jewish identity.

The Black movement was certainly very important to my consciousness. Getting involved in the Free Speech Movement whilst at graduate school was the transformative event for me, taking me from intellectual noninvolvement to total involvement.

The Free Speech movement was about the right to organize on campus for activity off campus that might be illegal. The university at Berkeley was telling the Congress of Racial Equality, for example, that it could not organize on campus for civil rights sit-ins it was planning against businesses that refused to hire Blacks. The students were arguing the illegitimacy of "prior restraint" of an activity—picketing for civil rights—that was not itself illegal. The first few days this was happening I walked by, thinking, "I'm a grad student. I'm not interested in student politics." Then the moment came when a police car came on campus to arrest the person sitting recruiting at the CORE table. Just as the police put Jack Weinberg—a Jewish activist—in the car, the students surrounded the car and sat down: so it couldn't go anywhere without running someone over. Some police are there to prevent the student being pulled out of the car; but they don't know what to do, and the university doesn't know what to do. Then Mario Savio jumps on top of the car and starts a rally, which goes on for twelve hours, with students using the car as a podium. This was the first big event of the Free Speech movement, and I realized it wasn't just a campus issue. Finally about two hundred fraternity boys arrived, surrounded the people sitting down, and started throwing beer bottles at them. The people sitting down were singing Civil Rights songs and the people standing up were threatening violence, and if you were sitting then everyone standing up was a potential threat. It was one of those moments when you have to choose a side, and so I sat down. To me it was clear: "here were these violent non-Jews, acting like proto-Nazis," and "here, protesting for civil rights, are the Blacks and Jews." There was no possible way you could be a Jew with any sensitivity to your own history and not sit down with the Blacks and Jews.

C.W.   Let me ask you, of the people sitting down how many were Black?

M.L.   Very few. Maybe ten or twelve.

C.W.   It's ironic, the relative absence of a Black presence given that it was issues relating to Black folk that sparked this thing. Although it's great to see a stand being taken on moral issues, including on what seem to be other people's battles.

M.L.   Exactly. From my point of view, I'm sitting there, twenty-one years old, and thinking, "What am I doing getting myself into trouble; I've got my career to think of." When I was growing up the police were the ones chauffeuring my father around: now they were the ones beating us up. What was I doing there? And the answer I got was—what did I expect from the German people? Whatever I was asking for from them, I had to do that same thing for Blacks here.

C.W.   And more for Blacks than for yourself as a Jew?

M.L.   It was for the underdogs, the Jews of that situation. Even if they didn't understand why it was in their interest. It wasn't my obligation to develop their consciousness, only to make sure they didn't get screwed over. The same goes for Germany. The Jewish community didn't understand the nature of the Nazi threat in the 1920s, but I wanted the non-Jewish progressives in Germany to figure out a way to stop that Nazism regardless of whether or not the Jews knew it was not good for them.

C.W. Given that the activity at Berkeley was spurred on by the Congress of Racial Equality and the Student Nonviolent Coordinating Committee, there is evidence that a significant number of Black folk had reached that level of consciousness and were taking precisely the stance and risk you took.

M.L. My relationship to Blacks was central to my moral and political development. Yet for me Blacks were still an abstract identity of an oppressed group. Yet personally I had few relationships with Blacks outside of politics.

C.W. In my own life, my interaction with Jewish intellectuals—not that I thought of them as such then—was critical in terms of my growth and development. The difference is that after the age of eighteen or nineteen that contact was concrete. We were at pizza parlors all the time—talking, reading. Whereas you, at twenty-one, have still not had a lasting relationship with Blacks. When did you have your first substantive, fruitful, productive, challenging relationship with a concrete Black person?

M.L. All those adjectives; you're asking for a lot! I would say I didn't have that until 1972. There were people I did political work with: Huey Newton, Cleaver. I knew them, we talked and had arguments, but I don't know how you'd describe the relationship.

C.W. I wouldn't call it friendship; maybe comradeship. In 1972 you were twenty-nine. Would you say that was typical for Jews of your generation?

M.L. Yes, because where would you meet them? This was before affirmative action consciousness had given the colleges an impetus to recruit Blacks. There weren't that many Blacks in college. The only way to do it was to consciously think, "I want to go out and have a Black friend." To me that was the wrong consciousness on which to connect with somebody. It was patronizing. I didn't want to have a friendship with someone just because they were Black; I didn't want instrumental friendships. It was only when I was teaching college at Trinity that I began to really develop a good friendship with James

Miller in the English Department, a friendship based on shared values rather than on some decision to "have an African-American friend."

Yet, I had much experience of close support from Blacks in the Movement days. When I was indicted by the federal government as part of what was called "the Seattle Seven" for organizing an anti-war and pro-Black liberation demonstration (on charges of "using the facilities of interstate commerce with the intent to incite riot"—a law that was later declared unconstitutional but which worked effectively in repressing the anti-war movement), and was sent to federal penitentiary for "contempt of court" (later overturned), I found that the people in the penitentiary who were *most* supportive and protective of me (from white rightists who threatened to assault me) were Black brothers. That made a lasting impression on me. Even though I was "out" as a Jew, and made it clear to people that my involvement in the social change movements flowed from my Jewishness, I found that the Blacks in that prison were able to see me as an ally and gave me needed support. That made a lasting impression on me.

Since then I was blessed with a series of very wonderful African-American friends like James Miller when I taught at Trinity College and Wilson Riles, Jr., when I set up the Institure for Labor and Mental Health, and now, you. People who have felt like soul mates on the path of healing and repairing the world.

CHAPTER 2

Past Oppression

It's impossible to understand the present without some perspective on the past.

C.W. A dialogue like this is so very important because you and I represent such distinct traditions. Lodged between the American Jewish community and the Afro-American community are issues that separate and distance us, but that must be dealt with, honestly and candidly. Yet at the same time there is overlap and convergence between the two, a real commonality that should be highlighted as well.

M.L. I agree. It's important for the Jewish world because part of the conservatism that has emerged in the leadership section and some of the more activist elements is rooted in a disillusionment with our relationship with Blacks. When you push the conservative/liberal debate you often find people saying, "So-and-so in the Black world said such-and-such . . . Why should we remain liberals, when being liberal means helping the most oppressed, Blacks who are out to screw us?" Jews have been strongly affected politically by the fantasy that Blacks have switched to being hurtful toward them. Trying to sort out these issues seems an important reason for dialogue.

When we talk about the origins of oppression in both communities, it is often possible to look at the current reality, notice differences of economic and political power, and yet not to recognize the history that produced this reality. To Jews it appears as if Blacks are lumping us together with all whites—and not just any whites but the worst ones on the block.

We need to remind ourselves that both communities have histories of oppression, which may be different in form but in which there are historical overlaps. So that's what we have decided to explore first.

C.W.   In talking about the Black experience in this country, we have a legacy that dates back far further than that of most Jewish Americans, who go back three, four, five, maybe six generations. By contrast, 244 years of slavery leaves a legacy of dehumanization that is still struggling within us. When we talk about slavery we're not talking about an institution in the past that you can point to and say is over: you're talking about an institution that leaves a very deep imprint on Black minds and Black bodies and constraints on Black political and economic power.

Yet for me, the most crucial moment for Black people in this country was not slavery, but the failure of American democracy in the Reconstruction period. If there had been the kind of substantive expansion of democracy that was initiated by Reconstruction, then the whole history of American immigration would have been different. Black people would have been mobile, they would have been able to come North and move into those jobs that millions and millions of immigrants, including poor Eastern-European Jews, were moving into.

M.L.   Tell me what you're actually talking about.

C.W.   We're talking about Jim Crow; we're talking about sharecropping; we're talking about debt tenancy; we're talking about peonage status.

M.L.   Which kept Blacks from being able to move to the North.

C.W.   Kept them immobile—probably the most un-American word in the English language. That is why a major theme in Black history is "staying on the run" and "flying away" from white supremacist spaces.

M.L.   When I think of Jim Crow, I have a very narrow conception of what that meant. My conception is of discrimination against Blacks in Black towns. I don't connect it with not being able to move to the North.

C.W.   After the Civil War there was a tremendous struggle to keep Black people a dependent and disciplined labor force. This happens even before the Black Codes of 1865, 1866. And yet—boom!—Reconstruction emerges, and it looks as if there is going to be some possibility of breaking out. Symbolic political elites emerge. The Louisiana Lieutenant Governor is Black, a Supreme Court judge in South Carolina is Black. For the first time in the history of the world, it looks as if the slaves are being given more or less equal rights in one generation. For the first time, American notions of citizenship are defined in the Fourteenth Amendment. Because the question is, what to do with these newly freed Black men and women? It raises the question of what it means to be an American citizen, so it affects the body politic as a whole. For those twelve years (1865–1877) it looked as if the sun was going to begin to shine for the first time for Black people in the U.S.A. That's why when we talk about the history of Black-Jewish relations we can't focus solely or even primarily on slavery. We need to look at what happened when the wheels of democracy looked as if they were about to start turning in a fair way.

Yet, come 1877, the military troops are withdrawn and the white supremacist forces come into power. Jim Crow wasn't put in place legally until 1895, so it took twenty-two years of this slow process to begin to fundamentally shape the everyday lives of Black folk in a segregated way. Hence, the Confederacy lost the war, but white supremacy won the peace!

Black people, for the most part, were peasants, and they wanted what every peasant in the world wants, which is self-sufficient production, to be free of a market that coerces, and not to be servants. Hence their response is migration—or getting the hell out. Trying to go in search of land to the Midwest, to Kansas or Oklahoma: and if that didn't work, then emigrate.

On the other hand, the back of slavery had been broken and a halfway house emerged: sharecropping. Tenants who are in perennial debt to landlords and shopkeepers; who spend large amounts of their time working for a market and yet have a small percentage of their time for themselves. They have a little plot of land for growing their own little crops. So there is a tremendous struggle going on, but the result is the sharecropping system into which most Black people were locked. And this is just the moment in which industrial America is being built. This is the moment when labor shortages demand immigrants from around the world.

M.L.   Tell me exactly how the sharecropping system kept Blacks from moving.

C.W.   It kept them locked into a system in which they were deep in debt, and could not leave until they had paid it off. Each year, and from generation to generation, they get deeper and deeper in debt. They're still forced to pick the cotton, in some ways like slaves; but they're not slaves because they are on the free market. Which means they have to find their own housing, grow their own food; and the only way to do that is to be in debt to those who provide them with those items. When people are locked into such a Catch-22 situation, you no longer need laws to prevent them from leaving.

These are just some key points in a history of Black folks in the United States, to which Jewish Americans need to be attuned if they are going to overcome a lot of misunderstandings. It's not just a legacy of slavery: its a legacy of subordination of labor, of Jim Crowism, of lynching, of institutional and psychic terrorism that would be the case until the 1950s. What could have been done to these people that America, associated in the minds of most people with opportunity and freedom, would give Black people nightmares? We have to take seriously what Josephine Baker said in 1917: that the very idea of America makes me tremble, it makes me shake, it gives me nightmares. She is referring to her girlhood in East Saint Louis amidst its riot in 1917. It was an experience that echoed that of large numbers of Black folk between 1877 and 1915, who thought about America the way Russian Jews thought about Ukraine. This kind of terror is unprecedented in American history.

M.L.   It's probably useful for people in the Black community to know about the specificity of the oppression of Jews in the Western world. The standard line on Jewish oppression has been that it's rooted in Christianity. Certainly the Christian definition of Jews as the bad guys who betrayed and killed Jesus has been powerful. In the early centuries there was a tremendous competition between Judaism and Christianity that, as far as I know, shaped the way that Jews would be portrayed in the Gospels. Some of the Gospels may have been written by people of Hellenistic culture who weren't directly familiar with Jesus, who were trying to sell their version of Judaism— not that they saw it as such—to a non-Jewish world. They were under tremendous pressure. There were Jews around saying, "We knew Jesus. He was one of our boys, and we never thought of him as the Messiah." So, some of those whose task it was to convert people to Christianity in the early years found it advantageous to portray Jews as destructive, the enemy. Meanwhile the Jewish world was discrediting Christianity as a perversion of Judaism. In those days Judaism still engaged in proselytizing, so both Jews and non-Jews were competing for the non-Jewish audience.

This was the context in which the Gospels and the early Church were formed. There was a struggle going on, and both sides tended to see the other as a threat, particularly in areas where proselytizing was still taking place. The official Church was suffused with ambivalence toward Jews: on the one hand, Jews' testimony was discredited and they were portrayed as Christ-killers toward whom it was appropriate to direct a great deal of anger; on the other hand, there was a holding back from their total destruction since they were eventually to be converted rather than wiped out. Having that as the central legacy of European thought—being seen always as the Other—has been extremely destructive to us.

This was certainly a part of the picture of European anti-Semitism, but I think it underplays another root of antagonism to Jews: the fear of our revolutionary message. Even before Christianity emerged, Jews were a troublesome people to ruling classes of the ancient world, because they had emerged with a revolutionary message, articulated in the Exodus story: the message that ruling classes were not inevitable, that the world could be fundamentally transformed.

The historical experience of Jews is a legacy of anti-Semitism in the

West, rooted both in the New Testament—and in the role Jews play as potential disrupters and boundary-crossers. Disrupters partly because we don't accept the Christian Bible, and partly because our own Bible has elements within it that can read as a challenge to any established order. Boundary-crossers because it seemed to us that the way the elaborate theories set up to explain why the world *had* to be the way it is and why nothing could change could never possibly explain our historical existence as a free people who had once been slaves and subjected to this very same ideological assault that tried to convince us that we would inevitably always be slaves.

Not that most Jews through most of our history were consciously thinking, "Let's overthrow feudalism." But the thrust of our text, which suggested that the world was full of oppression and that it might be appropriate to struggle against it, made it difficult to accept the "God's in His heaven, all's right with the world" view of reality.

Jews were often uncomfortable with the revolutionary thrust of our own message, realizing that it put us in great danger, and that it made demands on us to live in the consciousness of a God that made for the possibility of radical transformation and hence destabilized all fixed categories. So Jews often tried to soften the message, play down, or run away from its radical implications (most dramatically spelled out in Torah's injunction to eliminate all debts each seven years and to completely redistribute land every fifty years, as well as in its insistence that we actively pursue justice and "love the stranger" by remembering our own enslavement).

Ruling elites who found this message disturbing did all they could to stir up their own domestic populations against the Jews, to spread vicious stories about us, to characterize us as devils or well-poisoners or people who lied, were sexually promiscuous and had large sex organs, and as people who would cheat everyone out of their money. Moreover, since Jews were not allowed by the Church to own land or work the land or join guilds and become craftsmen or artisans, they were forced into the most disrespected of all possible professions— traders, shopkeepers, and others who were not producing goods, but merely selling goods at a higher price than they had paid for them. The combination of indoctrination plus people's anger at those who traded goods rather than produce something tangible led to a long history of anti-Semitic feeling and ideas, which entered the modern world.

The shocking event of the modern world for Jews was the Dreyfus trial at the end of the nineteenth century. After the French Revolution Jews had thought, "We're being offered a new deal! Christianity is out; capitalism and bourgeois ideals are in. In the new secular nation state, we can be French, German, English in the public arena as long as we keep our Judaism behind our front doors." These hopeful fantasies were shattered at the end of the nineteenth century when a Jewish captain in the French army was charged with treason and betraying his country to the Germans—a charge that was later proved to be totally without foundation. He had been scapegoated solely because he was a Jew. The Dreyfus case was so shocking because it suddenly awakened Jews to the awareness that, even without an explicit religious base, anti-Semitism had been transmitted historically into the contemporary arena. What had happened was a classic case of the independence of ideology, in which hostility to Jews had spread to such an extent that it had taken on a life of its own. Even though it was no longer rooted in political, economic, or religious realities, the idea that Jews were to be hated had managed to survive and to have a mass base of appeal.

At that point, some Jews created Zionism as a solution—a way of saying that if the modern secular national states would not accept us, we would hook our own secular nationalist movement onto the long religious aspirations of a return to our ancient homeland.

Others turned to Marxism in the hopes that a revolutionary transformation of society would allow for the full acceptance of Jews. Still others intensified their efforts at assimilation, hoping that if they became less and less noticed as Jews, and less and less "offensive" (they imagined that it was Jewish behavioral characteristics that were "provoking" the non-Jews to hate us), maybe we could sneak through to safety.

Many of the Jews who came to the U.S. chose the assimilationist route but then were unable to follow through totally on that path. Hitler proved that even assimilation would not provide safety—because people whose parents had converted two generations before were still identified as "racially Jewish" and sent to concentration camps. There seemed to be no escape. And the creation of Israel gave Jews a sense of pride and feeling that perhaps they could protect themselves rather than abandon their identity.

And then, America had a tradition of legal tolerance of religious differences as long as those religions were kept out of the public arena and made a merely "private" issue—so Jews could remain Jewish on weekends in their homes as long as they didn't bring Jewish values into the world of work (which some did through their involvement in the union movement) or into politics (which some did through their involvement in Left politics).

Traumatized by the Holocaust, many Jews were all too eager to play down their Jewishness, marginalize it into an "ethnic identity," and make it in American society. But this raised a difficult set of questions about the nature of their identity for the next generation of Jews who were raised in the fifties, sixties, seventies, and eighties—namely, "If Judaism itself is not the core of Jewishness, what exactly is the nature of Jewish identity?" The further Jews were estranged from their religious identity, the more the identity in the post–World War Two era was focused on issues of defense (protect ourselves from new upsurges of anti-Semitism) or support of Israel (here we can have pride in being strong and recreating our lives after having been subject to genocide). No wonder, then, that Jews felt upset that Blacks did not provide much support for Jews in facing the Holocaust and that Blacks became prominent critics of Israel.

I think we need to consider the impact of the Holocaust on the state of Black-Jewish relations. In the years leading up to the Holocaust and during it, the Jewish experience was of everyone abandoning them. The abandonment took many forms. The Left's betrayal of Jews was very concrete: they had arms and ammunition which they didn't give us, and when we joined resistance groups they shot us. In most of the rest of the world it was more indirect. Jews were trying to escape and nobody would take us in. There literally were boats full of Jews going from port to port that none would let in, and that ultimately sunk. People in those countries could have taken a stand. Faced with this situation, neither Americans nor, as they were then, Negroes came out in support of Jews. Even on domestic anti-Semitism, Blacks would only identify with Jews against the Ku Klux Klan because it was explicitly anti-Black as well.

C.W. How can you say that when you know that Paul Robeson was appearing on platforms supporting the State of Israel? Or when W. E. B. Du Bois was writing editorials in support of Zionism? Or when Walter White of the NAACP was pushing for U.S. pressure against the Nazis?

M.L. But there was no mass consciousness about this amongst Blacks. Unlike Jewish consciousness when there was a Civil Rights movement.

C.W. That was different. You had television scenes portraying these struggles; the problem was visible. With the Holocaust there was a relative silence around the world, not only because of anti-Semitism but also because of mass paranoia. It was a question of communication, of credibility. Even the Jewish community was unsure whether to take it seriously or dismiss it as propaganda.

M.L. And after the war, when it did become known, the Black community was not exactly supportive of the Zionist movement's attempt to establish a national home for the Jews.

C.W. There was very little understanding. In 1948, 65 percent of Black people were living in rural areas in the South. Given what they were up against, you weren't going to get any deep grasp of what was going on for world Jewry. Yet Black leaders were quite supportive of Israel, as was Ralph Bunche.

M.L. In Africa, also, the anti-colonial movements were very insensitive to Jewish issues.

C.W. Because they perceived Israel as part of American imperialism.

M.L. It was impossible in 1945 to '48 to perceive that. The United States was not supporting the Zionist movement, there was an embargo of arms, and American Jews were being prosecuted for smuggling weapons to Palestine.

C.W. Most African freedom fighters read the Zionist struggle against the British imperialists like the Boer War. Their perception was of Afrikaners fighting against European imperialism, but first settling the land of people who were already there. I do think the African Nationalists had some ground for criticizing what Britain and the U.S., as imperial powers, did to help the founding of Israel.

As regards subsequent trade links between Israel and South Africa, I think there's been a lot of misunderstanding and misrepresentation. It's true that Black people tend to pick out Israel, as opposed to a whole host of nations in the world that had relations with South Africa during apartheid, including Black African nations. On these other nations there was silence. Some of this was anti-Semitic and some was morally motivated in a targeted way. Jews understandably think they are being unfairly treated in having the limelight cast only on them. I think they should expect to be measured with one measuring rod, like everyone else.

M.L. Israel's connection with South Africa was deplorable, and we at *Tikkun* magazine publicly exposed and opposed it, just as in the U.S. we supported disinvestment as long as apartheid persisted. But we also pointed out that Saudi Arabia and Germany were heavily implicated, too. South Africa runs on Saudi oil. But you heard no discourse of anti-Islamic or anti-Arab sentiment among American Blacks for the same crimes for which they indicted Jews.

C.W. The United States has close relations with both Saudi Arabia and Germany as well as Israel. So we're talking analogous situations with regard to relations with the U.S. empire.

M.L. In a sense, Israeli trade with South Africa was similar to the drug trade. There you've got a lot of Blacks who are pushed into selling their souls to the devil and end up selling terribly destructive drugs to their fellow Blacks and to many whites as well.

C.W. You are saying that Israel's motivation behind selling arms is to make money. They will sell to anyone—left wing, right wing, centrist, South America, China. It's not a question of supporting white supremacists or political affinity. They will sell to whoever is on the market.

M.L. Even to Iran's Islamic fundamentalist regime! Imagine that. They sold to people who bombed them. Black America needs to hear this. The same market mechanisms that lead so many American firms and so many European firms to sell arms wherever they can find a market, without regard to moral consequences.

C.W. Hence the perception that Israel may be losing its soul. Israeli morality as shown in its barbaric treatment of others within the Occupied Territories is a challenge to many Jews' self-perception, to their assumption of higher ethical standards than others. Of course, every nation has engaged in barbaric behavior toward other people. Yet there was a surprise and horror in seeing Israelis doing so. I think Jews need to acknowledge their faults and foibles, and not to fall into the trap of self-denigration. To act like other humans under such circumstances is not to be subhuman. But you're going to be picked out for moral criticism if you've projected expectations that are somehow above those of other nations.

M.L. The notion of Jews as a chosen people is part of a religious system that requires Jews to act with a high level of morality toward each other and other people. I wish that every other people in the world would similarly see themselves as chosen. There's nothing in Jewish texts saying that God didn't make any deals with other peoples, or that only Jews were given the duty of moral responsibility.

As to us projecting expectations, I think there's a difference between Jews having a higher expectation of themselves, and others having it of Jews. If one is part of the theological community that accepts Torah, then one has a right to put special demands on oneself and one's own community that one would not put on others and that others outside the community who do not accept its theological assertions have no right to place upon us.

Non-Jews and assimilated Jews, two groups that do *not* accept the theological claims of Judaism, should not suddenly pick this one part of the theological discourse, privilege it, and tell us that suddenly on this issue of higher expectations they want to accept our language and hence judge us more harshly than they would judge others who are held to a lower standard. They should treat Jews the same as anyone else, and not impose on us a higher standard. It is inappropriate and anti-Semitic to put higher demands on the Jewish people than are put on other nations. Yet in the days when I was publicly opposing the Israeli occupation of Gaza and the West Bank, and organizing others to publicly condemn Yitzhak Shamir's government for its insensitivity to Palestinian needs, I was disturbed to find among many non-Jews and assimilated Jews that the level of outrage toward Israel was much higher than that toward many other attrocities going on in the world.

Jews have an obligation within our own community to live according to a higher standard, but if you think that that tradition doesn't bind you for anything else, because it's not your tradition or one that you believe in, then it seems to me to be wrong to invoke it only for the purpose of putting Jews down.

I find this equally troubling when it comes to assimilated Jews— Jews who feel no obligation, for example, to identify themselves as Jewish when they are doing positive political work on behalf of feminism or gay rights or peace or environmental concerns, and hence never ask others to give *credit to the Jewish people* for its disproportionate contribution to the transformative social change movements of our time. These assimilated Jews who only claim their Jewishness in order to invoke a "higher standard" to judge Israel than they judge others are, in my view, acting inappropriately, even though I agree with the substance of their criticisms of Israel myself. There is something deeply "off" in this pattern of claiming one's Jewishness only when Jewishness is something to be critiqued.

C.W. I know you say that as someone who was, during the Begin and Shamir years, himself identified as "public enemy no. 1" by parts of the Jewish establishment, precisely because of your outspoken criticism of the Occupation of the West Bank, and your role in organizing full-page ads to protest Israeli policy during the Intifada and again after the slaying of Palestinians in Hebron in 1994. Even today *Tikkun* magazine doesn't have any funding from the Jewish establishment or from many Jews who are liberal on other issues just because of the courageous stands you took on Israel—even though today those policies are the policies of the government of Israel. So what you say on this account is important to hear.

Still, I'm not sure that invoking a higher standard is only anti-

Semitism. It may be partly that and partly it's the reality that if you project yourselves as more enlightened and moral than other nations you are going to solicit attention. The myth of chosenness means that Jews and the world at large tend to judge Israel by a higher morality.

M.L. So if someone like Kahane were to come to power in Israel, publicly reject democratic norms and establish a theocratic society, people would say, "Now that the Jews are saying that they reject democratic norms and saying that they want to be just like Saudi Arabia, we won't judge them by a different standard."

C.W. It's not so easily dismantled. The moral expectation goes all the way back through the history of the Jews. The Israeli declaration at the founding of the State in 1948 sounded much like the United States. Even if, God forbid, some religious fundamentalist came to power, this would in no way downplay the expectations that people have. When Weizmann, Golda Meir, and so on put themselves forward as a model of democracy, they increased certain levels of expectation.

There's no doubt that Israel has been radically more democratic than most Third World nations. This does not excuse in any way the atrocities perpetrated on the Palestinians. It's like with America, which was more of a democracy than any other nation in the world but still perpetrated atrocities not just on Jews, Catholics, women, and workers, but especially Asians, American Indians, and Blacks.

M.L. It's part of the long history of anti-Semitism that anti-Semites have justified their hatred of Jews by demanding they be higher than others and then "discovering" that they aren't higher: which justifies their anger at Jews. We don't hear from Blacks in this country any agitation about the non-democratic nature of African states that is vaguely comparable to the amount that progressive American Jews agitate about the lack of democratic equality in Israel. Even though the level of democracy in Israel is higher than virtually every African state. Yet African-Americans make demands on Israel.

We have a genocidal slaughter of hundreds of thousands of people in Rwanda, and yet African-Americans have more to say about the undemocratic nature of Israel than they do about the oppression of

Blacks by Blacks in Africa. I don't see Jews going around saying that African states should be eliminated, or that they don't have a right to exist because they oppress minority groups—even though there's a long history of minority groups being oppressed in African states.

C.W. I don't think anyone should claim that the State of Israel should be eliminated.

We're just trying to contest some of the moral claims Zionists put forth in terms of it being somehow distinct due to having a Jewish, and therefore democratic, character. If Zionists were to claim their democratic operations were constrained, that they weren't a secular nation state, that would be an act of intellectual honesty. Just as some states—like Idi Amin's Uganda at the time—say right out that they aren't interested in democracy.

M.L. Is there any Black state that you know of that is trying to be democratic?

C.W. Ivory Coast and Senegal have relatively stable democracies. But then none of them claims to be such in the way that Israel does. Jamaica has been a democratic state for three decades. Needless to say, Mandela in South Africa looms large, too.

M.L. For over a decade I've favored working out an accommodation with the Palestinians, which gives them real rights, real self-determination, and real land. I've supported the creation of a demilitarized Palestinian state, and though I believe that Jews have a right to remain in the West Bank as long as they are willing to live peacefully and fully obey the laws of that Palestinian state, I've also called for the dismantling of those West Bank settlements that are clearly not willing to live in peace with their Palestinian neighbors.

But I want to build peace in a way that doesn't paint the story as a classic case of oppressor versus oppressed. It is a deeply complex reality in which the Jews jumped from the burning buildings of Europe and landed on the backs of Palestinians. We jumped because we had to. America's doors were closed to us starting in the 1920s, and we unintentionally hurt others when we landed. When we hear Christians referring to Jews as oppressors, it rings very hollow in our ears.

C.W.   Well, it shouldn't ring hollow in your ears. We know oppressed people have the capacity to oppress if they are in a position to do so. You can't invalidate the critique.

M.L.   I don't invalidate the critique: I invalidate the critic. These Christians haven't even dealt with their own history as oppressors. It would be different if I was hearing about Blacks going to church and learning about anti-Semitism, being upset about the history of Christianity, and then articulating it. Meanwhile a whole continent of Black folk are oppressing each other whilst Black folk in the U.S. don't give a damn—but they know about Jews and our shortcomings. This is wrong.

C.W.   But you know why they know about Jews. Because the press writes from the vantage point of America and its interests. The relationship between America and Israel is much more intimate than between America and any African nation. You don't get much information in the press about Africa. You can't expect Black folk not to focus on Israel when that's what the papers cover. The major issue Black people fear is white supremacy; and what scenario do you find? White Jewish Israeli society—we see very little of Jews of color and Sephardic Jews—with an anti-Arab mentality trading with South Africa: which takes you back to the U.S.A., that other hub of white supremacy in the world.

M.L.   The first thing I want to say about that is that Blacks should know better. You're telling me Black consciousness is shaped by the press. I don't know if you'd feel comfortable if I used the same argument to explain Jewish racism toward Blacks. Suppose they were racist because all Jews read about Blacks concerned crime and rapists. It would be an explanation for racism but not an excuse.

As for Black Jews—60 percent of the population in Israel are people of color. They are Sephardim from Northern Africa and Spain, Mizrahi (which means Eastern) from Arab countries like Yemen and Iraq. If these people were in this country you wouldn't call them white. Their culture isn't white; Europe doesn't mean a thing to them. They don't have the European history of equality and democracy. The fact is it's the Jews who come from Arab lands who are the most anti-

Arab. In terms of skin color, you can't tell the difference between most Palestinians and most Israelis. That's why they need those identification cards.

C.W.   Most of the elites in Israel aren't Sephardic Jews. Those are the Jews we see on television. When you see images of Jewish elites, they are "white" or light-skinned persons. When you look at images of the victims in the villages, you see dark-skinned persons. It could be that the images are wrong, but that's what's available.

Because of the Old Testament and because of a perception of Jewish unity and homogeneity they wished they could emulate, I think Black people have actually identified closely with Jewish history. But having identified with them, Black people now find it looks like these Jews are victimizing a darker-skinned people, the Palestinians.

M.L.   Black-American ignorance about Israel and about African nation states is not just a fact of nature: it reflects the failure of the Black leadership and of Black liberation struggles. Black progressives spend more time educating American Blacks about what's wrong with Israel than about what's wrong with African states.

C.W.   There are reasons for that. One is the blindness of the Black leadership. Another is that Israel, like South Africa, provides a parallel with what is happening here in the U.S. in terms of a light-skinned people victimizing a darker-skinned one. Your point about Sephardic Jews is not generally understood by American Blacks. It's not really hard to understand why Black people here identify with those in South Africa, or with Palestinians. Although the sheer turn-away from African barbarities is highly problematic, the attention to Israel is comprehensible.

M.L.   It would be comprehensible if American Jews spent all their energies focusing not on the Palestinians but on Idi Amin.

C.W.   Some do. *Commentary* magazine talks about African barbarism every other issue. Politically conservative American Jews focus on the barbarism of Third World nations all the time, often in cruel and vulgar ways, but touching on the truth in ways that to me are significant.

M.L. We who are pro-Zionist critics of Israel have been in the forefront of critiquing Israel when it has treated Palestinians poorly, and pressuring Israel with demands for a Palestinian state.

C.W. I have no argument with that. That's the reason why what I call "progressive Zionists" are still my comrades. We have so much common ground in our acknowledgment of Israel's need for security, the quest for Jewish identity, and the struggle for justice in Israel, Gaza, and the West Bank.

M.L. I can't say that progressive Blacks have been at the forefront of critiquing African states, even though they claim some relationship to them.

C.W. It's a very distant relationship. But you are right that there has been an unjustified silence, though Trans Africa has voiced criticism. I'm not sure that you yourself consider yourself on the cutting edge of critiques of African states.

M.L. I don't claim any special relationship to African states.

C.W. You don't need a special relationship. It's just a moral critique we make of any nation state that's mistreating its citizens.

M.L. I agree. But my special critical emphasis is on those places that I have special caring for. What troubles Jews is when Blacks seem to put this special emphasis on Israel, without a corresponding caring. It feels like you are acting in an unfair way.

CHAPTER 3

Cultural Identity
and Whiteness

*Jews are sometimes lumped together with other ethnic groups
from Europe and labeled "white." Yet the assumption that
Jews are white may itself be part of the tension between Jews
and Blacks, because labeling some group "white" may not be
an impartial descriptive judgment. But does the desire to
reject whiteness belie the reality of Jewish economic privilege
in the U.S.?*

C.W. The Jewish quest for identity presupposes a European
background, an experience that had been ugly and by the 1940s had
become incredible in terms of the depths of evil. This, and the huge
numbers of Jewish immigrants coming to the States between 1880 and
1920, made it trans-American in a fundamental way. In contrast, the
quest for Black identity has rarely been trans-American in a substantive sense. Yes, there has been a lot of rhetoric about Africa. But when
you look at the content and substance of it, even in the Garvey movement—the largest Black mass movement—it's very difficult to give
that trans-American identity any sort of concrete palpability. Afro-
Americans have been bogged down by their American experience in a
way that makes it hard to get beyond the borders in a substantive way.

When we look at some of the uglier stereotypes of Black people,
one of their more telling features is the absolute denial of the capacity
for critical intelligence. When we look at the stereotypes of Jewish
people, some might be concerned with aesthetics, but rarely is it a
denial of access to critical intelligence.

Why this is so has partly to do with the fact that Jewish people have been forced to sustain their sense of community by focusing on text, textual interpretation, and commentary. It's thus very difficult to float a myth about Jews as lacking critical intelligence—the history is too great. But when you look at Black people in the modern world, for whom access to literacy was forbidden, you begin to see the quest for Black identity as having a different sort of weight. Critical intelligence is one of the most desirable features in the modern world: it thus becomes fundamental to the Black quest for identity. Oftentimes, the Jewish quest for identity, crucial as it is, can take for granted an access to critical intelligence, since there has not been a systemic onslaught against it. So whilst both groups are seeking an identity, their very different histories give the quests different trajectories and weights.

The Jewish stress on critical intelligence puts a consequent emphasis on education as a requisite for success in the modern world. As Jews began to push back the anti-Semitic barriers, their preoccupation with the value of education enabled them to gain access to skills and therefore resources. This, again, differs from the Black quest for identity. There has been education for Black people—especially for the Black elite within Black colleges—and much of it has been due to American Jewish philanthropy, as well as evangelical Protestant church mission efforts to found and maintain Black colleges. But it is much harder to come to terms with the ugly racist assaults on Black people's capacity to attain skills, and acquire self-confidence. These assaults work in a deep way. And even when one gains that self-confidence, access to higher learning institutions has been difficult since the racist barriers against Black people have been much weightier than the anti-Semitic barriers against Jews. Of course after about 1968, we have another story: but up until then racist and anti-Semitic barriers were in place, albeit with different weights, different gravities.

M.L.   At Yale, for example, the Jewish quota was strongly in place until the 1960s.

C.W.   Until about 1953 Princeton only allowed a small, select number of Jews into each entering class. After that, numbers slowly increased. Princeton was even more anti-Semitic than Yale or Harvard, given its Southern influence. Yet Princeton did not admit its first Black student until the early 1940s. Around 1968, 1969, things began to explode with struggles for affirmative action. Given the premium on education within American Jewish subculture, Jewish women became significant beneficiaries of affirmative action. Once certain kinds of gates open up, those who are prepared to use the opportunities will benefit.

M.L. I want to say something about the role that education plays in Jewish self-understanding and in the conflict with Blacks. In a way, education in the ancient world became the realm in which Jewish machismo could get played out. Let me explain. The dominant culture of the ancient world was built around military power and sports. The Hellenistic society that had militarily conquered Judea tried to impose the gymnasium and the sports arena on Jewish society: if you like, its "friendly fascist" face. The unfriendly face was that of the Roman legions. This friendly form of oppression said that to be a real man was to be a warrior or at least a sportsman, someone who was into cultivating their body. Jews fought back by rejecting Hellenistic ideas about the body. This is one reason why circumcision became so important as an attachment to Jewish ritual. The Romans and Greeks were absolutely horrified that Jews would mutilate their bodies, when the highest value in their culture was the glorification of the body.

So where does a Jewish man become a man, if he can't compete on the same grounds as the dominant culture? The answer is, he does it by becoming a scholar, a reader of texts, or a scribe, someone who can act out his prowess in the realm of written words. Some of the Talmudic debates seem very silly, and it's hard to imagine why people put their energy into them: they are the product of a people for whom textual debate was the only realm in which they could excel without coming into conflict with the dominant society.

Jewish intellectuals invested their energies in building a system of laws designed for a society the Jews weren't living in. The Talmud recorded these ongoing debates that focused on planning for the time, if ever, when we got Judea back. This way no one could find what the Jews were doing subversive. Here was a safe realm in which some

Jewish men could succeed. After about two thousand years of practicing this kind of mind development—the creation of the fantasy world of the Talmud—the intellectual skills developed enabled Jews to be successful in the intellectual, cultural, and economic pursuits that are rewarded in the modern capitalist world.

Jews then asked, "Why don't Blacks just do the same thing? Isn't our success here basically a function of our own virtue?" I want to make two cautionary points here. Firstly, the textual choice was based on all other options being blocked for us. It's not clear that, given freedom from Roman oppression, we would have chosen education as our highest value. It was a reaction to our powerlessness.

Secondly, we were privileged in having communities that could create schools and generate this kind of internal, intellectual life. The degree of the systematic destruction of Black community through the experience of slavery really undermines the possibility of conveying a shared intellectual tradition. It is impossible to expect the Black world to have developed these kinds of intellectual skills as a way of dealing with its history of oppression. Consequently it makes it all the more unfair when Jews buy into the notion of meritocracy, the dominant ideology of capitalism, which says you can make it if you really try. It assumes that we're all entering into a competitive race at equal places at the starting gate. Jews enter, yes, with great disabilities, but with the advantage of having adopted a response to oppression that now gives us useful skills for competing in contemporary America.

C.W. It's also important to note the way in which Americans, and Afro-Americans in particular, lean toward a certain anti-intellectualism, and therefore ideas tend to be given a crude instrumental value. That's very different from what I see in the Jewish subculture, especially fifty or sixty years ago, when ideas were not simply linked to a crude instrumental use but had a life of their own in which one could revel.

But in addition to that there's also the history of educated Afro-American persons who, roughly between 1895 and 1950, as so-called "uppity Negroes," were often viewed as the most likely organizers of resistance and were therefore watched more closely. Many of these uppity Negroes were lynched as they tried to move in the direction of critique: so that in this period some Afro-Americans could not see much value in being highly educated and therefore more readily under the surveillance of the white supremacist powers-that-be. Under these Jim Crow segregated conditions one tended to be reticent about the real value of being an educated Negro, and this sent signals to the younger generation of Black folk, yet many persisted anyway. It amplified the anti-intellectualism already rampant in American culture.

M.L. It's extremely difficult for Jews to understand how Blacks could see us as oppressors given the overwhelming ways in which we have been oppressed. Often this situation is made worse by a Left that hasn't given adequate attention to or understanding of the dynamics of Jewish oppression.

C.W. One of the reasons for that is that the Left focuses on underdogs and has a certain conception of oppression. This makes it very difficult for Jews to acknowledge the degree to which, even whilst they are middle dogs and some top dogs, they are still linked to a history of oppression.

M.L. When the Left denies our actual oppression, it makes Jews feel all the more that no one understands us. So it's harder to delineate when the real oppression has ended and when we have ourselves become oppressors, because the Left thought we were oppressors when in fact we were being murdered.

C.W. This is a very important point for Blacks in the Black-Jewish dialogue. A comparable situation is the Middle East, on which some Blacks are pressuring American Jews to admit to some complicity in oppressing Palestinians in the Occupied Territories. Usually this is put in such a way as to push aside the larger circumstances. Jews say, "You're looking at this solely by focusing on the plight of people who, if they could, would drive us into the sea." It's because of this vulnerability that you, Michael, sometimes claim that Jews aren't really white. So to what degree do American Jews perceive themselves as white?

M.L. Whiteness is by and large a social construct, not a description of skin color. There are Blacks—admittedly not many—whose history of rape and so on means they look white and can "pass." Similarly there are many Jews whose skin color is more Arabic than European. To be "white" is to fit into the social construct of the beneficiaries of European imperialism, whose relationship to the world has been one of conquest. Far from being such beneficiaries, Jews have been the primary "Other," have been socially and legally discriminated against, have been the subject of racism and genocide, and in those terms Jews are not white.

Many Black activists understand this at one level, and that is why they often go out of their way to include Arabs in the category of non-whites, because they want to identify with the history of Arab oppression under the thumbs of Western imperialism. Yet Arabs come from the same racial stock of Semites as Jews. So the category is about something else besides skin color—it's about one's relationship to oppression. And by calling Jews "white," Blacks are in effect denying our history of oppression.

C.W. My question then becomes, how do you account for my thesis that Jews have been beneficiaries of white skin privilege? I can accept your analysis about the European construct of whiteness and Christianity over and against Jews, but by the time you get to America the situation is quite different. Even amidst anti-Semitism, the anti-Black situation confers white-skin privilege on Jews.

M.L. The white-skin privilege here is the privilege to renounce one's Judaism. By and large the way to get into this system is to take off your *kippah,* cut off your beard, hide your fringes; in other words, to reject your entire cultural and religious humanity. In that sense, Jews could have given up their Judaism in the Roman world and then we would have had Roman privilege. Or we could have fallen in with European Christendom and developed exactly the same genetic makeup, and we would have been doing better. Conversely, you get an interesting experience when you try resuming all the external markings of Jewishness. I remember an incident in Berkeley in 1982 when I decided to start wearing my *kippah.* I wanted to see what it would be like to be "out" as a Jew. About three days after this decision I was walking down the street and somebody ten feet ahead of me says, "Take the cap off, kike!" in a really hostile, angry voice.

Jews have worn distinctive garb throughout most of our history. The Bible requires us to wear fringes on the corners of our garments —they're called *tzitzit*—as a reminder of the commandments. You knew someone was a Jew not only by what he looked like but by what he was wearing. Yet once Jews got to the U.S., or within at most two generations, Jews had shed all their distinctive garments. To go out into the world was not obviously to go out into the world as a Jew. The inner dialogue amongst Jews is about whether or not this ability to pass is indeed true. Are we rather always going to be seen as Jews, and hence endangered? Once again we have to remember the experience of the so-called assimilated German Jew.

C.W. This renunciation of religious identity is a possibility for Jews, but not for Blacks.

M.L. If, fifty years from now, it becomes possible through genetic engineering to change your hair and skin so that black families can produce white babies, I don't know that you're going to feel you have white-skin privilege. It's a narrow conception of benefits: one that confers material rewards but does not acknowledge the cost of the psychic trade-off. It's not only the anxiety that goes with the renunciation of identity: it's also a denial of self-worth.

C.W. You have to have them both. You get the anxieties when you get access to material means in the richest country in the history of the world. The psychic pain for Jews is real; yet the material deprivation and psychic pain for Blacks are hellish.

M.L. But I don't hear anyone on the Left acknowledging what the psychological costs are for Jews in becoming American.

C.W. That is true. All I'm saying is that you have a choice people of color don't have.

M.L. I know that. I just want to point out that the cost of hiding one's identity has been a terrific psychic trauma. The only reason Jews don't talk about it more is that they already felt their religion had been distorted in a world of oppression. The pain of Jewish identity, from the Spanish expulsion of 1492, through the 1648 massacres and up to the Holocaust, has been so excruciating that Jews have sought to get rid of their own Jewishness. It was an opportunity to run away from a Jewishness tied to oppression, murder, rape, and destruction. If Blacks could have run away from slavery by hiding their identity, you might have chosen that too.

C.W. I still have to say that the choice to gain access to material prosperity, even at the cost of escaping from one's own identity, was a choice the white supremacist country with its caste system would never make available to Black folk.

M.L. It wasn't a simple choice in the way you are describing it. It had to be struggled for and won in a fight in which there were very severe anti-Semitic elements.

C.W. But it was made available. And any Jew could choose to move into the mainstream at any time because of the white supremacist construct. Isn't that right?

M.L. It's true to the extent that the more one appeared not to be Jewish, the greater one's options. Just as to the extent one appeared less Black, with lighter skin color, one had greater options. I'm not denying that it's harder for a Black to pass than a Jew.

But I'd like to take another angle on this question. There are many ways to come up with a description of reality, and "white" may be one of them. It helps the poor and downtrodden in the white community to feel they still have benefits that are greater than this other group. It takes their attention away from their own misery and social and psychological oppression.

Thirty percent or more of the Black population is middle class, doing considerably better than these white folk in economic terms, living in states with no legal restrictions against Blacks and not suffering much discrimination. Yet the construction of "whiteness" as a way by which people are encouraged to process their experience leads many economically oppressed people—even those on welfare or a minimum wage—to feel in a superior position to Blacks who provide them with someone to look down on. Meanwhile, "whiteness" helps the various supposedly white groups to forget their own history of oppression that led many of them to these shores in the first place, and gives them a way of thinking that makes them feel solidarity with ruling elites who benefited from the exploitation of their parents or grandparents. So the social construction of reality which emphasizes whiteness is of particular service to the established order, and we need to construct a different reality.

C.W. We don't want to lose touch with the reality that today whiteness confers privilege in a way Blackness does not, even in these days of affirmative action.

M.L. We don't want to lose touch with what the reality has been. But we also don't want to reapply the past into the present so as to make impossible the transformation of the past into the future. It's a subtle tightrope to walk. This is the difference between a descriptive sociology and a transformative sociology. In my view, a transformative sociology is one that cuts up reality in a way that helps us see the potential that exists in the present as we move toward our shared liberated goals. White-skin privilege is a category that undermines social change, because it emphasizes what the majority of people have in common with the white ruling class. It deemphasizes liberatory potential and emphasizes instead the way all white people "benefit" from oppression of Blacks.

But these "benefits" are largely illusory, because they tie people to a social order which actually brings them a great deal of alienation, loneliness, non-recognition, breakdown of community, and psychic pain. And, of course, in the case of Jews, we are not "white" in the eyes of many American hate groups that preach white supremacy.

C.W. White-skin privilege is also used to blind people from seeing what they have in common with others.

M.L. I don't deny that. It's a question of where your primary focus is. You, Cornel, have been for years a national leader of the Democratic Socialists of America. What I keep coming back to over and over again is that the message coming from the social change movement for the last thirty years discourages people from being a part. Often they unintentionally convey the message to the very people that they say they want to organize or reach that, "You people are really bad people and your only hope for salvation is to renounce who you are or feel bad about who you are." It tells them how much privilege they have, how they are just like the ruling class. And this, because of something about the color of their skin, something they can't possibly change! "Sure, you are oppressed, but you are not the *most* oppressed, and don't you forget that." The message that gets communicated to most Americans is: "Your problems aren't worth a tinker's dam, because it's only psychic pain that you experience, and you are doing so much better than Blacks or Third World peoples."

C.W. You can convince white folk that you are concerned about their pain and their anxieties. You can talk about why it is so difficult for them to see what they have in common with the oppressed. You can speak about white privilege. But the feeling from the Black world is that you will downplay it. You'll admit it's there, but you'll avoid putting it in their face.

M.L. I do believe that white-skin privilege is a category that the ruling class in this country benefits from disproportionately. Perhaps another example will show why I think this category is destructive. I'd like to put forward another similarly destructive category—namely, imperial privilege. Imagine if I began to talk about an American imperial privilege that is just as significant economically as white-skin privilege. A Black person, I could argue, living on welfare in a ghetto in the United States has social resources available to them that puts them at a higher material level than a large segment of people living in the Third World. Those material resources, this argument would suggest, derive from the U.S. having been part of a larger colonialist imperial system that has set up the exploitation of Third World peoples, maintains it now through the supposedly impartial workings of an international economic system and the machinations of the International Monetary Fund, and materially benefits from it. So every time a Black person points to inequalities here, if I were to follow this path, I could point out that s/he has been benefiting from an imperial system.

C.W. Only in relation to Third World countries, not in comparison to American whites.

M.L. And it's the same thing with Jews. Jews are not overwhelmingly members of the ruling class in this society. They have benefited more than Blacks, but by and large they are not controlling the corporations.

C.W. They do much more than the majority of the society.

M.L. Alright. But the facts are that Blacks, even in the ghetto, have benefited much more here than people in China or India, most of whom are living at a far poorer material level. The question is, how to construe those facts. Highlighting certain kinds of privilege tends to make those who are told that they have these "privileges" feel that their own struggles are less legitimate, and that they are being self-indulgent if they focus on the forms of pain that they *do* experience as a result of being part of the contemporary capitalist society, like alienation or psychological, spiritual, and ethical frustrations, which I call the deprivation of meaning. You are implicitly saying, "You people are white, whites are privileged, you are privileged, so don't tell me about your pain, because you have so much privilege already that the only moral thing you can do is focus on somebody else's pain." It's like saying to Blacks, "You may be wanting a higher cut, but we can't deal with that right now because we have more pressing issues. Thirty million kids in the world are starving to death each year. So don't tell me about your situation as Blacks because you have American imperial privilege and your demand for a restructuring of this society involves shutting your eyes to the pain of people who are a whole lot worse off than you." Politically, what that implicitly does is to undermine the ability of people to struggle.

C.W. I don't see how that follows at all. If you were to tell any relatively impoverished group in the United States that their situation is still so much better off than someone in India or China, it doesn't follow that you undermine the legitimacy of the struggle. It does relativize it in terms of acknowledging their participation in a larger global system.

M.L. You're telling me that intellectually it doesn't require that conclusion. And I'm telling you that psychologically and politically it creates that conclusion. By highlighting how much better the American situation is than others', you undermine the ability of people to feel like it's worth struggling, to take risks in their life. That's why ruling elites teach Americans the mantra that Americans are better off than everybody else in the world.

C.W. But that works only if you believe that legitimate progressive struggles ought to focus solely or primarily on those who are absolutely the worst off. If you begin with that premise it will paralyze you.

M.L. I'm saying that this is what *has* been happening in the social change movements of the past thirty years where the emphasis has been on "who is most oppressed?" It's just the same as in this conversation when you keep saying, "You Jews have more options" and so on. I'm saying this is a variant of the "You guys are better off than us" line, which psychologically depoliticizes that group.

C.W. Wait a moment. The argument is not motivated by the claim that Black people are the worst off and demand sole attention. If we want to talk worst off, we should be talking about indigenous people. Very few Black folk would fail to acknowledge that indigenous people get a worse deal than them. But the point is that we must keep track of the facts and the way certain kinds of privilege operate. So when you talk about American imperial privilege, I think you are absolutely right. But just pointing out the facts of American imperial privilege, white privilege, male and heterosexual privilege in no way undermines the legitimacy of the struggle against white supremacy, male supremacy, class inequality, and homophobia.

M.L. You keep coming back to the fact that there isn't necessarily an intellectual counterposition. Whereas what I'm saying is that from the standpoint of my experiences in the Movement, the dominant dynamic has been a victimology in which issues get shaped around the question of who is most oppressed. People are constantly trumping each other over this both in individual arguments and in terms of framing what it is we should be working on together. In fact, many of the struggles around identity politics revolve around the dynamics of claims to oppression. The result has been to push away many people who feel inadequate to press their claim to being most oppressed.

Comparative victimology becomes the coin of the realm.

Either we must reshape politics so that this is not so important; or we must expand our notions of oppression to include the spiritually, ethically, and psychologically debilitating consequences of the competitive market. Then more and more people will see how there are various ways of being oppressed and that they are equally valid, politically and psychologically.

C.W. The kind of victimology that you are talking about is certainly destructive and prevents the kind of alliances that you and I want. And we know that the conservatives see this as a real gold mine because that's all they see in the Left. In the form you describe it, you are absolutely right. We have to struggle against it. That's one of the reasons why I stress the moral character of our commitment as much as our experiences. You want to include other rubrics of oppression than just material oppression, from which we can embrace peoples not normally considered oppressed. But we can't overlook that alongside the victimology game there are still certain facts. They don't allow one to infer that the most oppressed should play one-upmanship against the less oppressed. But they do exist in terms of different kinds of privilege, different kinds of power, both psychic and material.

M.L. The meaning of the facts is not in the facts. The meaning is value-driven. Inequalities of income can be seen as very important, somewhat important, or unimportant, depending on a larger claim of meaning about what the relative importance of income is to a good life.

C.W. Every attempt to invoke facts is driven by a value-laden framework that discerns the weight those facts have. You are talking about psychic facts.

M.L. Exactly. I'm trying to tell you that in the Jewish community where the Right is continually focusing on the murder of Jews this century and arguing from that value-framework—the framework of who is most likely to be wiped out—that Jews have a better case than Blacks for claiming they are most at risk. Whilst I recognize their argument, and understand that it has an internal logic (more Jews have been killed than Blacks in the twentieth century), I also see it as a construct of facts that makes it less likely that we will build a social change movement that can accomplish my goals—namely, to heal, repair, and transform the world. By emphasizing victimology, people are distanced from what needs to be highlighted in political consciousness: that they are *also* being oppressed by the same social system that oppresses others who might be potential allies.

C.W. I think the Jewish Right has an important point that, given past and recent history, the possibility of Jews being attacked is as high or higher than any other group. We're talking about perennial vulnerability.

Now, there's been no systematic genocidal attack on Afro-American people, though the number of Africans murdered by imperial power in the twentieth century is staggering! What there has been is a caste—like subordination of Afro-Americans, the legacy of which is still operative, even though there have been breakthroughs in the last twenty years. These are two very different issues.

M.L. I understand that. A full descriptive sociology should include these differences, just as it should include the American imperial privilege that every Black has in comparison with a Third Worlder, or that middle-class Blacks have in comparison with those poorer than them. Any serious political movement must acknowledge these differences.

C.W. So we agree.

M.L. No. It's not just an abstract intellectual question of what should be acknowledged. It's a question of what the experiential culture created by that movement feels like to the people it is attempting to recruit.

To most people it feels like the Left is putting them down. By focusing on their relative privilege and ignoring their own oppression by the social system, it has driven away millions of people who came into the Left at the height of the anti-war movement. If the Left is continually making people feel bad about themselves, they will clearly want no more to do with it. And that's what has actually happened in the past twenty-five years.

C.W. This is where our fundamental disagreement lies. I myself come out of the American Left which at its best was not pointing at white folks to make them feel bad, but trying rather to cast the freedom struggle on a level that didn't only acknowledge the facts but made a moral appeal. So the Left you are talking about is not my Left, even though it is a Left that has played a disproportionate role in the last twenty-five years or so.

But I have to say again that if you want to bring people into the Left without acknowledging white-skin privilege for fear of driving them away, there will never be a Left. The Left must provide meaning to those facts in such a way that the beneficiaries of privilege recognize their role but are not solely defined by it.

M.L. Absolutely. I've been arguing for the Left to add another category of oppression, namely anti-Semitism, so that people coming in can learn about Jewish oppression just as they learned about anti-Black racism.

But I do agree that anti-Black racism cannot be pushed aside. Otherwise we face the problem of the populist movement in the early twentieth century, in which racism continued to abound despite its appearing to put itself forward in the interests of the American majority. But there's something else the Left is lacking; the ability to help those people who have seen themselves as relatively privileged to become conscious of the ways in which the existing social system oppresses them also.

Right now there is almost no awareness on the Left that the psychological, spiritual, and alienation pain of either whites or the middle class—you can construe it either racially or economically—need to be spoken to, their problems addressed, their pains validated, or that they should be involved in the liberal and progressive movements. These movements need to undergo a transformation.

What I've tried to do in developing a Politics of Meaning is to suggest ways this transformation might occur. People experience pain in having no control over shaping what they do all day, problems in sustaining loving relationships, frustration at being part of a society governed solely by materialism. By focusing on these impacts on their lives, such a politics can make people conscious that the same system that has destructive consequences for the Third World and the most economically oppressed has destructive consequences for other segments of the population.

C.W.   You're talking about a kind of cultural politics.

M.L.   Right. And it's not one that downplays racism or anti-Semitism. People need to understand how these are destructive to their interests as well: how in order to have more fulfilling lives they need to be in relation to these other struggles that they previously perceived as someone else's problem. Yet this consciousness has almost no role on the Left. If you raise that question, you are almost labeled a racist or anti-Semite for deflecting attention from the levels of oppression being dealt with. Whereas I'm saying, "I don't want to deflect attention from your levels of pain. I want to change your levels of pain." To do that I need to have an alliance with these other people. Otherwise we will have a Left just composed of the most oppressed, who can't provide healing for that pain.

C.W.   We know the kind of politics you are describing has been used by the Right. Do you know of any historical examples where it has been enacted in a progressive way?

M.L.   The clearest example I can point to is the disproportionate involvement of Jews in the Civil Rights movement. Jews have identified with Black pain more than any other sector of this society, even though they have not suffered the most oppression here or exploitation from imperialism on a world scale. Why is this? Because Jews' cultural politics, our construal of our own history, has highlighted non-economic and political rights factors, an obligation to other peoples, so as to lead us to identify with the oppression of others.

C.W.   But how long will this last among American Jewry in the prosperous suburbs? A great fear in Black America is that Jews will become simply the "typical white Americans" with an indescribable Holocaust in the past used to preclude criticism of their complicity to privilege and power in America. When you look at issues of police brutality over the last fifteen years in Black America, you'll see more Chicanos demonstrating than Jews. I'm not saying that most Jews aren't against police brutality. But for Chicanos, these are issues that they themselves have directly experienced.

M.L. That's just my point. In order to build the kind of alliance we need to change the situation of the oppressed, we need to bring into the Movement people who don't share the same kinds of oppression. Otherwise you'll never have the political clout to end police brutality, because it will remain a concern of a minority of Americans.

I'm not saying that we should deny the actual differences that exist in our economic circumstances, but rather I'm asking, "Where should we place the emphasis?" And *that* question does not ask for "an objective account of reality," because reality is multilayered and complex and would take an eternity to adequately describe—but rather, it is a question that asks, "By what principle should we decide what aspects of reality to give our primary focus?" To which my answer is "those aspects most conducive to empowering us to heal, repair, and transform the world in ways that will maximize our ethical and spiritual and liberatory capacities." When you cut up the world that way, introduce categories using that as the criterion for which categories to emphasize, then you immediately see why "whiteness" itself is a problematic category, and why, at the very least, liberals and progressives should insist that Jews are not white.

Today there are well-financed groups who are attempting to move the Jewish world even further to the Right. Elliot Abrams, the son-in-law of Norman Podhoretz and Reagan's Assistant Secretary of State for Central American Affairs, who left government after having been implicated in the dishonesty surrounding the arming of the Contras, has joined with many other Jewish neocons to champion conservative politics inside the Jewish world. They bought an ad on the op-ed page of the *New York Times* in December 1994, in which they congratulated Newt Gingrich and argued that traditional Jewish values favor conservatism (a claim frequently refuted in *Tikkun* and more systematically disputed in my book *Jewish Renewal*). The triumph of conservatism that these neocons are attempting to facilitate will further polarize the society, give greater credence to fascistic and anti-Semitic forces that have always found their primary base of support within the Right and its anti-immigrant, racist, and xenophobic nationalist proclivities. By the time these right-wing Jews realize what they've wrought, America may be plunged into a resurgence of hatred and reaction far more pernicious than anything we've experienced since the thirties. Although they represent only a small percentage of American Jews, their impact is magnified because they represent the worldview of the richest Jews, they can fund their magazines and political organizations, their circles have disproportionate access to the most influential media, and they are overly represented among orthodox Jews and Jews in positions of leadership in the organized Jewish community.

The power of these neocons is increased the more that Jews tend to think of themselves and their interests as indistinguishable from that of the majority of American middle-class, suburban whites. Those on the Left and those in the African-American world who insist that Jews think of themselves as white are the best allies of these neocon Jews, who want the same thing. We who want to fight the Right want Jews to think of themselves as Jews, with an historic mission of *tikkun olam,* of healing and transforming a world in pain because of its alienation from God and from the God within every human being. To the extent that we positively affirm that Jewish task and Jewish destiny, it will be hard for us to identify with the ethos of selfishness that has become so central to the meaning of being white in contemporary discourse. For similar reasons, we have reasons to want many other groups to disidentify with "whiteness" and to develop an identity based on their relationship to their own highest sense of purpose for their communities.

CHAPTER 4

The Civil Rights Movement

If we wish to start a process of healing and repair between Blacks and Jews, we are going to have to come to grips with the fallout from the ending of the Black-Jewish relationship during the Civil Rights movement of the fifties and sixties.

M.L. I've heard some radical Blacks deny that there ever really was an alliance between Blacks and Jews. From your standpoint, Cornel, was there a Black-Jewish alliance in the Civil Rights movement? And if so, what happened to it?

C.W. I think there was definitely an alliance, but we have to first define what we mean by an alliance. By an alliance, we mean a coming together for a particular cause. There is no doubt that there was significant coming together of liberal and progressive Jews and liberal and progressive Black folks, to push for legislation regarding civil rights, voting rights, and later, housing rights. The question is: what was the nature of their alliance?

M.L. Why are we asking this question?

C.W. We're asking the question because, as the tension and friction between Blacks and Jews in this country has escalated in the last ten years or so, that alliance has been unraveling.

M.L. So you find people saying they wished they had that alliance back, and others saying it didn't really exist. What do you think the reality was?

C.W.   We had a significant coming together, based on a number of different things. First of all, you had a social movement which began in the belly of an apartheid South: King, Dixon, Rosa Parks, and others.

As it began to manifest itself, it began to solicit attention from a number of persons outside the South. And early on, some prominent Jewish intellectuals and activists got involved. These were the rumblings and stirrings of what would result in this alliance that we're talking about, and many were Jewish. Cynics would say that those who became involved were those whose motivation was simply self-interest.

M.L.   What do you mean "cynics"? Who are these cynics?

C.W.   Some Black Nationalists, though by no means all of them. Supporting the Movement is being seen as a matter of self-interest, because maybe focusing on the xenophobes in the South is a safeguard against those persons focusing xenophobia against us.

M.L.   The self-interest is supposedly, "If we don't stop it, it will affect us also." So it's in the self-interest of the Jews, because if Blacks are oppressed then Jews, too, will be oppressed.

C.W.   The cynics argue that white folk in the South are also anti-Semitic. In which case Blacks and Jews have a common enemy, who just happens to be focusing on Black folk.

M.L.   And therefore Jews don't deserve any of the credit for being a part of the real alliance?

C.W.   But this cynical view is basically wrong. Self-interest was involved, but much more was operative here. I think that it's a matter of trying to look at how American Jews were trying to come to terms with their heritage at a particular moment in industrial America. That heritage is one that puts a premium on the moral ideals of justice and freedom, especially as it affects the underdog. The struggle for Jewish self-understanding did result in a profound empathy with the American underdog in this particular moment of American history.

That prophetic element within Jewish tradition that always said no to injustice, no to hypocrisy, that saw the gap between the ideals and practices of a nation, and then acted on it, actually did achieve something. This is an element we cannot overlook. We talk about the disproportionate number of Jews who supported that movement financially, personally, bodily; giving money, giving time, giving energy, giving life.

I don't think that the Civil Rights movement was some grand Golden Age because of course you always have some tension and friction between human beings. But certainly it was an age in which there was a significant coming together for a moral cause, a political cause.

M.L. I agree, and think that ought to be celebrated. But if that's true, how do you explain how it could be possible for so many Blacks today not to understand the moral significance and importance of this alliance and of the willingness of many Jews to become involved in this Movement?

C.W. I don't know that they don't. Most Black folk are not persuaded by the particular cynicism of certain Black Nationalists. Part of the problem, and it's true for most Americans, is that history means so very little in America.

M.L. Here you have a very interesting convergence between the neoconservative *Commentary* crowd and their reading of history, and the Black Nationalist crowd. The *Commentary* crowd would also like to reduce the moral meaning of the Civil Rights movement to a moment of rational self-interest so that it can proceed to say that it is now, in the 1990s, no longer in Jewish self-interest to be involved in alliance with African-Americans. The calculation has to be made in pure self-interest terms, because "that's all there is" according to all of those who have let the crude mechanisms of the competitive market shape their thinking about how to conduct our public and private lives.

In fact, once this way of thinking is established, the neoconservatives can ridicule the liberalism of the Jewish people as an anachronistic hold-over from an earlier historical period, since it can no longer be shown to be in the narrow economic self-interest of most Jews. Their lament was summed up by one neocon article analyzing liberals' continuing commitment to liberal political candidates in the 1980s this way: "Jews earn like Episcopalians, but vote like Puerto Ricans." That is to say, if Jews were to vote their economic interests in the narrowest sense, they'd be against liberal candidates who support programs that call for taxes that will take some of their money and redistribute it to the poor. While most other ethnic groups deriving from European ancestry tend to vote along these more narrow self-interest lines, Jews have not.

What infuriates the neocons and what confounds all the theorists of narrow self-interest is that Jews seem to have our behavior determined not only by self-interest, but also, as a kind of independent, and sometimes decisive, variable, by Jewish historical consciousness and by the values that derive from the Torah tradition, with its powerful moral injunctions and insistence on recognizing the needs of the poor. This reality is hard to understand for anybody whose ontology of the world says that people can only be motivated by self-interest. Because the Torah tradition says that you have to be morally sensitive to the needs of others, even if it's not in your self-interest. There's nothing in there that says, "Look, if it's in your interest, love your neighbors, but if it's not in your interest, screw 'em." It's just not what's in the Torah.

Jewish neocons, then, have to reject a Torah perspective, even if some of them dress themselves in religious garb, observe all the ritual commands, and position themselves as "more religious" than the Jewish liberals. At the core, these people *refuse* to take Torah seriously, and instead in their actual lives in the economic world and in the politics they support they identify with the crudest "reality"-oriented way of dealing, deriving their ethics and politics not from the spirit of Torah but from the spirit of the cutthroat world of competitive market economics.

In my view, Jewish neocons became obsessed with "reality" and its imagined injunction to "look out for no. 1" *not* because of the Holocaust as much as because of their desire to fit in to the selfishness-oriented dynamics of American society and to get their share of the emotional and material rewards that "making it" (in the tragically self-revealing and his-generation-revealing title of Norman Podhoretz's autobiography) could offer.

This self-interest philosophy, so fitting to the Reagan/Bush years, ironically became the underpinnings, in an inverted way, of the multiculturalists who proposed a new moral relativism based on the notion that any form of universalism was necessarily oppressive and a "hegemonizing discourse" aimed at cultural domination. Every discourse was motivated only by the interests of those putting it forward, and each cultural community had incommensurable discourse with that of other communities, and hence could not be subject to some universal standards.

Though this approach seemed radical, because it challenged the dominant elite of white Anglo-Saxon Protestant men who ran the society, it ironically had a demobilizing and politically enervating consequence. Jewish neocons could fully endorse this way of thinking, and then say, usually more implicitly than explicitly, something like this: "Fine, we have incommensurable discourses. We like to spend our money on our suburban homes or fancy East Side of New York City apartments, and to have a well-to-do lifestyle focused on satisfying our own needs, and the needs of fellow Jews. You people in the ghetto have a different discourse that says you think people should take care of the poor. We recognize your right to your discourse, and we hope you will recognize our right to our discourse. We understand that your discourse is motivated by self-interest, just like ours is—because that's all there is. And the Black nationalists amongst you are right—because they understand that that is all there is. So call us when you poor people or oppressed communities have something to offer us, and then we will see how much it's in *our* interests, and then we can talk about deals and alliances. Till then, buzz off, or we will call the police, and the only legislation we want to pass, [bravo, Clinton], is that which builds more prisons and puts more policemen on the street so that those who have some resentments about our lifestyle will be prevented from acting it out against anybody but themselves." Nobody actually says this, of course, but I'm trying to unpack in simple terms the logic of their position.

From the neocon standpoint, Jewish liberals are soft and mushy-headed for talking about wanting to build an alliance or engage in political activity not based solely on self-interest but based on concern about eliminating oppression. Liberals are implicitly saying, "It may turn out that there's nothing in it for us to fight oppression, other than whatever satisfaction we get in living a moral and Torah-based life. Nevertheless we have an obligation to do so."

For the neocons, this is the kind of naive thinking that gets us dragged back to Auschwitz. Caring for the other makes nice religious sentiment, but it has no application in the real world. Whereas for those of us who are trying to build a Jewish renewal in the Jewish world, a renewal that reclaims the deep spiritual/political integration that was once central to Judaism, the whole point of God's message is to *not* accept the real world, but to transform it. That's what *tikkun* means—to heal, repair, and transform the world. From the standpoint of the Jewish renewal sought by *Tikkun* magazine, the task of the Jewish people is to proclaim to the world the possibility of this kind of transformation, and to be witnesses to the God of the universe that makes for the possibility of this transformation. That's what it means to believe in God, and so the "realists" and cynics—in the Jewish world, among those Blacks who reduce everything to self-interest, and of course in the dominant culture of American society—are all idolators at the deepest and most profound level.

C.W. You have to admit that the Jewish neocons and the Black nationalists do have a point. Self-interest or group-interest is an inescapable, unavoidable element in one's calculations. It is an element because, given the fact that we live in a world in which cynicism is the dominant ethos, those who appeal to conscience, morality, and sensitivity as a major element in human motivation can be easily cast as naive. Where you and I agree is that self-interest is not the sole element.

M.L. Exactly.

C.W. The question then becomes, how do we balance the inescapable reality of self-interest with some moral vision, some self-critique, and a critique of the status quo? That's what's so very difficult to do in this cynical moment.

M.L. All the more reason why we should honor those who acted from a real moral commitment when they became involved in the Civil Rights movement, and why it's important to recognize that the majority of those who Blacks identified as "whites" in this movement were actually Jews.

The young Jews in SNCC or CORE started going down to the South and risking their lives in an alliance with Blacks. These young Jews were frequently those people who had critiqued the conservatism of the Jewish community. Conservatives often denigrated these liberal Jews as "being universalists who care only about the needs of everyone else, but don't really care about the needs of your own Jewish community." Many of the Jews who went South or who became Movement activists felt that they had to break with the existing Jewish community, though some were inspired by people like Abraham Joshua Heschel and Joachim Prinz and other Jewish leaders who insisted that their involvement in the Movement flowed directly from their Jewishness.

What conservatives said to these principled and dedicated liberals was something like this: "You people will learn exactly what a previous generation of idealists in Europe who trusted in the good intentions of the German and East European working classes learned—that when push comes to shove, all these other people whom you think you are helping will have nothing but contempt for you. They will spit in your faces."

The tragedy is that that's exactly what happened to many of these activists. After years of self-sacrifice, SNCC in particular and Black militants in general turned on their erstwhile allies and told them to get out of the Movement, accused them of attempting to dominate and manipulate Black organizations, and acted as though all they had offered was worthless. This had a powerfully debilitating impact on Jewish liberalism and universalism that gave tremendous credibility and power to the Jewish neocons. The very Jewish liberals who had been critiquing the Jewish community for not doing enough to support Black causes are now being devastated by the Black movement, which is telling them to get the hell out of there.

C.W. Let's be fair. Black Power advocates were saying that whites could best fight white supremacy at this particular stage in the struggle by going into the white community. That was the form of the proposed alliance. Now, you see that that project doesn't occur for the most part. The whites really wanted to get closer to the Black folk to fight white supremacy. Why not go back to fight white supremacy in the white community or Jewish community? It was less fun, more lonely.

M.L.   I wouldn't deny that that's a part of the dynamic, although another part is that the Jews who are the majority of these organizations don't think of themselves as white. These are college students or people who are in their early twenties. They don't self-consciously think of themselves as Jews, and some of them have even done everything they could to distance themselves from the materialism and conservatism of the suburban Jewish communities in which they had been raised, but nevertheless they have imbibed a Torah tradition, as well as some of the problems of Jewish identity as a vanguard and as separate. So when Blacks turn to these secular Jews who are activists and say, "Go back to the white community," they are at a loss because they do not feel that they have more in common with the WASPs down in, say, Castro Valley or Simi Valley or Glencoe or South Boston or Westchester than they have with the Blacks in the city. "What are you talking about? That's not my community."

C.W.   But a lot of them grew up in the white suburbs. They were going to elite universities like Harvard, Yale, and Columbia.

M.L.   But in that context they formed a subculture that was Jewish in everything but name and official tradition. It was Jewish by being committed to civil rights and by being universalist. That's what being culturally Jewish was: to be moral and universalistic in your approach. Then they're being told by Blacks to get particularistic. To which their response is, "But I don't want to be in the Jewish world; that's why I'm a secular Jew. I should be a particularistic *white?* What are you talking about? I don't have any connection with these white people. I don't know where to go now because you've thrown me away from the one place that seemed to be my community: namely, one struggling for a universalistic, moral goal. That was my community and you Black people are now telling me it is yours alone because right now you are the real victims of oppression."

C.W. In a way that makes Malcolm's point. Namely, that if it's that difficult organizing against white supremacy in the white community, then what kind of alliance are we talking about?

In any event, I'm not convinced that what you are pointing to were the fundamental factors that account for Jewish conservativism. Without the perception of Black betrayal, do you think Jewish liberalism would have remained stronger?

M.L. If Blacks had treated Jews who had been in the center of that movement in a really respectful way, it would have helped. If SNCC had said in 1966, "We want to thank the Jewish communities of this country for what they've done for us *and* tell them why we now need to go in a separate direction. But we realize we got more from this community than from virtually any other ethnic community in America."

C.W. But that was done though, Michael. It was done by leading Civil Rights peace spokespersons. Every time they spoke at major events they made sure the Jewish community was represented.

M.L. But these Jews were people who had shared the same risks on the battle lines. They had gone to these communities and some of them had been killed—

C.W. Now you can't say they shared the same risks. When you look at those students who came from the North—Jews, whites, and Blacks—they stayed for three months. The Black activists and the Southern white activists were there all year, right? So you can't say they shared the same risks. Freedom summers are one thing, but to be down there every day year after year is another.

M.L. The distinguishing factor between those who were treated right and those who weren't was not how long they stayed or what risks they were taking. What distinguished them was the color of their skin. If they were white they were being kicked out.

I always had the feeling that for Jews this alliance was a really big deal, and the disillusionment was a lot more important, too. Whereas for Blacks—except for a handful of Black nationalists now who like to beat up on Jews, so they deny there ever was an alliance—this alliance was never anything that really got into their consciousness in the first place. So they don't feel the absence of it, and they don't feel betrayed by Jews for having abandoned it. For them, Jews are just a species of whites, so they're unimportant. Am I right?

C.W. There's a certain element of that. Black folk didn't come into a movement so they could be congratulated, or to keep alive their connection with their heritage, or to soothe their agonized conscience. Black folk in the South faced terrorism and looked for allies. When allies came, they didn't say, "Here are the whites, here are the Jews, and here are the gentiles." They said, "Here's some folk in America who give a damn about people who have been mistreated for ten generations."

And among those whites who came South, some seemed to feel as though they knew more, or knew all. The paternalism was tangible. You see it depicted in *Meridian* by Alice Walker and in other texts. Southern Blacks sometimes felt overwhelmed by the fast talking as opposed to slow talking; by the cosmopolitan sense of what the world is like out there, as opposed to a conventional and provincial, collo- quial, pedestrian sense of our small little world. That's a major clash. Because the struggle was against Black degradation, that clash was going to be highlighted no matter how subtle it was, and no matter how well intended persons were. Any instance of a subtle perception of Black degradation would get a response—sometimes an excessive one.

I think that we have to make a distinction between the period before 1965–66 and after. By this I mean that King and others knew quite explicitly that the alliance they were forging was with Jews as well as whites, for they did in fact encounter Jewish leaders and Jewish themes. King was talking about Abraham Joshua Heschel, and he knew he wasn't just another white person. He knew that this was someone with a deep Jewish tradition and heritage. In that period it was fairly clear that Jewish support was quite strong, and it was ac- knowledged as such. The Blacks were quite gracious about it in their gratitude.

Once the issue of identity hit hard against the younger generation, then the excessive rejection of *any* manifestation of white heritage was almost predictable. In no way was it meant as a betrayal of Jews. It was a matter of moving to the next stage of the struggle. One which is Black controlled, with Black leadership across the board and with Black—sometimes separatist—solidarities.

Personally, I've always recognized that multiracial alliances are indispensable. But there were many voices in the Black community who disagreed with this particular perception of the next stage. What is upsetting to me is that large numbers of American Jews are making SNCC—the Black organization that did seek to throw whites out of their organizing activities—the only authentic Black voice of the late sixties, as if there were not other Black voices critical of SNCC, still hoping to make an interracial alliance.

M.L. For Jewish activists, it was these SNCC people, and those whom they influenced in the Black movement, who had been their colleagues in the South and who were the people that these Jews most respected. Moreover, the impact of SNCC's move of excluding whites and Jews was enormous among young Blacks on college campuses—the other place where young Jews in their twenties were most likely to encounter or potentially interact with Blacks. So the effect of SNCC's move was enormous. Most Blacks whom young Jews met were influenced by the SNCC mentality, not the Blacks who were influenced by any kind of Southern Christian Leadership Conference–Martin Luther King mentality.

C.W. But simply having had limited experiences does not allow one to assume that SNCC was speaking for the whole Black community. If 95 percent of young Jews had an experience with SNCC, that still does not allow them to infer that Black America as a whole somehow "rejected us when we supported them." It just doesn't follow. They've got to broaden their sense of the multiplicity and diversity of Black voices.

CHAPTER 5

Black Nationalism

In the period after the decline of the Civil Rights movement and the alliance it generated between Blacks and Jews, nationalist forces in each community have pushed against greater cooperation and toward separation. In this chapter we explore the meaning of Black Nationalism and its role in this dynamic.

C.W. The evangelical churches associate the Jewish people with a notion of chosenness. This notion is more predominant than the anti-Semitic stereotype of Jews as Christ-killers, and leads to a certain feeling of kinship with Jews as the people who have a special kinship with God.

M.L. That might be why the strongest Black element of anti-Semitism comes rather from the Muslim world, the Black Nationalists.

C.W. Actually, you don't get an explicit articulation of anti-Semitic feelings in the Black Islamic world until you get a close relationship between particular Arab culture and African-Americans. It's a political overlay on a religious base.

M.L. How do you think the Christian-Jewish dynamic relates to the Black-Jewish one?

C.W. It's like this. In the Black Christian world there is in a significant sense an accent on a love that is universalistic and internationalist. This is a quite different emphasis from most or much Christianity in the United States, and opens up the possibility of multiracial alliances. King's movement was one manifestation of this. It's Christianity's universalistic ethic that enables it to make it in the jaws of defeat and still afford some sense of agency or possible moral action, which is important since the Black sense of the tragic is very much at the center of Black Christianity.

I don't expect to see racism eliminated in American life, but we still fight against it. Never give up combat till the end. Betterment is always possible. And no matter how secular Jews are, they still have core elements of a progressive worldview that means they would not want to give up on human amelioration in history. There's no doubt in my mind that those who will be on the cutting edge of Black-Jewish dialogue on the ground will be the prophetic Black churches.

M.L. The Black churches have elements of Black Nationalism in them also, don't they?

C.W. Not too much. We have to make a distinction between Black cultural distinctiveness and Black Nationalism.

M.L. Tell me about that. What is Black cultural distinctiveness?

C.W. It's a history of Black styles and mannerisms: ways of singing, praying, worshipping, and communicating that have created a certain sense of community and sustained sanity. There's no doubt that in syncopated styles, rhythmic styles, and repetitive and antiphonal styles one sees a distinctiveness among Black folk in the United States. The Black Church plays a crucial role in the creation of these styles and mannerisms. This is not Black Nationalism because nationalism is an ideology.

Louis Armstrong had a Black style. How he walked, talked, blew his horn and so forth: but he wasn't a Black nationalist. Wynton Marsalis in the same way comes deeply out of a tradition of Black cultural distinctiveness. In many ways he recognizes the degree to which Black styles and mannerisms have influenced his sense of who he is, but he's not a Black nationalist. You can't assume that anybody who revels in Black cultural distinctiveness is a Black nationalist.

M.L. So a Black nationalist is usually somebody who says what?

C.W. A Black nationalist is somebody who says that Black people must close ranks, be suspicious of others, and even hold them at arm's length. Primarily they stress Black unity, solidarity, togetherness in a quest for a Black nation—a place of Black safety and self-determination. It's probably a good thing to have a certain healthy suspicion of others, because Black people can be used and abused, but if you want to get people to change, you have to give openness a chance.

M.L. Many people say that a primary task for Blacks in this period is to discover their own Black authenticity and their own identity. That the primary way in which Blacks have been undermined, and continue to be undermined, is by the cultural materialism of the dominant society. And that Black nationalists are taking a leadership role in trying to reestablish a struggle for Black authenticity. I wonder if that's true. Where does this struggle for Black authenticity and Black identity fit into your picture of what needs to happen for Blacks?

C.W. Where I agree with Black Nationalism unequivocally and wholeheartedly is the attempt to provide a sense of the history of African people—a history that's either been denied, marginalized, degraded, or denigrated. In that regard, Black nationalists are certainly attacking the vicious legacy of white supremacy, and I agree with that entirely, as would you yourself. We want to strip the past of white supremacist lies that have so often regulated much of Western historiography about people of color who come to America—especially Africans.

Now of course in a market culture where a sense of history is increasingly farfetched and distant, it's no accident that the sense of history can easily be displaced by very crude nostalgic myths about the past. Some Black nationalists have fallen into this trap: of just generating romantic conceptions of the past to undergird self-esteem. I think that's short-sighted, and I think it undermines the capacity of Black people to critically confront our past.

This sense of history that the Black nationalists call for, I agree with it, very much so. I don't like the term "Black authenticity" because it implies that's there has been and is one Black essence, one Black core, one Black center—and that one group has a monopoly on that center. That's precisely what history is not. History is about the multiple strands of various traditions, about communities clashing, quarreling, appropriating. Talking about "authenticity" is a way of trumping any serious discussion about the Black condition, past and present. Black nationalists can fall into traps of nostalgia and romanticism as they attempt to generate their own myths, their own fictions.

M.L.   We have those same things in certain versions of Zionism.

C.W.   It's true in every group, every tribe, and every nation. Look at the history of America in terms of all the celebratory lies that tried to hide the realities, truths, and facts they didn't want to confront.

M.L.   The question is: what can replace that nationalism and still retain a commitment to validating the needs of people for a cultural identity that is not defined solely in terms of their relationship with the capitalist market? What's the answer to that? It seems to me that the consciousness of the Black community today is unbelievably permeated by the capitalist market—and this gets reflected in popular culture in an obsession with fancy clothes, sexuality turned into a commodity, and salvation through consumption—with the possible exception of the Black churches.

C.W.   Yes, we have in the Black churches a community that sustains members. We have a style, form, and level of content, definitely so. But as you know, it isn't completely unaffected by the market. There's a lot of market religion in both the Jewish and the Black community. T. S. Eliot was absolutely right when he said you don't inherit a tradition, you have to obtain it at great labor. The only way you preserve a sense of history is to have a community and tradition struggling in the present to keep the best of the past alive. That's one of the real paradoxes in our understanding of the past: it stays alive only to the degree to which persons in the present keep it alive. Many church communities in the Black community and religious communities in the Jewish community are able to do that. Not them alone, but they are the dominant ones. Needless to say, market religion that effaces the past is growing in both Black and Jewish communities.

The struggle is amplified by the degree to which market forces become more and more powerful, more and more erosive of historical memory. In place of historical memory you get either nostalgia, a "fossil-collecting," antiquarian sensibility, or a kind of icon selection of the past, where you simply talk about the "greatest hits"—the great figures who come back out of context solely as the icons before whom you worship, rather than as live figures whom you learned from, criticized, and sympathized with.

Although it's sometimes hard to acknowledge it amongst narrow Black nationalists, there is actually such a thing as progressive Black Nationalism.

M.L. What's the distinction?

C.W. A progressive Black nationalist is like a progressive Zionist. They have a real solidarity with their people, but they also want to accent the humanity of others who are engaging in humane interaction across groupings. Their nationalism has an internationalist, universalistic dimension. However, there's a big tension between the universalism they expound and the nationalism they are forced to defend, so they are rarely the ones in power. They are, rather, the prophetic critics of their fellow nationalists.

M.L. How can we get people to spend less time listening to Farrakhan and more time listening to progressive people?

C.W. We've got to institutionalize progressive voices in both communities so that they become more visible and effective. There are a number of persons who right now sympathize with and even follow Minister Farrakhan, who in the early part of the twenty-first century will be radical democrats. These people are fundamentally concerned about Black suffering; they go into Farrakhan's organization because they are concerned about this suffering and in the end they feel that it doesn't provide enough vision and insight and analysis. So they end up as progressives. This is the trajectory of persons such as Malcolm X, Amiri Baraka, Sonia Sanchez. There is a struggle going on over the minds, bodies, and souls of young Black Americans, some of whom will go through Minister Louis Farrakhan's organization and end up as progressives. How soon? It's hard to say. The progressive Black nationalist position is the closest I come to, although I personally don't consider myself a nationalist of any sort.

M.L. Can you summarize your position on that?

C.W. Any kind of nationalism, for the most part, will be used in a way that ends up dehumanizing folk. We all need recognition and some form of protection, but usually in these dominant forms the quest for group unity results in attacking someone else. The history of nationalism seems to be part and parcel of the history of tribalism. It tends to be deeply patriarchal and homophobic with little sense of our common humanity. Black Nationalism has come to be problematic because every Black nationalist has to sooner or later have some relation with territory or land. Black people in America are a people without land, that's part of our heritage.

M.L. Do you ever have a longing for land?

C.W. Yes. We have a house in Ethiopia. When I go to Ethiopia I feel in some sense at home. I could certainly envision living there, because racial tension is virtually nonexistent. It's not romantic, because tribal strife does exist: it's just a question of being in a country where Black humanity is taken so utterly for granted. But I'm still an outsider there.

M.L. American Jews have programs whereby they can go to Israel for a year, or maybe just for the summer. What would be wrong with having similar institutionalized ways of bringing folk over to Africa?

C.W. I rather like that idea. But there is a trap of which I'm leery. There are very positive things about Africa in terms of being comfortable, but negative things in terms of being New Worlders in the Old World. A lot of Blacks have localized sentiments about African identity, and I would want to fight against that. It's the same with Jews. You think you can go to Israel and, lo and behold, all the tensions of being Jewish in Chicago or New York disappear. Or it's a guilt trip, almost an appeal to machismo: "Come to where the real action is." This is an idolatrous trap, because of course you want to contribute to Jewish survival, but its easy to cheapen that and not recognize that all of us are born into circumstances not of our choosing. You can't leapfrog out of your circumstance in order to grab hold of some easy identity.

M.L. So, on a personal level, do you feel you can be part of this society?

C.W. Yes and no. After 244 years of slavery and 87 years of Jim Crow, I think Black people in America will always have some sense of being outsiders. Yet there's a sense in which I am a part of it, because the nation is unimaginable without Black people in the culture, either past or present. It's the tension between being an outsider, and being more integral to America than 90 percent of Americans. It's what Du Bois called "double consciousness." I'm thirteenth-generation American! That's about as integral as you can get.

M.L. The twentieth century has been full of horrendous and disgusting national struggles. Right now we have a picture in our mind of Serbs and Bosnians killing each other, and we see the possibility of the same thing re-emerging throughout Eastern Europe. A progressive person might explain Black Nationalism as a response to the failure of society to give Blacks equality: a distorted response, but one they can understand. When Black Nationalism pops up in America today and manifests in anti-Semitic ways, Jews have a lot of questions about it. Was Black Nationalism flourishing when Blacks were slaves? Was there nationalism in Africa?

C.W. Nationalism per se is a modern phenomenon. It's a post-Napoleonic development in modern Europe. Once organizing activity began to take place for the purpose of promoting self-determination among Black people, nationalism became one of the more attractive ideologies that could attempt to mobilize them.

M.L. When did it happen, this activity to organize Black people?

C.W. Slave insurrections, hundreds of them. They were proto-Black nationalist efforts. But organizationally speaking, Black Nationalism doesn't really take off till you get Chief Sam's "back to Africa" movement in Oklahoma trying to constitute a nation in a serious sense. By "serious" I mean talking about land and territory, because so much of Black Nationalism avoids this fundamental issue. Chief

Sam's movement organized people to go back to Africa: they actually went back to Sierra Leone.

M.L.   When was this?

C.W.   Right after the attempt by a group of Blacks to make Oklahoma an all-Black state between 1900 and 1905. It wasn't successful, but it left a legacy. The first part of the legacy was Black municipalities scattered all over Oklahoma. The second part was the founding in 1896 of a Black/Judaic religious institution. That institution in Boley, Oklahoma, still exists today, but it isn't as visible because of the Black Hebrews in the urban centers. That Black/Judaic movement had a significant impact on Black group thinking. It was nationalist thinking, but it used a Jewish model for organizing Black people, with their own Temple, their own rabbis, and so forth.

M.L.   They self-consciously modeled themselves on Jews?

C.W.   It was very much based on the Old Testament—they shunned the New Testament. Curtis Caldwell is writing the history of this fascinating group. Now as I said before, Chief Sam was the third part of the legacy of the attempt to make Oklahoma an all-Black state. He had a real impact on Marcus Garvey, who reached the conclusion all Black nationalists reach, which is deep pessimism regarding America's will toward racial justice. They give up on the possibility of ever living lives of dignity and decency in America, and they leave. This brother, Chief Sam, organized folk in such a way that he took off in a boat with sixty-five people: which means he was more successful than Marcus Garvey. Garvey never saw Africa, though he talked about it every day. But when Garvey arrived in the States in 1915, he put together the largest mass movement among Black people ever. And it happened to be a thorough-going Black nationalist movement.

M.L.   Why did it catch on?

C.W.   Garvey was able to speak to the deep sense of disillusionment and disappointment of uprooted Black people after their participation in the First World War. Many had risked their lives. Of course we can't forget the major race riot in East St. Louis, July 1917. Tulsa, Oklahoma, 1921, another race riot. In fact in the summer of 1919 there were over twenty major race riots. Now keep in mind that at this period, "race riot" means white Americans murdering, pillaging, and plundering in Black communities.

M.L.   Not like today's race riots which are largely Blacks acting in response to their oppression.

C.W.   You started getting Blacks on the aggressive on a grand scale with Watts in August 1965. Though it's true there were exceptions, as in Harlem in 1943. Or, in Tulsa, Oklahoma, you had a number of Black soldiers who organized and began shooting at policemen. This was just mind-boggling for most of white America. Anyway, there were Black people becoming progressively disillusioned in terms of the promise of American democracy, and giving up.

M.L.   After the compromise of 1876, when Reconstruction was dismantled, why were Blacks disillusioned then?

C.W.   There was a majority of Black people in the South, but it was difficult, if not impossible, to organize politically. Because they were silenced by terrorism. A number of voices emerged, but they ended up swinging on trees. The level of terrorism was instilling fear into Black hearts and Black souls, so that it was impossible to overcome it in order to get them to organize. That is one of the reasons why Garvey's movement was centered in New York and the North. Garvey himself had to meet the Ku Klux Klan in order to let them know that there were going to be some Universal Negro Improvement Association branches in the South, and they ought not to mess with those branches. Because these branches were afraid to meet. The NAACP, too: it was basically an illegal organization, and if they met, the white reactionary forces would come down hard.

M.L.   I'm not sure I understand. What do you mean, "if they met"?

C.W.   If you formed an NAACP branch in one of a large number of Southern cities, the space would be torched, the individuals would be hunted down.

M.L.   So why would the Klan listen to Garvey?

C.W. Well, that's very interesting. In some ways they were similar. Both believed in segregation; both believed Blacks ought to leave the country. Garvey continually made the same three points. One: "You are a mighty race, you can do what you will." Two: "Our basic problem is disorganization. Black people must organize and mobilize." Three: "Don't ever be duped into believing that your white allies are reliable. Under conditions of economic, social, political, and sexual competition, every white person is a potential Klansman." When he invited the Klan and the Anglo-Saxon club to Liberty Hall in Harlem he said, "This is what white Americans really think. Liberals don't want to believe it, but you push them far enough or desire their daughters and they'll say the same things." So Garvey's appeal to Blacks' postwar pessimism came at a propitious moment. Black Nationalism was predicated on deep pessimism, and on Black people understanding self-determination in a mode in which the issue of land was never seriously addressed. Garvey wanted to but could not really address the issue of land. He would either have to talk about colonizing Africa, the way it had been done with Liberia; or about getting the Africans who were there to invite the African-Americans over; or he had to go symbolic and talk about a state of mind rather than a nation-state, which is primarily what he did. "Decolonize your mind, your body, your soul." Which was very positive in terms of affirmation, and Garvey was not a Black supremacist. Garvey's movement, of course, was crushed by the U.S. government and the disillusionment remained, to emerge again with Elijah Muhammad's movement.

M.L. You seem to be giving Black Nationalism a pivotal role here.

C.W. Black Nationalism is an integral part of Black history, but I don't believe it is central to it. That is because the pessimism on which Black Nationalism was predicated was never fully embraced in an organizational sense. Black people usually still maintain some possibility for a multiracial coalition, for trying to extend the scope of democracy in America. I think the role of the Black Church has been crucial in this, because what it has done historically is steal the thunder from the Black nationalists. It highlights Black cultural distinctiveness and, despite calling for group cohesiveness, its message is universalistic. It has always been open to others willing to work with us. By saying that self-love and self-affirmation are key, it took center ground over Black Nationalism. So the Black Church is much more central to Black history than Black Nationalism.

M. L. Well, when Black Nationalism emerged in the twenties, it must have been offering something the Black Church wasn't. I'd like to hear more about how it developed from that time until today.

C. W. Garvey was wise enough to know that he had to organize his movement by appealing to the church. Over twenty percent of the people who signed his famous organization charter in the early twenties here in New York were preachers. It was an ecumenical arrangement, so that it would not be tilted toward one denomination. He also had a few Islamic groups. He tapped into the church by holding onto a universalistic view. Unlike among some Black nationalists nowadays, white put-down was not integral to his talk about Black build-up.

After Garvey collapsed, Black Nationalism was filtered primarily through non-Christian channels, because Christianity itself became viewed as part of the European, Western way of life. Keep in mind, Garvey was a Christian. So a host of different Black Islamic movements emerged, all of which, even Elijah's, remained very small until brother Malcolm came along, because they were apolitical on the domestic front. They would not allow their members to participate in the political process. They never voted; they couldn't demonstrate or agitate.

M. L. You mean they wouldn't allow themselves?

C. W. Elijah told them not to vote. He was consistent; he'd say, "I will give this government no legitimacy. In which case it makes no sense for me to participate in its organs of participation." So, no voting. He also wanted not to pay taxes, but he didn't want the whole movement to go to jail. As to land, their aim was to form a Black nation in the South, in Mississippi, Alabama, and Georgia. They knew it wasn't realistic, but it was principled, given Elijah's Black nationalist principle. It was Malcolm who upset things.

M. L. And Malcolm's arriving in the sixties.

C.W.   Malcolm arrives in June 1952. He leaves prison in 1952 and is standing on the street corner in New York soon after.

M.L.   He was a leader in the early fifties?

C.W.   Very much so. That's where he cuts his teeth. He's a die-hard follower of Elijah Muhammad. He's a young man, twenty-six years old, he'll die thirteen years later. But he's quite powerful. He starts the newspaper, gets out the word. Malcolm is the editor: a young, brilliant, self-taught brother, very narrow in his views, playing the Black supremacy game straight up. "White folks are devils," and so forth. But Malcolm—he's like Paul in the Christian story—he's the first actually to get the word out. He's emerging at a time when, with the social issues that are coming to the fore in Alabama, race is once again moving to the center of the national agenda. But Malcolm has no idea that his particular nationalism is going to become as influential as it did become, in the sixties especially.

M.L.   Why was it that in the fifties Blacks did not accept Black Nationalism more than they did? I've heard some Black nationalists claim it was because a lot of Black institutions were controlled by Jews. The NAACP, for example, had heavy funding from Jews, and so the nationalists assert, the board was trying to play up to them by not allowing nationalism to make a beachhead there. This kind of conspiracy theory is increasingly being heard by many Blacks today, both in the ghettoes and in African-centered Black studies programs at various universities.

C.W.   That's certainly not true in the case of NAACP, which was founded primarily by WASP progressives like William English Walling and Mary Ovington. Of course Jews played a disproportionate role in terms of supporting and promoting these organizations, but this is not the same thing as having control. These were very much multiracial organizations which behaved cautiously toward any leftist or Black nationalist politics that might render them marginal in terms of making realistic strides for Black progress. This strategy has limitations, but also strengths—as seen in the life and work of Thurgood Marshall. Malcolm couldn't deliver organizationally the way King or the NAACP could, partly because he hadn't spent enough time on that realistic level, talking about how to move step by step to enhance Black progress. Instead, on a rhetorical level, he was speaking to the psyche, the heart, the soul. Malcolm was first and foremost a prophet of the spirit and word, and we need such prophets. But that's very different from dealing with policies and programs.

M.L. So it wasn't until the mid-sixties that Black Nationalism emerged as an attractive ideology in the Black freedom movement. What do you see as the main dimensions of the conflict?

C.W. For one bright moment it looked as if America was actually concerned about the issue of white supremacy. President Johnson actually said, "We shall overcome." In 1964, that's serious business. And within the constraints of White House policy legislation, he really meant part of it. But in 1965, a week after Johnson signed the Voting Rights Act, you get the Watts explosion. Over the next three years you're going to get 329 rebellions in 257 cities as an expression not only of rage but of a re-emerging pessimism regarding America's will to deal with these problems.

M.L. How come it led to explosions then, when the rage and pessimism must be even deeper now? The Los Angeles riot was not primarily about race issues.

C.W. One of the big differences in Los Angeles between August 1965 and April 1992 is that in the sixties you'd had ten years of a social movement, some real successes and victories, and rising expectations. You had organizations in place in L.A. that could sustain a Watts rebellion for six or seven days. In April 1992, there are no rising expectations at all. We're talking about a nadir, a low point, with few organizations in place except gangs. They could sustain that sort of upheaval for only two or three days—half the time you had at Watts. And by the nineties the country had rendered much of Black social misery invisible, whereas in the sixties it was not invisible. It was on TV all the time. You had King articulating it with a level of eloquence we have yet to see again. Maybe now that things are heating up again, politically, we'll see that kind of upheaval again.

M.L. You're saying that Black Nationalism is the expression of the pessimism that even King was talking about in the last years of his life. What would you say was the positive side of the Black nationalist vision that has emerged since the sixties? Is there one particular vision that has emerged?

C.W. There's been an expression of a broad Black Nationalism that is very different from a narrow Black Nationalism such as Farrakhan's. Take someone like Manning Marable, whose *From the Grassroots* and *Blackwater* were important texts in the early eighties. They express a Black nationalist sensibility that is linked to democratic leftism. Marable, James Turner, and others tried to form an independent national Black political party in Philadelphia in 1980. This kind of Black Nationalism is broad in the sense that further down the road it would be open to a more traditional coalition; broad in that it's talking, as democratic socialism, about the redistribution of wealth and power in America and the world. But it also acknowledges the centrality of white supremacy, such that Black people have to come together first before they can become part of any coalition. Although, of course, I had my criticisms, I was there supporting Marable: it seemed the best thing to do at the time. This was a moment at which Black folk were being blamed for the decline of America, so the community had to consolidate its various views for sheer protection. Maybe there are similarities here with the early Zionist organizations. Both groups needed some shield against the white supremacist or gentile supremacist bombardment.

M.L. You are saying that the 1980 conference represented a more progressive form of Black Nationalism. What happened to it?

C.W. It just never got off the ground, because it was simply much too ambitious a level of organization. You don't just start off with a party: you've got to have grassroots organizations in place. That was one reason. Another was the class division within the Black community that simply cannot be concealed. Given the crucial role of a Black middle class that has more resources than other members of the community, they are likely to use the movement for their own ends. And that's in part what happened.

Two and a half years after the National Black Independent Political Party in 1980, you have the Jackson campaign. Now Jackson is a very courageous, jazzlike figure in terms of being improvisational, which at times becomes opportunism. By 1983 he sees a deeply outraged Black population looking for some channel to express that rage. He uses that rage as a means of pushing the Democratic Party, and even more of sending a message to the nation, which he does do. That's why in 1984 I enthusiastically supported Jackson. Unlike in '88, you'll recall that in '84 the Jackson campaign was very much a Black affair. All kinds of organizations in the Black community came together around it. The only ones who didn't were frightened members of the Black political class, those who had been booed for supporting Mondale. Otherwise Jesse was supported by the church, by Farrakhan nationalists, by broad Black nationalists, universalists, internationalists, liberals, and moderates. This partly reflected the United Front of the National Black Independent Party, but talk of the Party was shunned. Brother Jesse was center stage.

M.L. How come the Black nationalist movement thought it would get its fulfillment through a Black presidential candidate?

C.W. It just looked like the best option for sending a message and for hoping—in vain as it happened—that the Jackson campaign would help spawn grassroots organizations in the Black community.

M.L. Is that failure at a grassroots level why Black Nationalists didn't get involved in the '88 campaign?

C.W. That's one reason. It became clear that Jackson had never actually been very concerned about spawning grassroots organizations. It just wasn't his forte. He's not like Malcolm or King in that regard.

The situation was so desperate that Jesse wanted to play a variety of roles at the same time: prophet, politician, protest leader. Partly for psychological reasons, partly for moral, he wanted to make an impact. And he has made an impact. But one role he would not play was of facilitating widespread, gradual, substantive organizing. Yet for Black nationalists and a number of Leftists, that role was crucial; hence the construction of the Rainbow Coalition. Now, '88 is much broader. Jesse has become a full-blown Social Democrat. Which is why I supported him again, if critically. But now Black nationalists said that Jesse had sold them out last time, and I think some of their criticism was right on the mark. No Black organizations were being created, and it was more and more becoming a Jesse Jackson affair rather than an organizing effort for a plausible movement. By '92, newspaper editorials were attacking him for shunning accountability. The *City Sun,* an important Black nationalist voice, rejected Jesse as a loose cannon, as shunning responsibility.

M.L. It seems that, despite what you said, there are no ongoing progressive Black Nationalist organizations. Is that right?

C.W. No, there are a number. There are a host of local organizations, and the National Black United Front, led by brother Conrad Worrill, is growing. The UNIA still exists, although it's very small. In New York you've got Che Lumumba, headed by Elombe Brath: fairly pan-Africanist, and more open to leftist politics than most Black Nationalists. Its main focus is on the injuries of race caused by white supremacy. Brath put together and was the MC for the Nelson Mandela reception in Harlem, to which more than 25,000 people came. Che Lumumba is a broader Black nationalist organization than Farrakhan, though much less visible.

M.L. Broader in its politics or in its actual adherents?

C.W. Both. It's a pan-Africanist organization that is critical of the butchers in Africa, and is open to multiracial coalition, although it sees this as far down the road because Blacks need to get their acts together first. Then you've got Farrakhan's Nation of Islam, which is bigger than the others, partly owing to his charismatic ability. It is unique in being a national organization with networked branches, based on the organizational genius of Elijah Muhammad. Farrakhan has tried to keep this alive. With Muhammad's death in 1976, history turns. His son, Wallace, moved in a more orthodox and universalist direction. Farrakhan himself was initially ambivalent about keeping Elijah's legacy alive in the form of the Nation of Islam, but found a vacuum in the Black leadership that he attempted to fill. Since there was no national voice articulating a narrow Black nationalist ideology at a time of widespread pessimism, and because of the media preoccupation with sensationalism, he was able to surface. His movement has high visibility and many more sympathizers than followers.

M.L.   So it is the biggest. How would you describe it in terms of its influence on Black youth and intellectuals?

C.W.   Intellectuals, very small. Youth, highly significant. In the Black community there's some respect for the Nation's ability to create drug-free zones, which the police are unable to do. They have their own Black Muslim citizens' patrol, which lets the drug dealers know that if they intrude on their zone something negative will follow.

M.L.   If this is so successful, why hasn't this organization grown more rapidly? Why don't they extend the drug-free zones all over the place?

C.W.   I think large numbers of Black people have a schizophrenic reaction. On one side, the results relating to drugs are undeniable. On the other is the rhetoric and ideology. Most Black folks simply do not embrace either Islam or Farrakhan's political ideology. This places constraints on his ability to expand. For me, this is actually a good sign that there is still moral judgment in the Black community, even though it must be frustrating for Farrakhan. Fifty thousand people turn up to hear him speak, but he can't turn them into a mass organization or movement. This is something not given its due by the mainstream press. Most Black folk see a multiracial coalition as indispensable to their advancement, and reject the anti-Semitic elements of his rhetoric as simply too crude.

M.L.   Many outsiders think his anti-Semitism is what gives him the emotional charge that excites people. Jews interpret his success as due to his ability to identify for Blacks an external enemy that doesn't seem as overwhelming as the whole of American society. Blacks are more numerous and potentially tougher than Jews, who, coming from this Holocaust experience, are clearly scared of them in some way. Yet you are saying that his anti-Semitism has little appeal for most Blacks and is impeding the growth of his movement.

C.W.   My hypothesis is that if Jesse Jackson were in no way associated with any form of anti-Semitism, he would be a much more effective and appreciated progressive leader than he is. And the same for Farrakhan. Farrakhan is in the tradition of highly talented, articulate Black religious spokespersons. Ten, twelve thousand people come to hear preachers with far less than his level of rhetorical talent. So that if Farrakhan were in the mode of a King, he wouldn't just have fifty thousand people show up: he'd have a large organization. Here may be one of the few instances where doing the right thing goes hand in hand with expanding your base. That is not always the case in human history, as we know.

M.L. One could argue—and I'm not saying this is true—that this shows the depth of anti-Semitism among some Black nationalists. Hitler diverted resources from the struggle against the Soviet Union to engage in killing off Jews, and arguably weakened his ability to withstand the Soviet assault through his obsession with anti-Semitism. I'm not comparing Farrakhan with Hitler. But his people are prepared to hurt their cause through their deep commitment to hating Jews.

C.W. Yes, but Farrakhan's anti-Semitism is not predicated on a direct hatred of Jews the way Hitler's was. Farrakhan sees Jewish unity as a model for Black unity. That perception of Jewish unity may be romantic and idealized, but that's what he sees. And he sees that unity in the last twelve years as an obstacle to Black unity. Although he sees Jewish group interest as increasingly standing in the way of Black group interest, it's primarily his attempt to use the Jewish example as a Black role model that gets him into the Black/Jewish relationship in the first place.

M.L. Can you analyze where the anti-Semitism comes into play? Where I grew up in Newark the Blacks were always fighting the Irish, or the Italians, not the Jews. Why isn't it now a case of anti-Italianism?

C.W. There are a few points to make here. One is that the emergence of Black Nationalism around the turn of the century coincided with the appearance of Zionism. Fifty years later, after the Holocaust, the nascent and embryonic expression of Jewish national self-determination that was Zionism has become a nation state. Primarily owing to historical events, Jews were able to convince others of the Zionist case. At the same time, the Black nationalist movement is experiencing

more and more setbacks, even in persuading folk in the Black community. Marcus Garvey was a Zionist. Du Bois was a Zionist. King was a
Zionist. In their own words they expressed support for the Zionist
movement. By the mid-sixties, especially 1967 and the beginning of
the Occupation, the mood in the Black community slowly, but significantly, begins to be critical of Zionism.

The second point is that by the sixties you had an attempt to look
at Zionism not simply as an ideology of self-determination for a despised people but as a symbol of the tremendous power of a group to
push through what they want. This is important on the domestic front,
because in the eyes of some Black people Zionism is simply a metaphor for Jewish self-interest that worked.

M.L. We've talked a lot about options for Black identity through
nationalism. I still don't quite get what alternative you see as a way of
sustaining this authentically. First of all, is this a goal? Should Black
people strive to maintain an identity as Blacks? What's wrong with
assimilation into the American society if American society were open
to it? What if American society were ready to be changed in such a
way that in the next generation there are twenty million white women
who want to marry Black men and white men who want to marry
Black women. The white people are all saying, "We want you to be
welcomed in in the deepest sense. We want you all to move into our
families, we want to merge with you." Is there any reason why Blacks
shouldn't accept that offer? Is there any reason to struggle to maintain
a Black identity?

C.W. That offer is very farfetched given the escalating levels of
backlash and hostility from one side and the struggle and animosity
from the other. But I'd have nothing against it in principle. I simply
hope that we don't confuse a genuine and humane interaction among
Blacks and whites with a crude assimilation that erases blackness into
whiteness.

M.L. Well maybe it's not for the next generation, but what about
three generations from now? Maybe after three generations of multiculturalism and respect you'll get tens of millions of formerly white
Americans who are marrying Chinese, they're marrying Chicanos, and

they're saying, "Black people, come join the merge here." From the perspective of your theories of internationalism and universalism, is there any reason why Blacks should continue to maintain a cultural identity and a physical identity as a separate people in America *if* it is possible for them not to?

C.W.   Black people *as we are* are already mixed. About 85 percent of us have red blood from indigenous people, another 85 percent have white blood—some from the white male rapes of Black women. Biologically and culturally we're already a hybrid people, but we're still part of a history where we've been treated as a separate people.

M.L.   And you view yourselves as a separate people.

C.W.   Of course we've got to view ourselves as a separate people because we're treated as a separate people. You've got to be in contact with reality. If you're treated separately and degraded separately, then you have to understand that your own self-conception is going to be shaped by that.

M.L.   What I'm asking is whether Blacks should be demanding for themselves to be treated that way. Or whether Blacks should be demanding a social and cultural integration into American society such that years from now one would forget this category. Like today one forgets the distinction between WASPs who come from Scotland versus WASPs that come from England, or Germany, or Scandinavia.
Should progressives be striving for the elimination of blackness as a social identity and the acceptance of Blacks in such a way that two hundred years from now you'd say, "This one looks a little bit blackish and this one looks a little bit reddish, this one looks a little bit yellowish"? When I go down the street now I do not notice whether somebody's hair is blonde, brunette, or red, or what their eye color is —these just don't strike me as salient features.

C.W.   But just going down the street is not the example you want to use. If you were working somewhere like a law firm and someone were up for promotion, it would be very clear that one factor was what their ethnic background is and what their family history was. When it actually comes to making crucial decisions, even to this day, it's not as if people just say, "He or she is American." Not at all. They'd say in a law firm or on Wall Street, even to this day, "Another Jew. Another Catholic." Another so-and-so.

M.L.   But I want you to explore the hypothetical in order to understand more fully your position on nationalism. If it were possible for Blacks to become merely "Americans," is this something that's desirable for them? Do we want a Black identity two hundred years from now, or would we prefer to see a decrease in consciousness about who Blacks are? And if we want to see a Black identity, why do we?

C.W.   We have to look at what would be the conditions under which the Black identity would disappear. If it disappears in the form of being assimilated into the mainstream, then it means that we're simply reaffirming another identity—in this case it is a white American identity. I think the real challenge is not being able to preserve the Black identity, but to recognize it's not as fundamental as one's human identity. You can't talk about the humanity of Black folk, the humanity of Africans, without acknowledging their Blackness and their Africanness.

So the question becomes: is it possible to preserve Black identity, to acknowledge the Blackness, and at the same time render it secondary to human identity? The same for any other human beings—Italian, Jewish, Irish, or anything else. I do not think we can eliminate differences like that because you end up reinforcing some other dominant model, which presupposes that the dominant model is somehow more human than the other. That's precisely the thing to be resisted.

We see this all the time. I pick up *The New Republic* and I read a tendentious critique of August Wilson, reducing his work to merely talking about the Black experience. But of course Eugene O'Neill is talking about the *human* condition when he's talking about a particular Irish family. It's not just a question of the relative depth and profundity of O'Neill and August Wilson. It's because the subject matter of August Wilson still makes him ethnic, but the subject matter of O'Neill doesn't make him ethnic because the Irish—after Joyce and Yeats and others—have now reached a point where they illuminate the human condition as a whole. It's precisely that kind of thinking one has to reject.

Now the challenge is going to be: is it possible *only* in a highly miscegenated and assimilated world to do away with those secondary identities in order for the human identity to be active? That's a tough one because if we hold on to what I call secondary identities, then they take on a logic of their own. The human identity is also hard to keep track of, as we know, usually when it takes a nationalist or tribalist form. That's another reason why I'm against most forms of nationalism.

M.L.   Because it's harder to keep track of our human identity.

C.W.   Exactly.

M.L.   Here is a different way of understanding this issue. That the basis for understanding our human identity might be through a sensitivity to the experience of the pain shared in our separate national identities as oppressed groups. The criterion for which nationalities are worth preserving and fighting for and which nationalities should become assimilated is: does this national identity in its essential structure retain access to its history of pain and oppression, and an understanding of how that might link up to other people's pain and oppression? Or is the national identity so triumphal in its structure that it leads people in their memories to associate themselves more with the elements of the ruling elite, making it hard for them to see what they have in common with the pain and suffering of other people?

C.W.   That's one of the ways of generating what we're both after, which is empathy and compassion. There's a number of ways of doing that and that's certainly one I would not in any way want to push aside. It's spoken by a true progressive nationalist, by somebody who wants to hold onto a sense of loyalty and solidarity to a group, but in the name of a universalist ideal. But you are on a very, very slippery slope because most nationalists are going to cut so radically against your prophetic universalist ideals that, unless you keep them at work, you can easily end up being an apologist for destructive forms of nationalism.

At the same time, of course, one could say, "Prophetic internationalism is empty if it isn't linked to the reality that people do organize themselves in nation states. I know we have to deal with nationalist ideology, and nation states are a crucial way of organizing in our world, but I think it's part of that world's tragic character."

M.L.   From my standpoint I have my answer for why we shouldn't want to strive for the elimination of Black identity: because Black identity is one that emerges from a history of oppression and leads people back to understanding what they have in common with other oppressed groups. But from your standpoint, why shouldn't you be working for the elimination of Black identity, if you see the need to have it as a tragic reality?

C.W.   Because the tragic reality can't be confronted by means of elimination. Identities have to be understood in terms of the life and logic that they had rooted in the past and present. You have to try to highlight whatever progressive possibilities they had, even as one refuses to be a part of the tribalisms that have become dominant at this particular moment in the human adventure.

Anytime you call yourself a nationalist of any sort you are more than likely going to be defending aspects of that nationalism that are —from my vantage point—indefensible. Even progressive nationalism has built into it a certain apologetic element.

There's always a tension among progressive nationalists between their nationalism and their universalism. Usually progressive nationalists are forced to critically support or critically sympathize with forms of nationalism that are either progressive or conservative. You end up having to defend the positive elements of a nation state or certain kinds of nationalism, and criticize other elements because progressive nationalists are usually not in power: they are the prophetic critics of their fellow nationalists.

M.L.   How does that differ from calling yourself a Christian and having to defend a historical tradition that has at least as much to defend and apologize for as any nationalist position?

C.W.   As a nationalist you are defending a particular nation. As a Christian I am not defending any set of institutions. I'm only defending a certain prophetic conception of the faith that usually exists on the margins of Christian institutions and churches. There's more space for being a renegade, heretic, or prophetic critic in relation to Christianity because I am not defending a church, a pope, a bishop, or anything else. I'm only defending a particular prophetic interpretation of this tradition. And that prophetic interpretation is not institutionalized anywhere. Whereas when you're defending a certain nationalism, you are usually defending a set of institutions: namely nation states that are involved in securing, protecting, and usually subordinating and manipulating their people.

M.L. Not that protection is a bad thing. The Kurds need protection; the Jews need protection.

C.W. The Jews need protection and they get a nation state. There's no doubt about it. That's why I defend the *basic* aims of a nation: protection, security, and liberty. I defend those particular aspects of nation states that do these good things.

I defend those elements of the American nation state and its grand experiment in democracy—deeply flawed but also so precious—because those aims are very good ones. But does that make me a nationalist? No, not at all. It makes me a radical democrat who recognizes that nation states are at the moment indispensable. To the degree to which those nation states are radically democratic and libertarian, I defend. To the degree to which they are not, I object. You can imagine I end up objecting a whole lot. Every nation state we know has practiced some form of barbarism and every nation state we know has been involved in some kind of repression.

M.L. It's a truism that every specific human reality is going to be flawed in some way. But if you have the moral luxury of seeing salvation in some future world and not in this one, you don't have to get identified with some particular community.

C.W. I don't think salvation has anything to do with it. I can imagine a thoroughgoing secular skeptic who's a radical democrat saying exactly the same thing—and preserving a hope for social change.

CHAPTER 6

Jewish Nationalism

Jewish Nationalism and Zionism are often seen as contributing to a narrow particularism in the Jewish world that makes it harder to build connections with others. Yet a Torah-based nationalism may make connections with others a religious obligation.

C.W. Some American Blacks believe that the distance between Jews and Blacks was accelerated by a revival of Zionist and nationalist sentiment in the Jewish world in the wake of the 1967 Six Days War when Israel defeated Egypt and Syria and occupied the West Bank and Gaza. Can you explain why so many Jews have become fervent nationalists?

M.L. Jewish Nationalism was given its primary boost by the abandonment of the Jews during the Nazi period. If you were a Jew living between 1933 and 1945, you couldn't be sure you weren't going to end up as one of "the vermin that had to be extinguished."

Nationalism was a far healthier response to this oppression than that of the assimilators—Jews who felt that the reason that they were being picked out for persecution is that there was some aspect of Jewishness which objectively warranted this oppression. One of the ironies about *The New Republic*–style Jews who today implicitly blame racism on the culture of poverty is that a very short time ago this same thing was being done to Jews—we were being blamed for being offensive in various ways and hence generating our own oppression. German Jews often suggested that the problem was really based on the fact that there were all these crude and ill-mannered Eastern European Jews who hadn't learned proper manners, hadn't learned to speak quietly and be less pushy and aggressive. These Jews were an id that needed an ego to control it. West European Jewish inventions like psychoanalysis could help in that process. This way of thinking, of course, was an indentification with the aggressor—a phenomenon that we see today among some Black intellectuals who have teamed up with Republican conservatives to blame racism on Black behavior.

The assmilationist response was to try to become more like the non-Jew, in the hopes that if we looked more like them physically, perhaps we could "pass" as non-Jewish and avoid being wiped out. Psychologically, assimilationists were often responding to inner feelings of shame, of being the kind of people whom others were treating like the lowest form of life. After all, we lived in a capitalist society that taught us that what we received from the society was a reflection of our self-worth, so if we received racism the fault must be ours (the same logic behind current attempts to demean Blacks—witness *The Bell Curve*).

Zionism countered that by asserting that Jews are not bad, they are just on the receiving end of anti-Semitism and therefore need their own national self-determination like every other group. You can see why this kind of nationalism was a healthy self-affirmation.

For Jews to claim their right to a state of their own was an assertion of self-worth in the face of a world that had both oppressed and demeaned us.

C.W. What I'm hearing here is something often argued by my highly sophisticated Black nationalist friends. They claim that the sense of identity has to be linked with a Black nation state, a Black army, a Black navy, because these are the signs of power in the modern world. Otherwise there would be only disaster and ruin. That's why there's the attempt to link a people's quest for identity to the construction of a nation state that would somehow promote, enhance, and encourage that identity. Is that a fair characterization?

M.L. I personally am not saying that the only way Jews could ever get a sense of their value is through a nation state. For example, I could conceive of them having a strong sense of their value by really reclaiming their religious heritage. This is something I'm very much in favor of happening. It is difficult to assess how viable this option is for most Jews today, but it is much more viable now than it was in 1948, when Israel was born. In 1948, nothing was more discredited than religion, because God had not come through for the Jews during the Holocaust. Although some did argue that divine intervention took place in the form of the creation of the State of Israel.

C.W. I thought you were going to argue it took place in terms of the Russians and the Americans coming together to stop Hitler.

M.L. No, because by the time that happened we had been wiped out. There weren't very many of us left.

C.W. But the State of Israel also happened too late.

M.L. Not too late if you consider that anti-Semitism wasn't defeated in 1945. It might still have reoccurred in the Soviet Union and the United States, the two victor societies who had fought against German nationalism but not against anti-Semitism. They could yet have turned violently anti-Semitic.

C.W. That's a plausible argument.

M.L. In which case God's intervention was as if to say, "Well, it's happened in Europe, but I won't let it happen in the U.S. I'll create the State of Israel."

C.W. There's a problem with the assumption that the existence of a nation state does somehow provide protection.

M.L. My own opinion is that the ultimate salvation will involve the disappearance of nation states and the creation of an international universalistic order. Although that will not involve the disappearance of national groupings or, in particular, national cultures. But until that future moment, I'll support Jewish national aspirations to protect us from xenophobic nationalism and fundamentalism that still threaten to use the Jews as the "demeaned other."

C.W. Even though it's so farfetched from the reality, I'm on the same wavelength with you here. In this sense, others would call us "visionaries" or something less flattering. Though you share a vision of the elimination of the nation state, you justify it in the short run on prudential grounds, and as a vehicle for identity and hope. But my question remains whether the nation state becomes the only means by which Jews can have a sense of hope, identity, and security.

M.L. Jews to start with were not the leading champions of the nation state. On the contrary, it was presented to us as what we would have to buy into if we wanted liberation. But not our own nation state, someone else's. We were living in ghettoes or restricted areas until the French Revolution came along and offered us the possibility of escaping our position as second-class citizens. The price was to become a very good Frenchman, to identify with the nation state. As we talked about before, for much of the nineteenth century Jews thought they could manage this, by changing their appearance and behavior and by relegating religion to the private sphere. And part of that change involved creating an internal Jewish culture of denigrating Jewish characteristics because they separate us from our neighbors.

Having experienced what we did at the hands of other nation states, I think Jews are not going to be the first people to give up our own. I still want to see the elimination of nation states, but Israel should be well down the line in dissolving into some larger union, not the first to do so. We had the experience of trying to assimilate into nation states which promised to treat us equally and fairly, but that blew up in our faces. The only place that you might argue that non-Jews allowed us to assimilate is the U.S. during the last forty years— when ruling class preoccupations with the Cold War and with expanding its imperial interests gave it a group of external enemies sufficient to deflect interest from imagined internal ones. That dynamic might shift as the American economic empire contracts and it seeks new enemies to blame. Perhaps it will be African-Americans cast into this position, because there's such a deep historically rooted hatred of Blacks. But Blacks may be perceived by the ruling class as tougher fighters, not about to "take it" as much as Jews have historically been willing to take it when set up in this role.

C.W. I'd like to come back to the relationship between the nation state and visionary politics. What do you see as the link?

M.L. There was a prophetic minority amongst nineteenth-century Jews who, perceiving nation states as destructive, aimed to transcend them through a new universalism. That new universalism was the Left, the international Communist vision of transcending national boundaries and creating an international community.

Although most Jews didn't join the Left, a very large percentage of those joining the Left were Jews, certainly out of proportion to their numbers in the population. Our history has led us to be suspicious of the nation state and of any particular national groupings, proposing instead a prophetic vision of an international society in which "Nation shall not lift up sword against nation" and all peoples would worship together. Jewish attraction to Communist internationalism had deep roots in Jewish religious themes. Some were also attracted because they realized they weren't going to get real acceptance into existing national societies, and that the only solution to the Jewish problem would be an internationalism by which all nation states were dissolved.

Under Stalin, the Bolsheviks had a definition of the "national question" that validated national groupings for everyone except the Jews. The Jews alone were not defined as a nation state since they didn't own territory. Those who held on to their Jewishness were really holding on to a petit bourgeois prejudice. This way of thinking led to the suppression of Jewish institutions and religious practices, to treating Zionism as an enemy rather than as a liberation movement, and finally to the killing of Jewish intellectuals. It also led to a deep suspicion and anti-Semitism in the Communist party which culminated in the eradication of most Jewish leaders of World War Two resistance movements. The experience of Jews in both Stalinist Russia and then in the Soviet Union was of oppression, of negation of their particularity. In fact, the struggle inside the Communist party against Trotsky was in part waged against him *as Jew,* despite the fact that he himself, as the supreme internationalist, totally renounced his Jewishness.

C.W. That's part of the ugly czarist face of anti-Semitism that characterized Russian history as far back as the eighteenth century.

M.L. Yes, and the fantasy of the internationalist Jew joining the Communist party was that this anti-Semitic czarist tradition, rooted in Christianity, could be uprooted by joining with other internationalists who would accept them as brothers. The worst disillusionment was the European experience during the Holocaust, in which, when push came to shove, Communist parties, socialist parties, and resistance movements often proved more anti-Semitic than anti-Nazi. In incident after incident, culminating in the Warsaw Ghetto rebellion, Jews struggling against fascism could not get the support of the non-Jewish resistance fighters, Communists, and socialists, who turned their backs from a fear of losing their own base through association.

When, at the time of the Warsaw Ghetto uprising, the Jews desperately pleaded for support, the resistance fighters who were later to raise a rebellion against the Nazi regime stood by and did nothing. This happened over and over again throughout the resistance struggle against the Nazis. In the late 1980s, many of us liberals and progressives were providing sanctuary in the U.S. for people from El Salvador, even though the slaughter there was in no ways a wholesale, systematic genocide; but the Left in 1940s Europe did not organize any such process for saving Jews.

C.W. The Left would reply that they themselves were under attack, whereas these days they are suspicious of U.S. foreign policy and supportive of its victims.

M.L. It's certainly true that conditions then were much harder: yet there were many incidents of Jews joining the partisans in the forests and, far from being helped, being turned on and killed. There were many possible acts of support or resistance that were left undone, and that left the Jewish people feeling that internationalism had betrayed us.

From 1848 to 1933, the international movements of Europe had promised to encourage the working classes to see that it was more in their interest to overthrow the ruling classes than to kill Jews. Yet in the Nazi era large sectors of the European working class responded not to the internationalist appeal but to the fascist one, and wiped us out.

Isaac Deutscher, Trotsky's biographer and one of the greatest believers in internationalism, admitted in his book *The Non-Jewish Jew* that the people who believed in internationalism stayed in Europe and got wiped out, whilst those being denounced as narrow nationalists went to Palestine and survived. The international Left misled the Jews into believing that it was possible to transcend nationalism at this historical moment, that they didn't really need an army: and those who believed this fantasy are dead today because of it. Given this history, its extremely difficult to preach internationalism in the Jewish world today. If I say to my fellow Jews, "We have to fight for internationalism nonetheless, because nationalism leads to genocide," they say back to me, "That's a nice idea. Get any other nation state to abolish its borders and its armies first and we'll consider following suit."

C.W. Let me just sum up what you've been describing. You've put forward the assimilationist model, followed by the model of the secular state in which Jews tried to "pass." Then the internationalist minority on the Left which tried to transcend their particularism. Lastly nationalism, incorporated into the Zionist movement, which for the last forty years has become the most acceptable response.

M.L. And which we're seeing the limits of at this very moment.

C.W. Your argument is only persuasive when you ignore all that has happened for Jews in the past forty years. How can you argue that the attempt to become assimilated or to move up in a society that separates Church and State, public and private, has been unsuccessful? In America, there is certainly evidence that, even though anti-Semitism is still around, Jewish persons can indeed function and be accepted as relatively equal.

M.L. I personally believe it's time to trust non-Jews again, but in order to make that case plausible I have to first acknowledge what's reasonable in the case of those who still stand by their paranoia.

C.W. In Israel that paranoia is understandable.

M.L. Even in the United States, Jews are fed with their mother's milk a paranoia that runs the following way: "Everything you are saying now about the United States is exactly what people were saying about Germany. There was no society in which Jews seemed to have greater integration and acceptance. They were the leaders of culture: famous musicians, artists, and poets. German society seemed committed to the life of the mind and the spirit such that, despite currents of anti-Semitism, Hitler could be dismissed as an individual nut case. Even when he started passing anti-Jewish laws, most Jews dismissed it as an aberration due to the Depression, which would pass. The Germans would go back to their noblest and highest traditions. They themselves were fundamentally Germans, not Jews."

C.W.   There is a parallel in that present-day America is probably as decadent as Weimar Germany. But there is also a disanalogy. There is much less possibility of the U.S. producing a fascist leader who violates the rule of law across the board as Hitler did, due to America's longevity versus the fragility of Weimar German democracy. Our democracy is not what it could be, but it is much stronger than Germany could have ever imagined. Also, the presence of Black folk here, unlike in Germany, reduces the possibility of Jews becoming the scapegoat. That doesn't mean that Jews won't be included among the people of color, the gays, the women: but the targeting of them would be much less, even if Black and brown folk, given their anti-Semitism, tried to displace them.

M.L.   Plus, I don't think Chrisianity has the hold on this society that it had in Europe. The anti-Semitic traditions of the Church in Europe never permeated the secular sphere here in the way they did there.

Let's change the historical moment from one in which America is at the height of international and economic power to one in which there are no longer endless resources for the ruling class to buy off dissent. The society is in decline, facing a disintegration of its credibility. A militant movement of some sort is issuing a challenge, to which the response is, "We're not the ones screwing you up, it's the Jews. They own the banks, they're the big shots in the corporations, they run the news media. They're the ones you should be angry at." To the Blacks they say, "These Jews have been screwing over Palestinians and Arabs, and screwing you over, too. What society needs is a populist movement that blames the problem on the Jews." So that unfortu-

nately Blacks become that movement's leadership, articulating a populist anti-capitalism that supports a free market but blames the Jews for
wielding the power in it. Faced with this situation, I can imagine democratic restraint being somewhat less than impressive. And the rise of
the Christian Coalition makes many Jews wonder if politics will soon
be dominated by right-wing, Bible-thumping fundamentalists using
the most modern means of mass consciousness manipulation and
media-savvy spokespeople.

C.W.   I see the case you're making. It's certainly the case that any
people with a history of oppression, be it Jewish people or Black people, has to be suspicious of any present-day sanguine Pollyanna-ish
pictures of how nice things are.

At the same time I think that for anti-Semitism to happen at the
level you are talking about it would have to be linked with something
else, such as accusations of unpatriotism. It would have to be linked to
a neo-nationalism that excluded Jews from the national family, or to
some broad racism that tended to include as its target people of color.
So I think it's difficult to imagine Black folk being at its vanguard.
Most of your anti-capitalist Black folk would be more critical of and
less open to anti-Semitism than your pro-capitalist types.

M.L.   I'm not saying I believe this will happen, only that these
kind of paranoid fantasies are not totally crazy. They emerge out of a
real historical experience of oppression, and lead Jews to be very leery
of those who deny that as a reality.

C.W.   In the last forty years we've seen the boomtown entry of
Jews into the upper middle classes. So, many Black people would say,
"Yes, the Holocaust is in many ways indescribable, but what is the
link between the loss of one out of three Jews in the world and this
boomtown ascendancy of Jews into the middle and upper middle
classes? They may be psychologically traumatized, but at a socio-eco-
nomic level they're doing very well." It's a very narrow perspective
held by Americans and particularly by Black Americans.

M.L.   The Jews are an international people with a history—

C.W.   And that cuts against the American grain.

M.L. But it's how we have to look at ourselves. We can't look just at one little period in which things were groovy. To think ahistorically in that way runs counter to our whole trip, which is rooted in a redemption from slavery in Egypt 3,500 years ago. Jews in Spain thought things were groovy for hundreds of years: we called it the Golden Age of Jewish history. Then in 1492 they got kicked out and the Inquisition happened. Part of the problem these days in the Diaspora is the degree to which the Americanization of all Jews severs certain kinds of links to that history and to the Jewish past.

C.W. But what Black folk see is the reality of Jewish success.

M.L. There's something in the formulation of that statement that assumes that what is real is material success. The Marxists were unable to pick up on Jewish oppression, hence we were totally unprepared for the rise of fascism, which focused on anti-Semitism. Why? Because for the Marxists, the fundamental reality was economic oppression. Well, Jews seemed to be doing alright economically in 1920s' Germany, so Marxists didn't see them as a group whose interests needed to be protected. That's because Jewish oppression does not take the form of economic oppression. So does that mean they're not really oppressed? Or does it mean that Marxism's theory of what constitutes oppression is inadequate?

I opt for the latter. I say there are other forms of oppression that are spiritual, that are psychological, that have some resonance on other dimensions besides material deprivation. In its most crude form I would reply, "I'd rather have my people be poor today and not have had one out of three of us killed off fifty years ago. Speaking at a personal level, I'd rather have my sixty murdered relatives alive today and be in the working class, or struggling as a farmer somewhere." If I could make that trade-off, I would.

C.W. I understand. Your point is a good one. Yet is it reasonable to believe that institutional violence will strike middle-class Jews in the near future?

M.L. Only if you pay attention to our actual history. In the past two thousand years we have not gone for longer than a period of one hundred years before it erupted again. Given that there's a world of oppression, given how that world is structured and how there are ruling classes, we have gotten screwed over time and again. This has also had the effect of creating a certain kind of personality structure that generates more antagonism, because if you're expecting to get screwed over you act defensively, which leads other people to be angry at you. That behavior reaction, the development of "offensive" traits, is itself part of our victimization. It's part of our history of oppression. Israel's policy toward the Palestinians has been the tragic consequence of Jewish history, because we are acting out, in a paranoid and defensive way, what has been done to us.

C.W. I'm deeply suspicious of any form of nationalism that privileges a particular ethnic or racial group, the way Israel does in its Law of Return that gives special rights to Jews. When it comes to the Black context, I would never support a Black nation state on *moral* and *democratic* grounds that had a law of return primarily in order to preserve the Black character of the nation. With Israel, I would support it on *prudential* grounds, given the lack of alternatives. But I'd never call it a healthy *democratic* state—hence I'd try to democratize it.

M.L. In the context of struggling for a democratic world, there may need to be enclaves in which a particular group's historical pain is given special attention and requires special healing. I don't see that as antidemocratic, anymore than I think it antidemocratic that within a democracy there be individual families in which the needs of the members of the family are given higher priority or weight than that of the rest of the community. To support Zionism is simply to support affirmative action on the international scale.

Within the Jewish tradition the tension between particularism and universalism is not so great as many other forms of nationalism. In the United States I rarely find strong nationalists who are simultaneously emphasizing a universalist vision of fulfillment of all peoples. Yet I see that in the Jewish tradition, and as a result it has never been a surprise to me that those who came out of the oppression of Jewish history were led, from the ideological base of the universalist particularism, to create a secular universalist politics.

C.W.   But all progressive nationalists have a universalist dimension. That is why I call them progressive. Do you agree that to be a Zionist is to be a nationalist of a certain sort?

M.L.   To be a progressive Zionist is to have a commitment to a universalist perspective that makes us far closer to Karl Marx than to, say, Mussolini.

C.W.   But the halfway house is still in the nationalist camp, with universalist vision. You use a universalist vision to justify a particular form of nationalism.

M.L.   But out of my particular form of nationalism I came to believe that my own nation's best interests are served when all nations' interests are served.

C.W.   A lot of nationalists say that.

M.L.   Jews have played a disproportionate role in pushing forward universalist visions in the world not because our oppression throughout history was so much worse than that of any other oppressed group but because our nationalism was always connected to Torah and its validation that all people are created in the image of God, all deserve to be recognized, and that it is the religious obligation of Jews to love the stranger (and to remember that we were strangers in the land of Egypt). However much that message is being violated by some people on the ultranationalist or chauvinist religious Right in Israel, it is an intrinsic part of the heritage of Jewish nationalism. But how do you distinguish yourself, Cornel, as a universalist from a Black progressive nationalist? What is the difference between those two positions?

C.W.   The difference would be that a commitment to substantive and radical democracy is always primary and never to be subordinated to the interests of a particular group or nation or peoples. So a progressive nationalist would say, see I want to be as democratic as I can given my commitment to the survival of this particular nation. And so when those two are in tension—commitment to radical democracy vs. commitment to nation, and the tension does come—then you usually see the tilt toward nation as opposed to democracy. In that part of our debate about the State of Israel, the Law of Return, how democratic is

Israel, to what degree are their attempts to keep it a Jewish state and in some sense a democratic state, those are deep tensions.

M.L.   What you're saying is there is a principle that you put above the nation. That principle is democracy. I, too, put something above the nation, but it is not democracy, it's God.

There is in all human beings a part of our being that transcends the particularities of each and every culture and connects us to a God energy that permeates the universe, and from my standpoint the reason that a particular culture, for example Judaism, is justified is that it somehow resonates with and provides an access to that universal aspect of our souls. This is what the Torah means when it declares that all human beings are created in God's image. But having said this, we also must simultaneously acknowledge that Judaism is only one of many such avenues—and that is precisely what our Torah tells us when it tells us that every human being is created in the image of God.

I don't see this universalism as counterposed to nationalism because this universalism came out of this national vision. But it is a universalism, a highest principle, unlike democracy, which is more of a procedural principle for determining what to do. The nation only has rights or entitlements to the extent that it lives a moral life in accord with God's demand.

C.W.   Then there are two questions that come to mind. One is, is it the case that you are fundamentally a prophetic advocate of Judaism and secondarily a progressive proponent of Zionism? And if that is the case, then how does one translate on the ground in terms of those deep tensions between universalistic claims like democracy and particularistic claims like laws of return that tend to preserve the prevailing character of the nation state?

M.L.   Well I am not against nation states.

C.W.   The question is not being against them, the question is how democratic they are.

M.L.   How democratic they are depends on historical configurations at a particular moment, like at this moment I am for pushing

American democracy much further. On the other hand, I might not be for pushing some newly emerged state that hadn't had a chance to get itself together at all. I might say well, is it in a trajectory toward increased democracy?

C.W. Do you not believe that Zionism is a species of nationalism? A form of national self-determination?

M.L. Yes.

C.W. And you characterize yourself as a Zionist of some sort?

M.L. Yes.

C.W. Then you are a certain kind of nationalist.

M.L. I'm a religious Zionist. Religious Zionist means that I have the view that the world is governed and ought to be governed by God and that the nation has a relationship and a claim to the extent that it lives according to God's will.

C.W. Is that true for every nation or just certain nations?

M.L. I don't know about that. I want to hear what other nations have to say about their relationship to God.

C.W. But every nation we know has had some religious claim to God.

M.L. I'm not disputing that. I'm merely saying I know about my nation's relationship to God. I don't know about everyone else's relationship to God enough to try to make some general statement about what it is or isn't.

C.W. We go back to the issue of chosenness, the theological backdrop here, which means that there certainly is a unique covenantal relationship with one people and God, not because other peoples are less important, not because other peoples somehow deserve less value, treatment and so forth, but historically speaking there is this unique covenantal relationship that comes out of Judaism.

M.L. The thing is that the Bible doesn't use this word *unique*. Unique makes a claim about what God's relationship is to us in comparison with what God's relationship is with others. And I don't have any religious basis for knowing about God's relationship with others. I just don't know about it. I am not making a claim one way or the other.

C.W. But we know from the Hebrew Bible that God's relationship with the Caananites is different from God's relationship with the Israelites. Isn't there a difference there?

M.L. I know what God's relationship is with us. I don't know what God's relationship is with the Caananites.

C.W. Well, what would you infer? We don't have to have too much evidence.

M.L. For all I know, God had the exact same relationship with the Caananites and they made, at about the time that we entered that land, the same kind of moral errors that got *us* thrown out five hundred years later. What the text says is that this is a land that vomits out its corruption, and for all I know there have been one after another of these screwed-up peoples of which Jews are only one in a long list of screwed-up people.

C.W. The Christian claim is we are all in some fundamental way screwed up, but the difference is that this particular person who emerges out of the Israelite lineage actually has a different kind of status than another kind of person who came out of the Caananite lineage. So that if Jesus shows up out of this people who have this covenantal relationship that you can vouch for, even though you won't vouch for the Caananites and the other folks, but he comes out of that lineage, then there ought to be something distinctive about them from a Christian point of view.

M.L. Distinctive about them?

C.W. Yeah. Namely that they have this covenantal relation.

M.L. We have a covenantal relation to God. I just don't like claiming that nobody else does. I don't know about whether anybody else does.

C.W. Wait now, for the most part, people don't.

M.L. Well, you know that. I don't know that.

C.W. Why would you not know that?

M.L. Because the way I understand the covenant is a way of people getting a certain revelation from God.

C.W. Did other peoples get that revelation?

M.L. A lot of other peoples might have. They might not have used that language to describe what was happening because what this revelation is, is a certain turning to the source of being of the universe and understanding that they are commanded to see other human beings as created in the image of God and commanded to treat other human beings accordingly. I think that when this revelation happened to the Jewish people, somewhere between 1200 and 400 B.C.E., there is some energy coming into the world, giving Jews that message. My guess is if you look, this is the same time as Buddha, and Lao-Tsu and Confucius, this is the same time as some of the great teachers of Greece and other peoples as well. This energy was getting picked up by a lot of different peoples in a lot of different languages and I don't think necessarily that the Jews are the only ones who got the revelation. The part of the revelation that we got that might have been different from others was that we got the idea that the world could be fundamentally transformed.

C.W. That is a very important difference. There is a sense in which I would probably be much more willing to talk about the distinctiveness of the Jewish people than you would. That is to say, that when you organize your life and community around revelatory claims that the world can be changed, the world can be transformed, there is a fundamental identification with oppressed people with a stress on justice and mercy and righteousness and treating the stranger with kindness. That is not what Socrates is about, that is not what Plato is about, that is not what Lao-Tsu is about, that is not what a whole host of other religious or non-religious thinkers with whom we associate intellectual prowess, wisdom and so forth, that's not fundamentally what they are about. That doesn't mean what they are about is thoroughly negative, but it does mean what they are about positively is not about what was at the center of Jewish life, ideas about human dignity and about economic and social justice that feed on into not just Christianity but on into so much of the best of the modern world in terms of democratic notions and so forth. Now there I think we can just be explicit about that and just say look, this is distinctive.

For me the ultimate culmination of this prophetic viewpoint cuts against any form of nationalism. I say unequivocally as radical democrat and Christian, nationalism is a form of tragic tribalism. We are stuck in it but it is idolatrous for the most part. Now you would say, I am a Zionist, a religious Zionist. Zionism is a species of nationalism, but I'm critical of forms of nationalism from a religious point of view.

M.L. To the extent that they all have the possibilities, including Zionism, of being idolotrous, to that extent all nationalisms, including Zionism, should be carefully scrutinized and should be subject to vigorous critique.

C.W. Okay we agree on that point. Then where is our disagreement?

M.L. Just how we are labeling.

C.W. But the difference is probably that you are still willing to view yourself as part of a nationalist camp.

M.L. Yes, I like this people. I identify with this people and its project because . . .

M.L. Well I identify with Black folk, but not as a Black nationalist.

M.L. For a religious Jew, nationalism is always in the context of the struggle against idolatry and so our commitment to this people is consistent with warning this people that it must be subordinate to

God. For some ultra-nationalistic religious Zionists who became part of Gush Enumim, God's will is supposedly shown by the victories of the Israeli army. So if the Israeli army conquers the West Bank, well, that must be God's will. But this is the opposite of the bibical conception which says you can have lots of power but still be totally messed up from God's standpoint and in the end God will throw you out of your land of Israel—because our claim to possess the Land of Israel is totally dependent upon our ability to live a morally and spiritually sensitive life in that land.

C.W.   I think we are very close here. One of the choices which is a bit farfetched but analytically may help to sharpen this a bit is: if, in fact, you had a choice for the democratization of the nation, as opposed to preserving the particular character of the nation, what would you choose? I can imagine a Black nation created because the U.S. nation state has chronically failed over time to protect Black people. I would support that Black nation on prudential grounds. The same way I support Israel on prudential grounds for the security of Jewish people. Europe and other parts of the world have proven they can't treat these people right. Would I defend that nation on democratic grounds? No. Would I defend a Black nation on democratic grounds? No. If I had to choose, then, at a particular historical junction between the democratizing of that nation or the preservaton of the Black character of the nation, or the Jewish character of the nation, I would choose the former, no doubt in my mind. We are talking at particular moments. The question would be, at particular moments for you, would you certainly envision yourself thoroughly promoting democratization rather than preserving the Jewish character of the state of Israel?

M.L.   Yes, but the reason for that is that the only way to have a Jewish state is to have a democratic state. There are two meanings of a Jewish state. One would be a Jewish state where a lot of Jews live, which in that case we could have that in New York City.

Or you could say a Jewish state is a state which is actually a manifestation of Judaism, and in that case from my standpoint it can't be a Jewish state unless it's based on the assumption that every human being is created in the image of God and infinitely precious and valuable. Now you can't have that and subordinate the interests and needs of some minority population there, as currently happens to Israeli Arabs within the Green Line (the pre-1967 borders of Israel). So the reason I am a strong advocate of human rights and democracy is that these are concrete political manifestations of our fundamental belief in the sanctity and specialness of human beings as created in the image of God.

But one could use democratic mechanisms in such a way that the state that was Jewish in terms of population and Jewish in terms of commitment to human rights and democracy would still *not* be a Jewish state in terms of the choices it democratically made (e.g., if the people democratically decided that they loved capitalism so much they wanted to work seven days a week and buy and sell seven days a week. If it gave more attention and priority to accumulating wealth than to responding to the universe with awe, wonder, and radical amazement, it would be substantively so far from Jewishness that it would be hard to consider it a Jewish state).

From my perspective, the central element in a Jewish state is a state that is committed to the healing, transforming, and repairing of the world, which is the heart of the Jewish vision. Just as a Judaism that becomes a mere ritual-governed activity and that loses its focus on *tikkun,* on healing and repair, isn't authentic from my perspective (and I'm a supporter of ritual, not someone who feels that they necessarily limit or oppress us), so too a Jewish state that has all the other elements, including democracy and Jewish cultural observances in place, but does not commit itself and its resources to *tikkun olam,* to healing the planet and transforming the world to make it a place of justice, peace, and love, is not a Jewish state, but merely, like New York, a state where there are lots of Jews. So I'm only a Jewish Nationalist if Jewish Nationalism is conceived of as substantively dedicated to serving God, and by that I don't mean how often it uses theological language, but how much its energies and culture and intelligence and resources are committed to doing God's work of pursuing justice and maximizing love and peace and bringing healing to this world.

In the historically specific circumstances of Jews living in North America in the late twentieth and early twenty-first century, those flowery terms have to translate directly into the struggle to end the economic and political oppression faced by African-Americans in this country, just as in Israel it has to translate into ending the Occupation and rectifying the injustices that have been done to Palestinians. But as a person who deeply loves my own people, I insist that the process of rectification and repair be done in a way that does not endanger my fellow Jews, does not demean the Jewish people, and does not deny our right to seek our own well-being as a people.

CHAPTER 7

Jewish Racism and Black Anti-Semitism

The sad truth is that racism and anti-Semitism are realities in each community, and our task is not to deny but to explore how and why this is the case.

C.W.   Given the experience of the Jews in Europe, any manifestations of anti-Semitism deserve attention and legitimately generate concern. But you have to be very clear about the scope, depth, and numbers involved so that you don't give the racists and anti-Semites a bigger platform than they deserve. The ADL and some of the other supposed defense organizations have made a big mistake in focusing on Black anti-Semitism as if to imply it's much more important among Blacks. Of the 1,800 physical attacks on Jews last year, very few of them were by Blacks. That kind of deep hatred is still a marginal phenomenon in the Black community. I think it is much more prevalent in the white Christian world, and not just among fundamentalists. Yet the publicity of the mainstream media responds to the way that ADL focuses on specifically Black anti-Semitism..

M.L.   The ADL, like the Simon Wiesenthal Center in Los Angeles, has built its financial appeal to Jews on its ability to portray the Jewish people as surrounded by enemies who are on the verge of launching threatening anti-Semitic campaigns. It has a professional stake in exaggerating the dangers, and sometimes allows existing racial or political prejudices in the Jewish world to influence how it will portray the potential dangers. As a result, there are voices among

American Jewish liberals who question the special emphasis that ADL has placed on Black anti-Semitism. But you have to understand this as part of a larger political pattern, because the ADL was also involved in denigrating people on the Left, including Jews on the Left, who critiqued Israeli policy. In the name of defending Jewish interests, these organizations often end up defending a particular politics within the Jewish world and imagining that anyone who does not agree with those politics is a threat to the Jews, including fellow Jews with whom they disagree. Their power is that they continue to attract Jewish donors and members who are fearful of the undoubtedly real threats that do still exist, and which ADL sometimes is able to document.

Though I personally feel that ADL's impact is often pernicious, I don't want that to be the basis for you getting off the hook on this issue. Because even though the ADL may exaggerate the problem, the anti-Semitism that *does* exist in the Black community is shocking for Jews—so I'd appreciate your explanation of it.

C.W.   It has a number of different sources. The first is religious: the Christian tradition that the Jews are Christ-killers, from which the Black Church is not exempt. The second is economic, coming from interaction with the small numbers of Jewish businessmen and women active in the Black community. The third is cultural. Historically there has been an association between Black and Jewish people, who have tended to measure themselves in the light of Jewish achievement. That Jews have been able to move so quickly up the American ladder generates a deep sense of resentment and envy. Black people see a discrepancy between the claims that anti-Semitism is so pervasive in American society and yet this tremendous ascendancy of Jews into the upper middle classes. Whereas the Black people who are making the same claims about racism are not in any way being able to ascend in the way Jews have. So religious, economic, and cultural factors combine to produce a certain type of Black anti-Semitism. On the other hand, I think it's amazing the degree to which Black anti-Semitism is not as universal as people think. There is also an acknowledgment, albeit ambivalent, of the tremendous contribution Jews have made to the Black struggle in this century.

M.L. Your account of why this same resentment doesn't exist toward other immigrant groups that have made it—say, Japanese Americans—is that there's no history of religious anti-Japanese sentiment.

C.W. There may be resentment of Asian upward mobility, but the greater preoccupation with Jews is generated by Black identification with them.

M.L. Are there some areas where you feel Black anti-Semitism isn't being adequately addressed by the Black community?

C.W. Yes. First, I don't think Black churches have adequately reflected on the potentially anti-Semitic element in the Christian narrative. Second, I don't believe progressive Black nationalists have acknowledged the degree to which anti-Semitic elements have been built into the Black nationalist tradition. Not that every Black nationalist is an anti-Semite, just as not every Zionist hates Palestinians. Another source of tension is connected to gender consideration. I would like to see some comparison of attitudes toward Jews of Black women versus Black men. I do believe that anti-Semitism has an element of machismo: that the degradation of Jews has been linked much more to male virility and power than to what we've traditionally understood to be female roles. Such research would also include examining the relationship between Jewish and Black women, as contrasted to Jewish and Black men. Some Jewish men are also dealing with their own notions of machismo, and one wonders about the impact on this in a white supremacist society of Black males' reputed sexual prowess. Stereotypes of Black women are demeaning in a different way.

M.L. Do you have any suspicions about what you'd discover here? What is the psychoanalysis of Black-Jewish relations on the sexual level?

C.W. When you have a culture that has put such a premium on critical intelligence—what Freud would call the ego—then you do get a preoccupation with the id: the irrational, pleasure-seeking forces of the body and sexuality. Jewish culture has revolved around education to which Blacks often were denied access. There's no doubt that in American culture there has been a certain Jewish preoccupation with the id in a variety of forms, one of which is a fascination with Black culture and the Black body. A special relationship has evolved between the two groups, which functions on a deep cultural psychosexual level. It's not rational: it's to do with need. The Jews need to feel they have a special relationship with the people associated with id. The Black community needs to have a special relationship with the people associated with ego. This is just speculative food for thought.

M.L. I think it has also been a need for meaning and purpose. Secular Jews of the fifties and sixties were rejecting their own community of meaning as presented within the framework of a depoliticized and assimilated Judaism, and were attracted to the Black world, which seemed to have its own meaning and purpose.

Black resistance to oppression was attractive because it provided an alternative image to younger Jews about how a powerless people could deal with oppression other than the (distorted, but nevertheless prominent) account of Jews as having been weak and powerless and led to slaughter without significant and sustained resistance.

C.W. It can be historically shown that there was something distinctively Jewish in the Jewish propensity toward the Black movement. It had to do with the strong socialist sensibilities that their ancestors brought with them from Eastern Europe and Russia. Their quest for Jewish identity was an affirmation of something that was there in their parents and grandparents—a critique of injustice. Even radically secular young Jewish students were acting on a history of culturally leftwing responses to oppression.

Meanwhile in the sixties two themes were becoming prominent in the creation of a mass youth culture: sexual prowess and music. Music became a metaphor for sexual liberation among young people around the world. Now, the history of the Otherness ascribed to Black people tends to highlight sexual prowess and musical talent.

The culture revolved more and more around the centrality of popular music, which increasingly was Afro-American in origin, and around sexual prowess that had been linked to stereotypes of Black people going back hundreds of years. So it's not surprising that non-

Black youth would feel that somehow these Black young people had an advantage in terms of status within the mass youth culture. It's likely that this culture, and the perception of Black sexuality, played a role in how young Jews understood the Black quest for identity.

M.L. Of course, Jewish youth in the fifties, sixties, and seventies was divided between the majority who did not get involved in social change, though they sympathized with the goals of civil rights, and a very large minority who went beyond sympathy to active involvement, including in many cases a kind of idealization of Blacks as having a salvific identity. That idealization lasted for a decade, and then shattered as Jews started to meet Blacks who were not part of the Movement, and from whom they experienced antagonism that led many Jews to recoil and return to the path of their parents, who had by the mid 1970s made a major transition from the cities to the suburbs, in part to escape the perceived problems brought to neighborhoods by some of the African-Americans who were moving in.

C.W. And meanwhile they and their parents in the mainstream Jewish community are moving toward more subtle anti-Black racism, which persists to this day.

M.L. I certainly wouldn't deny the existence of anti-Black racism in the Jewish community. Most of this is a transference of general white racism, which Jews have bought into increasingly as they've assimilated American values; some of it is based on encounters with Blacks in which either violence has been experienced, or in which Jews have not respected the values that seem to dominate in Black culture. That culture is often a response to oppression, and Jews want to know why Blacks don't deal with oppression the way Jews did. Jews, however, never faced a breakdown in family and community in any way comparable to hundreds of years of slavery, so they don't understand why Black culture can't embody Jewish strengths. They find the answer in American society's assertions of Black inferiority, which fits a tendency amongst Jews toward *goy*-bashing: putting down non-Jews as somehow less than them. This is partly a product of Jewish defensiveness, self-protection against living as a denigrated minority in a Christian world. We turn it around and say that precisely because of the way they treat us, they are inferior. It is especially easily applied to Blacks because even the white *goyim* say this about them.

C.W.   It often takes the form of focusing on Black crime.

M.L.   Jews have experienced more direct confrontations and tensions with Blacks than with many other groups in American society, because we were the last ones living in the ghetto before the Blacks moved in. If, from their suburbs, the Jews now turned around and focused on crime amongst Blacks, their experience of crime would give us a reason for doing so, but not justification. It would still be wrong.

C.W.   Every discussion of crime in the U.S. that I know about has focused on Black crime.

M.L.   Yet it's not true about the Jewish community. When you go to a meeting on crime at a synagogue or a Jewish Community Federation, you won't hear a focus on Blacks. You won't encounter the analogue of a progressive Black rally talking about Jewish crimes in the State of Israel. There's plenty of racism amongst Jews, but it's not manifested by trying to deal with America's crime problem as a Black problem.

C.W.   I can't see how a Jewish meeting, as opposed to any other meeting, could fail to acknowledge Black crime, since some Blacks are disproportionately committing it.

M.L.   One-on-one amongst Jews you'll find some blaming of Blacks, but in public forums there's a little more sensitivity about racism.

C.W.   A small percentage of Black people are committing a disproportionate amount of crime. There's nothing racist about pointing that out.

M.L.   An even larger percentage of violent crime is perpetrated by men, but rarely do people talk about "male crime." Talking about "Black crime" is done to imply that the blackness is the explanatory feature, the cause, and that *is* racist, and leads people to fantasies of solving crime by throwing more Blacks into jail, and leads inner city policemen, even Black policemen, to imagine that every Black teen-ager they see is probably a criminal.

Jews in the U.S. have been on the cutting edge of supporting liberal forces that say the problems of the ghetto must be solved not with more law and order but with jobs and economic equality. In every election, Jews in overwhelming majorities have voted for the liberal candidate. We're the only group in America except for Blacks to do this.

C.W. Don't forget that you also have strong neoconservative Jewish voices which are as much for more prisons and police as any other conservative group. But when it comes to the majority of Jewish voters, you are absolutely right. I think that's something that needs to be acknowledged and highlighted.

M.L. It isn't acknowledged by Blacks.

C.W. That's not true. It's acknowledged by former Congressman Bill Gray, Elaine Brown, by Jesse Jackson. It could be veiwed as opportunistic, but it's not as if Black leadership hasn't recognized the degree to which Jewish voters have helped put Black mayors and state legislators into office.

M.L. Sure, those Blacks who seek Jewish economic or political support acknowledge the role, if pressed. But from most Blacks, including most Black intellectuals, Jews rarely get a feeling that we are recognized for the disproportionate support we've given to causes close to the heart of the Black community. Instead, we sense a special hostility coming at us from Black intellectuals and professionals who seem most interested in making these critiques of Israel.

C.W. Some Black professionals, finding themselves in workplaces where Jewish professionals wield power over them, do have a special hostility toward some Jews. Others react negatively to what they perceive to be an ideological shift in the Jewish professional world away from previously progressive perspectives. More Jews are Republicans every day. Black folk are wondering what the hell is going on.

M.L. Of course I've been arguing that this phenomenon is not independent of the movement of Blacks toward anti-Semitism.

C.W.   Black anti-Semitism is not the major factor why you're getting more Jewish Republicans every day. I think it has as much to do with class position, or with U.S. foreign policy. It might be one factor among others, but my hunch is that on a scale of 0–10, perception of Black anti-Semitism would rank at about 1.5, and class considerations probably at about 4.

M.L.   One argument is that people's objective class situation tilts them toward selfishness. Yet their Jewish ideology tilts them toward caring about Blacks. So there's a conflict here. The more the dominant society moves toward selfishness as its common sense, as it did in the eighties, the more people are inclined in that direction; but their identification with their Jewish history and Jewish culture pulls them back toward caring about the Other and caring about the oppressed. Now along come Black anti-Semites and provide people with exactly the excuse that they need to be able to say, "Oh well, my Jewishness shouldn't count against my being a Republican or my selfishness because these folks for whom I'm trying to not be selfish hate me!"

C.W.   In your view, what weight would the perception of Black anti-Jewish sensibility have in pushing Jews to the Right?

M.L.   In my view, it has been critical since the late sixties.

C.W.   On a scale of 0–10?

M.L.   It's not like that, because it's not an independent variable. It's a variable that fits into a pattern, a total picture, in which there's already a conflict between people's desire to hold onto their past and the ideology of Judaism versus their desire to be like Americans, to fit in. So Black anti-Semitism becomes an important legitimating factor in moving in a direction of selfishness. But I don't know how it weighs. It could be the straw that breaks the camel's back. It's not that heavy a straw, but it's the one that when everything else is exactly in balance tilts the argument in a particular direction.

C.W.   Would you say, absent the Black anti-Semitism, that there would remain a movement to the Right?

M.L.   I think there would be a much more significant Left in the Jewish world, and that that Left would be much more attractive to younger Jews. The Right is able continually to say to the Jewish Left, "You guys are self-hating. You want to ally with these people? Open your ears and listen to what they are saying. They're saying, 'We don't want you. At best you Jews are a problem for us, at worst you're the enemy.' "

C.W.   If you had a Black community in which King's legacy was thoroughly hegemonic, wouldn't the Jewish Right come up with some other excuse?

M.L.   It would, but it wouldn't have as much appeal. Because the Jewish Left wouldn't be so much on the defensive. The Jewish Left would have a lot stronger basis if we had another community that was our real ally. Since we don't have that we're in a very defensive position, because we keep on saying, "Care about these other people, these people who are getting screwed over by capitalism," and these people who we're saying we should care about are turning around and seeming to spit in our faces.

C.W.   But it's such a small slice of the Black community—

M.L.   It's not that small a slice! Not in terms of the experiences of kids on college campuses. When you're a Jewish kid on a college campus who hasn't met any Blacks growing up in his or her white suburb, and isn't meeting any in graduate school, certainly not in their profession. Their main encounter face to face with Blacks is on campuses, and it's there that this stuff is rampant.

C.W.   It's still a small slice, it's just that it's growing.

M.L.   In the sixties, if you wanted to reach out to Blacks, you could find a lot of Blacks to reach out to. I can't find them now.

C.W.   That's true for everybody in this society in relationship to everyone else. You can't reach out to hardly anybody. The Jews have trouble reaching out to Jews. Blacks have trouble reaching out to Blacks.

M.L.   Absolutely. There's been a breakdown of any kind of community, of shared vision. I'm saying that Black anti-Semitism has been a major factor in strengthening the Jewish Right, in making it more credible. When I speak to these kids on college campuses about these possibilities, they look at me like I'm totally crazy. They say, "Listen, we know who these Black people are and you don't. The Black people that we know on this campus hate us."

Now, I try to say to these Jewish college students, "There are other Blacks and you can find them." But what are they supposed to do, knock on peoples' doors and say, "Hey, you're Black. Are you open to me or not open to me?" It's very hard to do that if you think that you might have somebody tell you, "Oh, anti-Semitism, that's what you ripped off from me. There are no such thing as Jews, you're not really Jews at all." You just as much expect that to be the response as, "Hey brother, come on in, let's talk."

In that situation it's hard to be making the first move, particularly when Jews feel that it's not symmetrical. In other words, they don't see a Jewish demagogue like a Khallid Muhammad or a Louis Farrakhan getting, say, 20 percent or 10 percent of the Jewish students on campus coming out and saying, "These Black people have ripped off everything in America and are the source of our problems. You want to understand why Jews are in trouble in the world today? Why there has been fascism in the twentieth century? Because of Blacks." If we had that stuff going on at a comparable level of irrationality in our community, we'd say, "We understand their problems because we've got the same kind of nut cases here."

C.W.   When we actually look at the degree of anti-Black sensibility in the Jewish student community, what do we see? From the vantage point of some Black folk, the visibility of the Jewish Right is in some ways comparable to what you're talking about. It's not as overt or as explicit as Khallid Abdul Muhammad, but it can be just as effective in its more subtle and covert forms.

M.L.   It's mostly very invisible to Jews. I happen to agree with you that it exists but when Jews look around in their community they don't see it. You see it's one thing to say that there are messages that can be read as racist, for example when Jews turn their backs on Black suffering by saying, "These Blacks have brought their misery upon themselves." But you don't have a feeling that this is a racist statement because there are Black conservatives who say the same thing. Give them a Clarence Thomas or a Thomas Sowell and these right-wing Jews are totally embracing them and honoring them as Black intellectuals.

Meanwhile, I still don't fully understand your analysis of why Black anti-Semitism grew in the past two decades to whatever extent it did.

C.W.   I think what has happened is that the fundamental focus on Israel, together with the upper-middle class status of American Jewry, and the slow drift toward the center-right by certain elements, has made it difficult for people in the Black world to believe that the progressive elements in the Jewish world have the power they once did.

Yes, it would have helped if there had been that kind of reaching out from the Black world as Reaganism set in, talking about Jewish pain and oppression. But there were so many other things going on, such as the level of police brutality—you didn't see any major Jewish organization focusing on that. Those few Jewish progressives are always out there talking about it—*Tikkun, Nation, Dissent* magazine— but their voices are not heard that widely in Black America. So that what we see is programs pulled back, affirmative action attacked, police brutality, all viewed with relative indifference from the suburbs. There was a real sense that there was not too much reaching out to Blacks from the Jewish side. Hence the rift that has occurred. This is independent of any of the rhetoric we were just talking about; it's just everyday reality.

Look at the debate over the Holocaust Museum, which within the Jewish world has been quite intense. Now in Washington, D.C., you've got this powerful museum sitting at the very center of the capital of the nation. And you've got the series of evils which have historically sat at the center of American civilization uncommented on. When is America going to come to terms with its own legacy of injustice and evil toward indigenous people, the slave trade, Jim Crow, the suppression of the workers' movement? What that does for me is to raise the question, why this Jewish specific situation as opposed to these other specific situations? And of course the worst form of it is to engage in that algebra of blood that Camus talked about. Whose oppressions are worst? Why is their oppression gaining center stage and our oppression has no stage whatsoever? This is something of course that Farrakhan and others play on all the time with tremendous success, because it makes some sense.

M.L.   What do you say to that?

C.W.   What I say to that is to agree and disagree. On the one hand, they are absolutely right in terms of America's refusal candidly to come to terms with its own history of evils; on the other, the Holocaust is an evil that sits at the center of European modernity and is related to the other kinds of evil that we would talk about in the U.S. context.

I think one of the uglier sides of all this is the issue of power. The reason why you have the Holocaust Museum is not simply because the Holocaust was one form of evil, distinctive and unique, but that American Jews have levels of unity and influence and resources such that they can pull this thing off. Whoever really has the power to create such an event, that's who gets center stage. As long as Black people don't have the power to do it, nobody's going to give a damn about slavery, nobody's going to give a damn about lynching. But that takes the moral edge off it: it just becomes a question of who has the money. If you have the money to do it, you can keep your memory going; if you don't, you can't. And so we lose the deeper issues of how our injustices against humanity are linked.

M.L.   Of course one always has to make an important distinction between a segment of the people that has some power, and the people as a whole having the power. Just as Jewish progressives always insist that we should not be talking about Black crime, but crime of which a maybe disproportionate percentage is being done by a certain segment of the Black world. If I think that every Black person I see is a criminal because I've been talking about "Black crime," then that phrase starts to have racist dimensions to it because it seems to suggest that this is a phenomenon of an entire people.

Similarly, "Jewish power" has racist dimensions to it when it assumes that the rest of us have some kind of power or control over those Jews who have a disproportionate amount of money, or that they represent or speak for us.

C.W. This is precisely my point in terms of many Jews' perception of Farrakhan. If you hold that perception as a fact with substantiality to it, then it makes it very difficult to take the rest of the Black world seriously as a possible ally in a coalition, because you want to make sure that this substantial fact is thoroughly understood, contained, circumscribed, and controlled. Whereas your definition allows a certain fluidity to it, which means that it is always in process with a variety of other, potentially more desirable, facts that facilitate links.

M.L. In the course of the past few months I've been in synagogues in Tennessee, California, Oregon, Washington, New Jersey, and Florida as scholar-in-residence for the weekend. Over and over again, whatever I'm talking about, what do I hear? I hear, "Well all this is very nice, but don't you understand that those Blacks hate us?"

So when I hear this, I have to say to people, "Look, Farrakhan's not the whole reality of the Black world—there's Cornel West. You should know about West, about the NAACP, and people who think like them." Then they turn around to me and say, "Did you know that the NAACP invited Farrakhan to their meeting?" and I say, "Well, that's bad and they shouldn't have done it." And they say, "Do you know what else? Your friend Cornel West went to that Black leadership summit with Farrakhan. You're telling us not to worry about these other voices, but we're seeing that they are convergent."

My task is to convince people that that's not the entirety of the reality. If they believe it is, that makes it a lot harder for them to buy other parts of the liberal ideals they would like to respond to.

Meanwhile, like the rest of American society, there are a lot of Jews thinking, "Do I really want to pay more taxes? Do I want to pay higher health insurance in order to take care of these people? I'm reading in *The New Republic* that the reason why they're poor is because they are not willing to take care of themselves. They go out and have babies when they are fourteen years old and they don't care about the consequences. Then they tell me I've got to support them.

Well, sounds to me like maybe I shouldn't be caring so much about them and paying higher taxes when I could use that money for getting my kid a car."

C.W. "Or sending them to a private elite university."

M.L. "So why am I still on this liberal train? Because I'm Jewish. Well, what does my Jewishness mean to me today? Do I really feel that my Jewishness forces me to identify with the most oppressed? Maybe, it seems that these most oppressed people are irresponsible and hate me." Meanwhile, Jewish neocons covertly appeal to our selfishness by telling us that we'd actually take care of Blacks more if we were to end their dependency on governmental programs sponsored by well-intentioned liberals.

This kind of message requires that we suspend from our consciousness the fact that there aren't enough jobs to go around, and that Blacks desparately seek jobs at a decent wage, but that structural racism functions to ensure that unemployment will disproportionately fall on the Black community. But it's easy to forget that, when forgetting it coincides so nicely with the selfishness of not having to pay higher taxes to take care of our fellow human beings. Jews would have trouble doing this kind of forgetting, if they weren't assisted in the task by the honor given to a Farrakhan or a Jeffries in the Black community.

C.W. The more cynical voices in the Black world say that the argument about Black irresponsibility and laziness is actually about a need to account for Jewish drifts toward the center and the Right. That the focus on Black anti-Semitism and the obsession with Farrakhan become easy rationalizations to deal with an agonized conscience as one moves to the center and Right, rather than a major cause of that move. What do you say to those kinds of voices?

M.L. I'm not saying that Black anti-Semitism is solely responsible for the movement of some Jews in a conservative or selfishness-oriented direction. I'm saying that there is a dynamic struggle going on inside the Jewish people around these issues, just as this same struggle rages inside other non-Black Americans. Black anti-Semitism contributes to the mix that leads people to be more despairing of transformation, and hence to feel more legitimate about going for the self-interest like everyone else. Part of the reason the white media focuses so much on Black anti-Semitism is precisely because it plays so well into the dominant ideological cynicism of the media—as one more proof that *everyone* is out only for themselves, no one can be trusted, idealism is dead, and selfishness is king. So of course you are right that Black anti-Semitism can't be by itself the sole causal influence, but it can be a very important part of a mix.

C.W.   I think the same kind of struggle is going on in the hearts and minds and souls of a large number of Black folk. But I think what you actually get among Black pessimists—those who have given up on the possibility of coalition, given up on the notion that American society has the capacity to treat Black people like human beings—is a much stronger claim. Black anti-Semitism has in some ways always been there but is being highlighted now by Jews precisely because it not only rationalizes the Jewish move to the center and Right but is an attempt to hide and conceal the continual accumulation of more power and wealth and privilege among a sector of the Jewish world that itself is still relatively unaccountable to large numbers of Jews. The use of that power and wealth and privilege over against Black interests leads to a version of anti-Semitism which is obsessed with the uses of Jewish power vis-à-vis Black interests.

Black pessimists argue that very few people of any humane concern can actually live in a society with the levels of social misery being what they are. It's just so outside of the bounds of the richest nation in the history of the world. Over 35 percent of Black men and 51 percent of women unemployed, 51 percent of children living in poverty, 25 percent of young Black men either on parole or on probation or in prison: all this cannot be explained solely as a matter of individual behavior. So, since these generational layers of Black social misery still command very little attention in the larger society and less and less in the Jewish world, the argument is that the focusing on Black anti-Semitism must be a kind of looking away from, a way of justifying, the refusal to come to terms with that Black social misery.

M.L. Though Jewish neocons may be looking for an excuse, for most Jews there is a much more complex inner struggle going on, and many Jews are in inner turmoil, torn between the self-interest ethos of American society on the one hand, and their historical memory and religious tradition on the other. Moreover, no matter how much the conditioning of selfishness predominates in the larger society, there is something about what it is to be a human being that continually brings us back to a fundamental sympathy with and caring for other human beings. On top of that you've got the specific Jewish overlay of a tradition that validates that caring, that says, "Remember you were slaves in Egypt." Jews experience a special kind of tension in the obligation to remember our fundamental identity with the oppressed, because we were oppressed.

The selfishness in the larger society that is winning at the moment is not inevitably going to win forever.

It's always important to keep in mind how dynamic the issues are about what relative weight people are going to give in their own personal and economic and political lives to selfishness versus a willingness to make some sacrifices in short-term self-interest for the sake of others.

There's always this inner struggle in people between how much they go for their highest ideals versus how much they go for their selfishness. They look out at the world and are continually assessing what is going on with everyone else. Where the flow of possibility is. That's why vanguards become very important, because they are the groups that first tell you, "It's safe out here! We're the ones who jumped into the Red Sea and it started to split, so the rest of you can jump in. It's not going to kill you down here." Precisely because we had hoped for Clinton to be that vanguard telling us that it was o.k. to go for our highest ideals, his failure to do so in any overt and consistent way was more disillusioning even than anything that a Bush or a Reagan could have done to our hopefulness. Similarly, if the vanguard peoples—the Blacks and Jews, the two groups who have most consistently supported a progressive political agenda in the twentieth century—seem now to be saying, "We jumped down here in the water of hopefulness and now we're killing each other, instead of embodying a vision of hopefulness and cooperation and joint struggle against those who wish to privilege selfishness," then the others will say, "It's not so safe out there."

C.W. "I'm not jumping in *that* water."

M.L. "I'm not jumping into that water any more. It wasn't safe the last time I jumped in, in the late sixties," which is why so many people got out, "and now it looks like it's even more unsafe." So mine is a dynamic conception, one that recognizes that how people think about moral and political possibilities, and how much they are willing to risk transcending self-interest, is itself always in process, always impacted by their assessment of what is happening around them.

If we want Blacks out of poverty, they're not going to get out of poverty in a society in which most people share the ethos of selfishness. Most people are going to say to themselves, "If what counts is my short-term self-interest, then that means not paying more taxes. Maybe you're right that in the long run it would be better for me if there weren't poor people around. But if I can just pay enough taxes for more police, and more prisons, and stop there, I'll have more money in my pocket. So if the bottom line is short-term self-interest, screw the Blacks."

So Blacks have to say, "It is not in my short-term self-interest to live in a society where everybody's going for their short-term self-interest. I wish it were the white folks who were changing this first. But they're not! So I've got to worry about how to create a context in which they'll feel safe about moving toward idealism and caring."

C.W. Again though you can see a situation in which Black folk end up carrying more of the burden and having to do more of the work: especially if one fundamentally believes that there's only going to be a small number of white folk—albeit a larger number of Jews but still not hegemonic in the Jewish community—who are interested in allying with Blacks to change the larger context. Part of what fuels many forms of Black Nationalism, including the Nation of Islam, is the profound pessimism about the possibility of ever changing the larger context to one in which selfishness would no longer predominate in the white or Jewish population. But since only a very small slice of the white community, and a slightly larger slice of the Jewish community, are interested, it looks unlikely that a significant or substantive kind of coalition can take place. Therefore, in a context in which everybody else is concerned about their interests, the Black Nationalist point of view argues for being fundamentally concerned with narrow Black interests. This larger talk that you and I are putting forward about visions based on principled coalitions is something that is very rare.

Still, I like that dynamic conception of selfishness/caring. I think that your formulation of it is more convincing than the more mechanical one that simply says that people just look for whatever rationalization they can. I've always argued against Farrakhan and others that they ought not to be talking about Jewish power, especially in a conspiratorial form. You're talking about slices of Jewish elites who behave like any other set of elites. We shouldn't talk about Jewish power but about corporate power.

At the same time I would want to argue that persons in the Jewish world who are obsessed with Farrakhan ought to be just as or more obsessed with the Black social misery he focuses on. One of the reasons why Farrakhan does command a certain amount of attention is precisely what you said before. He focuses on Black social misery which itself has gone unfocused on for so long. There will always be Farrakhans as long as that social misery grows. If the Jewish world was to be as obsessed with the powers that be, the corporate and bank elites who often contribute to policies that perpetuate Black social misery, then that would be a way of speaking to that misery that Farrakhan himself focuses on with his own limited vision and truncated analysis.

Yet what one gets instead oftentimes is this obsession with Farrakhan and relative silence about the Black social misery that he focuses on. Hence the realities that we all ought to be concerned about are again rendered invisible.

M.L. I agree that the media and public attention too often ignore Black social misery, and the way it is connected to our economic and social policies in the U.S. There's a tendency to blame poverty on Blacks and to see poverty as the causal result of the "culture of poverty." And this is why I'm so upset with the Podhoretzes and the

Wieseltiers and the Peretzes: because they are the ones in the Jewish world who have legitimated drawing attention away from Black social misery and onto Blacks' responsibility for their own misery.

Their ideas are central to why this focus on misery doesn't happen in the Jewish world enough. Because they are legitimating a different discourse that says, "Yes, there is social misery, and you know who is responsible? The Blacks. They have brought this on themselves because they are irresponsible. We Jews didn't turn them into crack babies. And when we tell them they are irresponsible they turn around and say they hate Jews; that we are the ones who are doing this to them. And that's just further proof of how pathological these people are, that they would blame the Jews for something that they are clearly doing to themselves." When you read *Commentary* or *The New Republic* you sometimes get a feeling that they just can't hold back their delight at the prospect of throwing Black teenage mothers off of welfare or Black youth into an ever-expanding prison system.

C.W. Some of them are irresponsible. But you've got to link that to the larger social irresponsibility. Jewish conservatives, neoconservatives and neoliberals are part of a much larger movement. Their analysis is not prompted solely by their Jewishness, even though they do link their particular brand of politics to Jewish interests. That's what I mean by acknowledging their importance but not becoming obsessed with *them*. Although they play an important role—*New Republic* and *Commentary* are not to be sneezed at—they're still part of a much larger dynamic movement in the society as a whole.

M.L. I agree. All too often, however, Black intellectuals point out our Jewishness as the relevant factor to point to when they are denouncing Jews for activities that are engaged in by everyone similarly situated in the economic structure, but point to our whiteness when we talk about Jewish oppression. For example, when we say we want to have Jewish Studies or be included in the multicultural phenomena, a lot of Third World folk turn round and say, "What? You're not a separate entity. You're part of the white mass and you've already had your time." Which of course is ludicrous because the Jewish canon has been systematically excluded from the Western canon all the way through Western history.

C.W.   I want to know what you mean by "canon." Because so many highly influential Jewish intellectuals are part of the Western canon, especially the modern Western canon.

M.L.   You're talking about the last twenty years. My humanities course at Columbia didn't include a single Jewish author.

C.W.   You didn't read Marx, you didn't read Durkheim? At our college we read large numbers of Jewish writers, because it's just hard not to include them.

M.L.   The ones you mentioned, like Marx and Durkheim, are people who did their best to play down the fact that they were Jewish.

C.W.   They were Jews who happened to make certain choices but who nonetheless have contributed to Western civilization. You can't say, "Only my kind of Jews ought to be in the canon."

M.L.   I'm not saying that. I'm saying that the Jewish people have a rich history and culture and none of it appears in the canon. We've got a Talmud, we've got a Midrash, we've got a huge number of medieval philosophers and thinkers: and none of that appears in what gets defined as Western civilization. The Jews who are allowed to appear after 1850 appear not as Jews but as Western secular intellectuals. You can study Durkheim in a university and never know that he was a Jew.

C.W.   That's just because of the narrow way it's being taught. It's hard to understand who Durkheim was without understanding his Jewish origins, which no one would suggest fully accounts for his socialism or pragmatism. It's true that one can strip out these features—

M.L.   Well, they stripped themselves, because that's what the condition for entering society was for Jews: giving up their Jewish identity. You could keep your Jewish identity, as long as it was in the private realm. Not in the public realm: not in your realm as a philosopher or sociologist or psychologist or social theorist. That would be to bring something impure into the public realm. So Jews get to enter Western civilization only by denying or suppressing the Jewish part of their identity.

C.W. But denying or repressing it could be an occasion to high-light how important it is. So the fact that they also tried to strip themselves, and the fact that their subsequent reception has also downplayed their Jewishness, means that any serious understanding of who they are has to pay attention to what they repressed and how that denial was publicly validated.

M.L. I don't deny that. What I'm just saying is that it's hardly the same as the argument being used now by Black multiculturalists wanting to introduce Black curricula. They're saying, "We want to introduce these writers *because* they're Blacks. In other words, because in the Black culture itself there is something that we want to have represented in the multicultural agenda of the society. We want everyone else to learn about what it is that comes out of our people's experience, so we're not looking for the Uncle Toms to be represented; we're looking for people who are speaking as Blacks and writing as Blacks. You Jews, you've already had that."

Yet we *have not* already had that. We have not had Jews represented in Western civilization or in the great canon of the universities because they were Jews and speaking out of the historical experience of the Jewish people.

C.W. On the one hand, I think you have an important point. Even though you have autonomous institutions of learning that have sustained and expanded on that tradition, it has not been available to the mainstream. On the other, you've got Kafkas and others in whom you have to recognize just how prominent their Jewishness was, even in the denial.

When we talk about multiculturalism, there's no doubt you're right that there's been a process of selection in terms of what constitutes the canon that's downplayed Jewish voices, Black voices, Armenian voices; one could go on and on.

M.L. But my point is that when we Jews raise this issue, a lot of Black folk turn around and say, "Hey, you're white." But when we turn to the conservatism that is totally pervasive throughout American society, they turn around and say, "Hey, you're *Jewish!*" All of a sudden we're Jews. When we're doing something bad, we're Jews. Do you hear what I'm saying?

C.W.   I'll tell you one big difference. There's a difference between Jews who turn to conservatism and downplay Jewish identity and Jewishness, as opposed to Jews who turn to conservatism and highlight Jewish identity, in fact do it because of something called Jewish interest. This aggressive move over the last twenty-five years toward one's Jewishness and then casting it in a conservative mode has been cast in the mode of primarily pursuing Jewish interests. Now when you do that it's no accident then that Black folk say, "You're not just white, you're Jews because you're insisting on your Jewishness." When you cast it in a conservative mode it looks as if those Jewish interests are clashing with Black interests: and so you get an escalation of xenophobia on both sides.

CHAPTER 8

Economic Conflicts

Are there objective economic conflicts between Blacks and Jews and are they sufficient to explain the current tensions between these two communities, and will they remain definitive of the potential relationship?

C.W.   As Jews have moved out of inner cities and into the suburbs, they have tended to think like many other suburbanites. When we come to talk about urban decay, you're going to get suburbanites who are looking for *any* discourses that will rationalize their indifference and their apathy toward the plight of the city. To the extent that Jews have become more politically conservative and less interested in the plight of Blacks, this must be acknowledged as one important factor.

M.L.   That's true. Some Jews have not only moved physically but also spiritually, adopting the politics and moral attitudes of their neighbors in the nearly-white suburbs. Nevertheless, one of our tasks is to create a discourse that speaks to their interests and needs at the deepest level and shows them that what they need most in the world cannot be achieved by turning their backs on the plight of others who live in the city. That means showing them that they have a moral and self-interested set of reasons for caring about what's going on in the city.

C.W.   Yes, but not just the long-run self-interest, the short-run self-interest as well. They can't actually get a high enough level of security to protect their possessions. The plight of the suburbs and the cities is such that there is nowhere to hide. There are simply not enough security systems to protect their property as each year we carry on without facing head-on some of the deeper problems that contribute to criminal behavior. It doesn't mean that we don't need prisons and it doesn't mean that we don't need a fair criminal justice system that works. It does mean that as our cities continue to decay, the impact will be felt more and more in the suburbs at the level of crude self-interest, of fundamental needs. At the level of crude self-interest, what is fundamental are property, protection, and security. The suburbs will not and cannot remain as safe as we all want them to be.

M.L. There seem to be an awful lot of people who think at the level of crude self-interest whom I think have to be addressed on this point. They are saying to themselves, "We have to get more police; set up regulations to keep the city folks off of our streets; ensure that less of our taxes goes to these people." An important part of Clinton's massive 1994 Crime Bill got support from people who thought this way: "Those taxes we do pay should go for police forces, for an electronic fence, and for all kinds of ways to keep these people out of our suburban areas." The risk here is that we may move toward a class-segregated society in which, for example, they have their own television stations, and can do whatever they want on those stations . . .

C.W. . . . "We can live in a separate world . . ."

M.L. . . . "We can live in a separate world—a culturally separate world, a politically separate world, an economically separate world."

C.W. We have the figures. You see rising crime in suburban areas, both among young local people and among urban people going there for that purpose.

We see increasing fear even whilst security systems increase. We see a kind of Latin Americanization of American suburbs, in which you can build your walls high but you still live in fear. My hunch is that Los Angeles will become more frightful, more dangerous, and more insecure even as it acquires more police and a tighter criminal justice system. Those kinds of facts show that the particular set of strategies that some suburbanites support do not result in the desired kind of security. That's the bottom line. Building high enough walls and hiring enough police simply doesn't work. Chile is a case in point. Even the more conservative approach has been unable to produce results.

M.L. But the other way always seems to be one of systemic changes.

C.W. The other way is not only systemic change, but also on the road to systemic changes. Clinton doesn't have any systemic change in mind, but with support for public investment at least he's moving in the right direction. So far he's been halted by the dominant conservative wing of the Republican party, so we don't get more jobs, and we don't get better schools.

M.L. There are objective economic tensions here because suburban Jews may very well believe that their self-interest lies in getting their kids better schools rather than in giving some of that money to the inner city. They're being asked to reallocate their wealth, or some of what they have earned. There's a tension there and the question is: which way will Jews go? Which way will they identify? If they identify with the morally misguided strategies of conservatives who want to isolate the suburbs from the cities, they will bring upon themselves the anger of Blacks regarding their privileged circumstances.

C.W. Suburbanites also include the Black middle class.

M.L. So that this Black anger will also be directed at other Blacks who are living a better life.

C.W. That's the challenge of class. Even if the Black suburbanites still do vote disproportionately for a liberal candidate.

M.L. It is characteristic of Jews that those who are best off economically tend to have a higher degree of loyalty to traditional liberal causes, even when they are living in the suburbs. There are two reasons for this. One, they are motivated by a connection to Torah values and by their historical memory. Two, they have the cushion of greater economic superiority. Hence, they are voting less like their suburban brothers and sisters than you would expect based on economic figures alone.

Where Jews are closer to the lower middle class, like some who live in Brooklyn or Queens, racial hostilities are more intense and they tend to be motivated less by the legacy of Torah values, which they often dismiss as a luxury for those with greater economic and physical security. Ironically, and tragically for Judaism, some of these people *think* they are living religious lives, though when you ask them what part "love your neighbor as yourself" or "love the stranger" or other aspects of the moral commandments in Torah, just as explicit and clear as any commandment about kosher laws or about Shabbat observance, actually play in their lives, they dismiss this as irrelevant to daily life, act as though the strongly developed traditions of moral obligations have no relevance to anyone but Jews, and imagine that these moral commandments really have no application to their relationships to the poor. These are the Jews who voted for D'Amato, Pataki, and other conservative politicians who are anxious to further reduce programs for the poor.

C.W. In order to really get at some of the roots of this issue of "suburban versus urban," we have to talk about some of the ways in which suburbs were created. The way in which residential segregation was built in. The way in which mortgages were made available to certain groups and not to others. And hence the way in which suburbanization preserved a de facto segregated way of life. From the very beginning there were suburbs which were very much driven by a fear of Black people.

M.L. But you also have a flight of Jews from the cities, a flight that is based in part on fear of crime.

C.W. Fear of crime is synonymous with fear of Black folk.

M.L. They sometimes got mixed together in Jewish experience. Real estate interests created a panic in Jewish communities, causing them to believe that all of their property investments would go down the drain unless they sold their houses very quickly. There was a huge flight from the Jewish ghettos of Newark, where I grew up, into the adjoining suburban areas—tens of thousands of people, virtually the entire Jewish population, moved out in the course of ten years. That happened in part due to a strategy planned by a group of very opportunistic real estate people who saw the possibility of making a quick killing. Hillel Levine and Larry Harmon document this phenomenon in Boston. They also show how major financial interests helped manipulate this flight to their own advantage and to the disadvantage of the Black community.

It would have been very difficult to have done something about this dynamic without confronting head-on the interests of the banks and the real estate dealers—and that would have taken a Jewish leadership ready to raise questions about American economic elites whom they were not willing to confront and even had fantasies of joining.

C.W.   The failure of Black leadership is relevant, too, in not seeking a united front against bank and real estate interests. Achieving the united front would have taken a tremendous amount of organization, because alongside corporate interests, bank and real estate interests are the fundamental pillars of the American economy.

M.L.   Here you have a classic example of how opposition between the two communities is set up rather than generated out of our own spontaneous feelings, desires, or angers at each other.

C.W.   It's actually a divide-and-conquer strategy from above.

M.L.   Right. Once you get Jews running, then they sell their houses at a loss and they're angry at the Blacks for having undermined their investment. It's a self-fulfilling prophecy, because as some people begin to run, others feel like they have to sell their houses for less money than they thought they would get from another Jewish buyer. Because they have to sell to a Black family, everybody says to themselves, "I have to get out of here before prices fall all the way down, so I'd better make a compromise with my pride . . ."

C.W.   ". . . just to get what I can get."

M.L.   Right. This generates these falling prices, which then makes people angry that they lost their investment by virtue of Blacks moving into their neighborhood. Meanwhile, real estate companies and mortgage-offering banks and saving and loans made huge profits that would have been unavailable had neighborhoods remained stable, since far fewer people would have been seeking loans to make new housing purchases.

C.W.   In this process, negative perceptions of Black folk have been reinforced, because Blacks are seen as the cause of Jews losing the value of their investment in housing.

M.L.   And the irony here is that it was largely because of the negative perceptions of Blacks that the prices went down in the first place. On the other hand, that's not the whole story. The Blacks who have been oppressed in the larger society sometimes are actually bringing crime with them.

C.W.   That depends on what particular group of Black folk you're taking about. If you're talking about working-poor Black folk, then certainly you've got levels of criminal activity and behavior. If you're talking about stable, working-class Black people, there's much, much less criminal activity, even though they still suffer from the same stereotype. The Black middle class are often perceived as if they're the Black working poor in terms of their behavior. But actually their behavior conforms to that of much of the middle class in the country.

M.L.   When racist stereotypes are evoked you can't say, "Look, the prejudice shouldn't be towards all Blacks." The feeling is that as Black people moved in, crime went up, and we in the high schools experienced a new kind of hostility from Black teenagers in our daily interactions that often increased the level of fear and insecurity, so it appeared to many Jews as though the scary behavior of a *small* percentage of Blacks was being tolerated by the rest of that Black community. And that made some Jews distrust the whole Black community.

C.W.   The Black community hasn't tolerated it because they're being victimized more than the white communities. It's just out of control. They haven't figured out a way to stop it. It isn't as if Black people have any more control over eliminating Black crime than any other group. I wouldn't think that Jewish people have any control over Jewish crime or Italinan people over Italian crime. This is a public issue: the police are supposed to be doing something—but in the face of poverty, community breakdown, and despair, it's difficult.

M.L. I can tell you what the rap is among some in the Jewish community. It goes the following way: "When we were poor, back in the shtetls of Eastern Europe, on the Lower East Side of New York, in the East End of London, or the Jewish ghettos of Newark, people were starving or freezing to death in the winters. Our conditions were economically as devastating as those facing Blacks after Emancipation. Despite this we developed institutions of mutual support and caring that Black peoples can't seem to do." I'm frequently having to argue against this kind of reasoning.

C.W. Three points. One, there's a very rich history of mutual-aid societies, of Black support, in Black civil society from the churches to fraternities, sororities, and Masonic lodges. Between 1877 and 1920 an extensive system of social service provision was generated. It's important not to overlook that. Many of these still exist, although they're up against a lot.

Two, given 244 years of slavery and 80-odd years of Jim Crowism, Black people simply do not have the long history of independent and autonomous institutional development that Jews have, despite anti-Semitic persecution. There have been courageous and gallant efforts to do these things, but it's simply not comparable to what one finds in Jewish history. All through the Middle Ages and the modern world, Jews were frequently granted limited self-government and were able to develop and sustain a tradition of self-help institutions.

Three, it's important for Jewish Americans not to conceive in any way of Black people as wanting them to give them anything. We're talking citizen to citizen in this regard, we're talking about the quality of public life in society together. Money targeted for fellow citizens is not money given to Black people: it's money to provide possibilities for citizens to live together in a less violent, more loving way. Never is this a transfer from one ethnic group to another. This is important across the board, because tax monies involve Black money too. Once you break it down in a tribal manner, it degenerates into a no-win situation. Unfortunately the Republican party, given its racialized po-litical discourse, tended to reinforce this tribalistic mentality, so that

Blacks are recipients rather than fellow citizens. It's much more refreshing and positive to see Black people, *some* of whom come with a set of problems, as citizens who need more of a chance for us all to be able to survive on the boat together.

M.L. I definitely agree with you. What it reminds me of is an argument made by some Jews on the Left that the Jewish community should be aiding Blacks directly. Forget about government: on a community-to-community level we should be using our resources to help. Not just because they are fellow citizens, but because of their particular history of Black oppression.

C.W. The motivation is nice, because it seems to me they're trying to say that there is something distinctive about the plight of these citizens; and they're absolutely right. The racial caste system in American history is distinctive. It's different from ethnic discrimination, it's different from the degradation of women. The subordination and conquest of indigenous peoples was ugly and bloody and lethal, but nonetheless the racial caste system has its distinctiveness in relation to African people. So I understand what they are doing. At the same time I think there's a danger in collapsing *public* obligation, citizen to citizen, to the private concern of one individual ethnic group or racial group. This furthers the process of social and public space and public responsibilities being privatized.

M.L. A variant of this position calls upon Jewish liberals to argue in the public arena for reparations to Blacks for slavery, which haven't been delivered but should be. That is, Blacks not just as fellow citizens but as people who went through a particular historical experience.

C.W. That's an interesting formulation, though it's one about which I've always been ambivalent. It's difficult to dole out reparations as if there were a way of making up for slavery. I don't think it's possible for reparations in any way to begin to repay the depths of Black suffering and grief. Yet on the other hand, the American government is now making reparations to the Japanese, as the West German government did with Israel. So it might be something to explore. I'm much more concerned, though, about generating an active public sphere in which social provisions can be made independently of an appeal to a principle of reparations. One of the problems with reparations is that they may be a one-time affair. Once they're given, you figure you have no more obligation or concern. They're a soothing of the agonized conscience over a nation's racism, and therefore I'm a bit suspicious of them.

M.L.   Imagine, though, if the reparations took the form of giving every Black citizen a three-bedroom house and a job for twenty-five years. After that they would be on their own. Twenty-five years of employment would be a big jump: it's enough to start your kids off into a whole different reality. If they are at a high enough level, reparations don't seem so bad to me. And they are far more likely to reduce crime than the various repressive measures Clinton and the Republicans keep on dreaming up.

C.W.   I hear what you're saying, and although I would personally like to see happen what you've just said, because it would wipe out Black poverty overnight, it would still leave widespread poverty in the rest of the nation. I prefer to couch social reform and social change much more in principles that include the body politic as a whole. That could be naive and utopian, but it's what I'd like to see.

M.L.   I'd rather see a one-time major reparations than an on-going policy of affirmative action that sometimes seems to regenerate racial antagonisms. Where does affirmative action fall into your model of social reform?

C.W.   If a policy for affirmative action that is responsible for large numbers of Black employees is attacked with visible Jewish participation, it looks like naked Jewish self-interest versus Black self-interest. If Zionism is a metaphor for Jewish self-interest, then it looks like just a power game. No more appeal to moral principles. Zionism based on self-interest worked—you got a nation state. Hence the link with Jewish opposition to affirmative action based on self-interest. We also have to mention how the disproportionate amount of Jewish support for Black progress in the last sixty years is pitted against visible Jewish opposition to affirmative action. It stands in the way of that progress, and hence you get claims of Jewish betrayal. You couldn't do this with Italians. Italians have not betrayed Black progress because they were never significantly on board. All these factors make for tremendous tension and conflict. Now, as we know, there are Jewish voices for and against; there are Jewish voices everywhere. But the perception is one which downplays the role of moral principles, elevates naked self-interest, and therefore fans vulgar anti-Semitic charges against the Jewish community as a whole.

M.L. The maximum amount of Jews who voted for Reagan was 37 percent in 1980. No group opposed the Reagan/Bush years as consistently as Jews and Blacks.

C.W. That is still high for a group that twenty-five years earlier would have polled 8 or 9 percent right-wing votes. It's that 28 percent increase that serves as evidence of a Jewish betrayal. Take the Dinkins campaign. The Jewish vote still got him through in 1989. But if he'd run fifteen years ago I'm sure the Jewish vote would have been another fifteen points higher.

M.L. Well, he got the liberal vote among Jews, and for all the talk of Jewish desertion of Blacks, he lost only a small percentage of that vote when he ran for reelection in 1993. His loss was not a product of Jewish votes, but of the widespread sense of his incompetence (manifested not only in failing to quell the anti-Jewish riots in Crown Heights, but similarly in the way that he dealt with the fallout later). In the 1994 Congressional elections, 78 percent of Jewish voters supported Democrats—a higher percentage than Hispanics or any other supposedly non-white group, except for the 88 percent of Blacks who voted Democratic. Yet few Blacks recognize this objective alliance.

Similarly, Jews should be credited for supporting affirmative action more than virtually any other ethnic constituency that derived from European background. One reason this often goes unnoticed is that some prominent Jewish organizations opposed affirmative action (at least at the level of "quotas") and this got to be identified as representing the opinion of most Jews, which it did not. The media consistently quotes organizations like the American Jewish Committee or the Anti-Defamation League that are largely out of touch with the majority of Jews under the age of fifty. I've raised this issue repeatedly to editorial people at the *New York Times, Washington Post,* AP, and the major networks, usually to no avail.

C.W. But there are a disproportionate number of Jewish intellectuals who have identified themselves as Jewish who also identify themselves as politically conservative on issues affecting the Black community. For example, Nathan Glaser, Norman Podhoretz, or my friend Abigail Thurmond can critique and/or even attack affirmative action. Though Thomas Nagel or Gertrude Ezorsky or many writers in *Tikkun* subtly and persuasively defend it, the hard-core voices in the Jewish world get far more publicity in the *New York Times* and elsewhere. The Black community hears more Podhoretz-like voices than Michael Lerner-like or Irving Howe-like voices.

M.L. It's also true though that the Black community can choose which voices it wants to hear. Take *Tikkun* magazine, which has consistently supported affirmative action (though personally I'd prefer reparations, affirmative action is what we can obtain at this moment). In nine years it has become one of the largest and most influential Jewish magazines, and yet it doesn't get the quotations in the Black world. The Black world does not know about a liberal voice in the Jewish community; it doesn't hear the message that a lot of Jews do not support organizations that attack affirmative action. Some of them are Jews in Congress. Even you yourself almost fell into saying that all Jews were opposed to affirmative action.

C.W. That's why I was focusing on the visible Jewish voice—because *Tikkun* and other important liberal Jewish voices don't get the visibility they deserve.

The same thing happens in reverse. Take the silence over the killing of brother Yankel Rosenbaum. I received so many letters asking, "Why were you silent? Why was the Black community silent?" Yet this was a misperception. There were speeches. I wrote an article in *Tikkun.* Black preachers *did* speak out. But the Jewish community didn't hear those voices. They assumed there was a silence just as the Black community assumed there was a Jewish silence regarding affirmative action. The communication networks begin to break down.

The links between progressive Black and progressive Jewish folk become less and less visible. They are still there, but we could reach the point when people don't want to see them any more.

M.L. To the extent that Jews were ambivalent or opposed to quotas for affirmative action, that was rooted in our history in the earlier part of the twentieth century when Jews who tried to break into the mainstream of American society were faced with a system of discriminatory quotas.

Affirmative action programs were historically supported insofar as they were aimed at overturning those quotas that kept qualified people from entering any given occupation or profession. But Jews did *not* support the notion that rewards should be doled our proportionate to each group's relative size.

Jews had struggled against legal barriers to equality for a long period of time. Eventually this had led to their breaking down and to Jews becoming through merit doctors, lawyers, teachers, social workers, and so on in potentially disproportionate numbers. But when Blacks turned affirmative action from a strategy to break down discrimination into a program that mandated a certain percentage of Blacks in a given occupation, some Jews began to worry that, given that Jews make up 1.5 percent of the population, our struggle to achieve integration would be undermined and we would be confined to 1.5 percent of the available positions in the professions. Jews would then face a new kind of discrimination, a new resurrection de facto of barriers to our own previous success.

Acutely attuned to our history, we remember the external limits placed on us by societies that authoritatively allocated social and economic goodies, and we don't want to return to that, anymore than we want to return to the quotas that kept Jews out of many universities and professions in the past. So many Jews imagine that the free marketplace will be our salvation, because here our Jewishness will not be held against us and goods will be distributed according to some criteria of who is the possessor of whatever talents or skills that the society is currently valuing enough to reward.

My own work at the Institute for Labor and Mental Health convinced me that this picture of the free marketplace is largely distorted. In many workplaces, advancement is not dependent on intelligence but on one's ability to kowtow to the egoes or economic interests of those with more power. It remains true that access to certain educational opportunities, and being born into families that have rich social networks, may be more predictive of success than any innate intelligence or skill.

Moreover, the skills that *are* rewarded are determined *not* by what society needs most, but by what those who have power need most. So, aggressive personality structures, quick and aggressive verbal acuity, or ability to turn one's back on the suffering of others may be more "useful" to the powerful than, for instance, empathy, integrity, or a commitment to social-justice, though these might be more useful for the society in the long run. But because these latter qualities are not useful to the powerful, they will not get measured on "aptitude" or "achievement" tests, and those who excel in these ways may be severely undervalued as a result.

The classic defense of technocratic definitions of "merit" often went something like this: "Would you prefer a doctor who was more empathic and social-justice oriented, or one who had more technocratic skills to be diagnosing you or performing operations?" Supposedly, the answer was clear. But given the defeat of universal health coverage and severe market pressures to cut back or limit medical services given through health care plans, the answer today is less clear. By rewarding technocratic skills and giving no weight to empathy and social-justice consciousness, we've developed a group of health care professionals who have been willing to give disproportionate influence to the profit-makers and their needs, and hence have a system that is not available for many people, and is increasingly restricting care for many others. In that case, the general level of health care in the society may be lower than it would be if a different kind of skill had been rewarded. More people might be receiving health care today had the medical establishment adopted a health-oriented rather than profit-oriented approach in evaluating various schemes for reform. So, at least from the standpoint of those facing medical service cutbacks or no health care service at all, it might have been far preferable to have practitioners whose empathic and social-justice skills were given equal weight with technocratic skills that are proclaimed to be "neutral" or reflecting some kind of "merit."

Moreover, the kinds of practitioners we get when empathy is *not* a criterion for who can be a doctor are often people whose consciousness has been so shaped by the materialism and selfishness of the larger society that they feel cheated and "poor" if they are only making three times the median average income in the society. Their way of thinking fits well with that of the owners of large medical conglommerates whose powerful drive toward profits forces a reduction in the services being offered in health maintenance organizations, and the imposition of bureaucracies charged with ensuring that health care deliverers don't provide "too generously." I know many decent doctors who then find themselves being told that they can't offer treatments they want, or psychotherapists who must cut off treatment prematurely. Eventually, these doctors internalize the standards of the insurance companies or HMO bureaucrats, become less sensitive to their patients' needs, and this is another consequence of keeping the system running on the basis of a narrow conception of what kind of merit is being valorized—where moral merit is excluded. One of the reasons why "single-payer" plans were excluded from serious debate in the health care debates of 1993–94 was that the Clintons believed that the opposition of medical associations and insurance companies would be so severe that such a plan would be defeated (even though there are some groups of doctors who support it). So our thinking about "competence" has been narrowly framed in terms that make it impossible to even raise the kinds of questions about whether the society as a whole does benefit from the kind of standards currently defined as "objective."

Similar arguments may be made against contemporary definitions of "competence" or "merit" or the "neutral objectivity" of many entrance examinations to universities, graduate or professional training institutions, or into the professions themselves (the Bar, for example).

Jews have been particularly resistant to thinking about these kinds of considerations, since we have often felt that we were the great beneficiaries of the current definitions, and because we have been fearful that when other considerations would be introduced, we'd be back in the situation we faced for so long of trying to overcome quota systems that excluded Jews.

Few Jews want to deal with these more complex issues of *what* is being rewarded and who decides that because they fear that once the market gets politicized in this way the Jewish opportunities for advancement will be called into question, and they will be faced with the alternative of either trying to "expand the whole pie" (which seems to many to be utopian and unrealistic) or of settling for a smaller portion of the pie. It is these kinds of issues that come up for Jews when the spectre of affirmative action is perceived as meaning that rewards should be allocated roughly according to the percentage of each group's numbers in the population as a whole.

C.W. There was no notion ever entertained that the proportion of Jews in American society would be the benchmark for the proportion of Jews to get entry to any of the schools, jobs, or professions. To make that particular point is alarmist, paranoid, and hyperbolic.

There may be some legitimate fears that the very high percentage of Jews in academia or certain professions might find their numbers dropping if affirmative action were implemented in some serious way, but there has never been any serious move among Blacks to suggest that Jews should be restricted to their number in the actual population.

M.L. You're perfectly right to say that nobody contemporaneously advocated that. But if in principle one begins to encourage the society to evaluate social practices in terms of whether they do have the consequence of allocating positions in some rough proportion to one's numbers in the population as a whole, as people now do when they say that Blacks have 10 percent of the population but only 5 percent of the jobs, then this way of thinking could lead down a slippery slope to a future in which Jews would fear eventually getting screwed.

Meanwhile, even in the not-so-long run some younger Jews are going to experience some downward mobility if serious affirmative action were implemented and the pie were not expanded. For example, imagine that it were true that today 10 percent of those admitted to law school are Jewish and that as a result of affirmative action the pie of places going to non-African Americans decreased somewhat so that now only 8 percent of the admissions were Jewish. To someone who might want to go into this profession, the narrowing of admission is an economic threat. So they might oppose it *not* because they are racist, but because they are self-interested.

C.W. The major beneficiaries of affirmative action, we could argue, are Jewish women. Given the sexist barriers of the Jewish community and U.S. society, and given a culture evolving out of text. Once women's self-confidence escalates and the sexual barriers fall, women are going to flourish. The males had a prerogative; they had self-confidence and an access to education. It's going to be different looking at it from the vantage point of the women.

Black people have *not* been the main beneficiaries of affirmative action even though we've been at the center of the discussion. What's fascinating is that when we look at admissions practices and policies, there have always been certain kinds of new quotas at work. Like regional quotas. You've got to have a certain number of people from, say, Montana, and if there aren't too many Jews and Blacks in Montana, then they're not going to be part of that school. That's a given, no matter how many smart people you get from Connecticut, New York, or New Jersey.

M.L. Jews were excluded all along.

C.W. That will remain part of the practice because the policies have never been based solely on narrow, strict, meritocratic criteria and never will be, in part for reasons you've cited. Informal networks are always operating, and mediocrity from all the various ethnic communities manages to seep through.

It's striking the degree to which it's Black folks who are targeted in these kinds of discussions. They are on the receiving end of a stereotype concerning the devaluation of Black bodies in privileged white spaces. This is actually quite significant because we know that none of these top places have ever been able to provide the proportionality we're talking about. When we're talking about affirmative action, we're talking much, much less about proportionality than about trying to reverse discriminatory practices that have been quite operatively setting Blacks back. Those who have been discriminated against— Catholics, Jews, Blacks, women, whoever—are going to be the ones trying to undermine such tactics.

Affirmative action through using strong quotas arouses some suspicion because quotas have been used against Jews. This scramble over professional slots and benefits has to be looked at in the light of a much larger context. When you look at the vast array of discriminatory practices, from banks to the unemployed, then affirmative action in relation to Black folk tilts the discussion in a different manner. Because when we actually look at the numbers and the impact of affirmative action programs, Black folk are affected a whole lot less.

There have been a whole host of highly competent Black people who could not gain access to law school or medical school. In the same way, there's been a whole host of highly mediocre people who did gain entrance to them. So you've got to talk as much about the white male mediocrity that was able to slip through as you do about the competent Blacks, Jews, and women that could not gain access. The question then becomes: given that there is probably a pool out there of more highly competent people than can be given access, how do you select?

Take law firms. You have three slots for partnerships so you look at your forty associates. Out of forty, twenty would be highly competent. Now which three do they pick? The chap who was engaged to one of the boss's daughter's friends. All kinds of subjective elements come into play here. But once these three are chosen, the others say, "Two were chosen for their competence. But one of them is Black, so he must be incompetent."

It was interesting hearing Judge Ginsberg the other day. She said, "This is a nation whose history is one of fighting against discrimination." I was thinking, "What nation is she talking about? Is it America after 1964 that she has in mind? Is it the Ivy Leagues after 1969 that she has in mind?" The Ivy League schools have been around for 250 years, and in the last thirty they finally started fighting discrimination in a serious way. You can't give them credit for being on the cutting edge of fighting discrimination.

M.L. They would argue back, "Compared to what? Compared to the history of most societies, this one has done more. It also has provided legal remedies for many others to fight against discrimination."

C.W. That's like saying I can outrun George Foreman in the hundred-yard dash—courageous and talented boxer that he is. Therefore I somehow think I'm a high-class sprinter! Compared to what? If we're going to look at it solely in terms of what other nations do by thriving on discriminatory practices, then all right, it's a relative claim. We have to admit that in fact we have for the most part been very much like these other nations. Progressive elements have finally had some impact: but who knows how long the impact will last?

M.L. Let me just understand one part of the argument on affirmative action. We have so many thousand places that are going to be allocated for the entrance to Harvard or to the elite schools and up until now they have gone to white kids overwhelmingly. In part because Black kids—

C.W. Including many white male Jews.

M.L. Now you've got an allocation that requires reducing that number of white well-to-do males and increasing the numbers of other groups. That group of white males is going to say, "We have a worse chance now of getting in, merely by virtue of who we are. Not by virtue of having reduced our intelligence or our capacity to compete on objective tests or of working less hard in school. We personally are not responsible for the history of oppression in this society, but we're suffering from the consequences of that through no fault of our own."

C.W. But they benefited from the racial discriminatory practices.

M.L. In the past.

C.W. When they set the quota on Jews, more WASPs were able to gain access. As those quotas were taken away, fewer WASPs were able to gain access.

M.L. Right. What I'm attempting to do is understand the dynamics of the Jewish world whereby people can see this as counterposed with their interests. Their perception is, "You can talk a fine game about the abstract reality, but I know where I'm hurting."

C.W.   You can see how Black folk would say, "Wait a minute. What does this mean, 'I'm hurting'?" Already you've got a significant number of Jews in the professions. At Harvard you've got a significant percentage and you want more. Whereas Blacks have got a small percentage, and you focus on this group as though it somehow took a lot away from you—and were taking over the place.

M.L.   A significantly greater percentage of places are going to Blacks than ever did before. The child of a poor or working-class Jew, of someone who's been struggling all their life to try to make it, thinks, "My parents finally saved enough money up to send me to college and I can't get in." The bottom of the meritocratic ladder, so to speak, is where the tensions are greater and being experienced most directly.

You find that it's the Jews in Queens and Brooklyn and their kids who are feeling a lot more antagonistic than the ones who are living in Scarsdale, or on the Upper West Side of New York City. Those who are living in Scarsdale or on the Upper West Side may feel a little discomfort because their kid ended up in Cornell instead of Harvard—but when it comes down to it, it's not such a big sacrifice to go to Cornell instead of Harvard.

At the other end, in Queens and Brooklyn, you might be someone who's worked all your life to save enough for your kid to get out of the working class. Then you see that the possible strategies for getting out of the working class are significantly narrowed by new groups being included into the system—according to no very high standard. For example, in the City of New York such Jews could be eliminated by open enrollment.

C.W.   The only criterion will be a high school diploma.

M.L.   Yes, or a high school equivalency. At that point, the competition becomes much more stiff because you've only got a certain number of places. If you expand the number of students but you don't have any funding to increase the number of faculty, you're going to guarantee a low quality of education. Teachers who previously managed to stick with the students and work with them on their essays can't do that any more. There will be students who have a low level of literacy, whom you're going to find it exasperating to spend more time working with on improvements whilst you have the lowest level of shared dialogue in the school. Even the people who get in are going to feel that the school is not as exciting intellectually as it once was.

The tensions are very high for Jews at the working-class level. The Jews who live on the Upper West Side, in Scarsdale, and in Beverly Hills, look at these other Jews and say, "They are racist. Their level of consciousness is low." Whereas those working-class Jews are saying to themselves, "Wait a second. Those upper-middle-class Jews can easily justify affirmative action because they don't suffer its consequences."

C.W. Cutbacks in social services and public funding for education.

M.L. And so forth. Many middle-class Jews are not suffering the consequences of this. They don't understand what it's like to have worked all your life to get your kid out of the working class, only to find out that you're in an economic situation in which there's no way out because other groups are filling your possible escape routes.

All the more reason why we need to expand the hypothetical pie. Is it just inevitable that the pie is shrinking? Or does it have something to do with a set of social decisions that disproportionately structured the economy in ways that are not generating jobs but instead geared toward making as much profit as possible? To put those questions on an agenda raises the same kinds of issues about how you change the economic system so that it allocates funds for human needs in a way that guarantees quality education for all.

C.W. You had the courage to say why it is that they pointed the first gun at Black people: because in light of the cuts and of a number of different groups trying to gain entry, there is tremendous competition for actual spots. White working-class, Italians, Poles, some WASPs, some browns, Blacks, and Asians: all of them are trying to squeeze through, understandably so. But when 95 percent of the attention is directed at Black folk, then we have to look at the numbers, and we see that Black students have been the group that has decreased in number and enrollment in colleges across the board—from City College to Harvard. We're pointing fingers at these Black folk, who are wondering, "What's going on?"

M.L. You know what's going on. Racism is going on.

C.W. You also have to recognize that there's also going to be a number of other groups, as well as women, who are trying to get through this very, very thin tunnel. There's going to be a number of reasons why people are pointing fingers at Black people. But when you end up having a group whose numbers are declining and who have historically had the least possibility of gaining entry to these things, you say, "Wait, this criticism seems to be a bit myopic and xenophobic."

M.L. Many white people are worried about their jobs, given changes in the world capitalist economy that have led to the elimination of many jobs. Along comes the Left and seems to say to these whites: "Your advantages should be distributed equally among everybody." In which case what people hear is, "I'm going to lose my job for the sake of someone else." You have to have a development of consciousness which says, "That someone else really is somebody I care about, and their unemployment hurts me, because I'm fundamentally connected to them and they to me." If I'm thinking that they are somebody else who is relevantly different from me, for example because of their race, then I'm going to try and find some race-related excuse for why they should not have a job and why I should. But if I can't think of a morally relevant difference, then I am pushed toward thinking about systemic changes rather than how I can take care of myself and ignore their plight. This, by the way, is why the daily acts of turning our backs on the homeless on our streets is *not* just a little thing, but a daily training in moral insensitivity that eventually hardens us to much greater systemic moral insensitivity.

I know that getting people to think about systemic change is hard, because they know that it would involve a struggle with elites of wealth and power that they can hardly imagine beating. And though people have taken on those elites before, and won, as in the thirties and sixties, the media and history books have already done so much to distort our collective memory of those moments, to trivialize our collective power and pathologize our transformative movements, so that the empowerment we should have experienced in those victories—which might have led us to take on larger transformations—have been undermined. Part of our task, if we are ever to overcome racism, is to combat what I call "surplus powerlessness"—the ways that we make ourselves even more powerless than we actually are, given the inequalities of power in the society. Because unless we can imagine ourselves as potentially powerful, we will resist the temptation to expand our circle of caring, because we intuitively know that kind of caring implies obligation to end each other's suffering, and that seems too overwhelming. If we ever want to be serious about overcoming racism in this society, it is precisely this sense of powerlessness that must be overcome. Racism is partly a distorted way of dealing with surplus powerlessness—we can count on the existing market system to distribute unemployment disproportionately to the Blacks, and if our racism tells us that that is O.K., we are off the hook of having to confront the existing economic system, a confrontation which seems so overwhelming to most of us that we'd prefer not even to think about it.

The Politics of Meaning, with its call to change the dominant discourse from selfishness to caring, is a way of addressing the dynamics that undergird American racism. But it feels utopian because it leads to a challenge to the fundamentals of the market system. Yet, in my view, if you want to overcome racist consciousness in this society, you must challenge the selfishness-orientation of contemporary capitalism.

C.W.   Oh sure, I agree and I'm with you in that. But that's why it's so unlikely that we'll ever overcome racism. Because we'd have to bank on convincing the larger white lower middle and working class that somehow they need to turn on the powers that be rather than those beside or below them. We know from history that it's highly unlikely.

M.L.   So what are we going to do?

C.W.   We are going to continue to do what we progressives do. We are still going to try to tell the truth about the situation to as many people as we can. Convince them to be courageous enough to fight against it, but also warn them that by going systemic they're in a long-term fight. It's not overnight. In this sense, it's very consistent with what you're saying. Anytime you go systemic, you're going utopian. At the same time, we still don't have a credible option for how people should deal with their situation at this very moment other than to unite against white and male supremacy, vast economic inequality, homophobia, and ecological abuse.

CHAPTER 9

Current Tension Points: Crown Heights and Farrakhan

The riots that took place on the streets of Crown Heights, Brooklyn, by Blacks against Jews, was perceived by many Jews as an organized pogrom that was deeply frightening. Anger and suspicion from that still lingers among some Jews. And there has been growing fear of the meaning of the emergence of Louis Farrakhan as a national leader in the Black community. Ever since the Nation of Islam's Minister Louis Farrakhan achieved national prominence for his association with Black leader Jesse Jackson, Jews have seen him as a symbol of the tension between Blacks and Jews, because the Reverend Farrakhan has made a number of overtly anti-Semitic statements and has led the Nation of Islam to sell anti-Semitic tracts like The Protocols of the Elders of Zion *in their bookstores. On the other hand, many Blacks have pointed to the positive work that has been done by the Nation of Islam in providing some Black youth with a sense of dignity and in encouraging values like hard work and economic and family responsibility.*

In the course of doing this dialogue, West and Lerner found themselves on opposite sides of a picket line. West attended a National Black Leadership Summit in Baltimore in June 1994, convened by then-national NAACP director Ben

*Chavis. Lerner brought demonstrators from surrounding states
to protest the meeting. Though their public embrace was
caught on television cameras, their debate before and after the
conference is reflected here.*

C.W. Given the suspicions of the Black and the Jewish communities, I think there's going to be a number in each group who will be suspicious of the other, even though both Black people and Jews are being targeted simultaneously as the enemy and the vermin of our society. Yet, as Crown Heights indicates, it seems at times all too easy to get us to focus away from common enemies and toward issues that set us in opposition to each other.

M.L. Unfortunately, most Jews believe that there was very little in the way of public outcry in the Black community against what happened in Crown Heights.

C.W. I don't know. I think there was more Black public outcry than people realize. The vast majority of Black people in America unequivocally and radically denounced the anti-Semitic remarks of the murderers of Yankel Rosenbaum.

M.L. If there had been a group of Jews who had taken a march through Harlem throwing bricks through windows . . .

C.W. But the analogy doesn't work because in Crown Heights there is no Black organized hatred of others. Crown Heights was random activity in the light of what they perceived as revenge against the death of a young Black person, brother Cato. This wasn't the kind of organization that then plans and designs a march. The attack on brother Yankel by these unorganized young Black folk is in no way a parallel with an organized group. What if it had been a Black motorist in a Jewish section of town who had accidentally run over a Jewish child? What if a vast majority of the Jews in that community were unconvinced that it was accidental? Given that there was a history of very, very negative relations between Jews and Blacks in that context, what if Jews, feeling a sense of revenge, attacked a particular Black person?

M.L.   Wait, it wasn't just one person being attacked. There were three days of rioting. There were three days in which Blacks were on the streets of Crown Heights, during which time Jews felt terrorized. The police said that they were overwhelmed by the level of violence happening on the streets.

Let's say that it happened in reverse in terms of who the helpless were and what the ethnic group was. You can be very sure that *Tikkun* and other progressive Jews would have organized a demonstration the next week in that same community in support of the Black who had been attacked, and in opposition to the Jews who had done the attacking.

Of course, I did condemn Rabbi Schneerson and other leaders of the Lubavitcher community for not doing more to make a public statement of remorse at the loss of life of the two children. I believe that the Lubavitcher movement should have sent a very visible delegation to visit the family and to express sympathy and to make clear that this accident was one that saddened Hasidic Jews. Had Schneerson been the kind of morally sensitive leader that the Jewish people needs, he would long ago have created within the Lubavitch community a dynamic of caring about others, including non-Jews, that would have led them to immediately declare a day of mourning for the Black children that had been run over by the rebbe's caravan. But this criticism does not in the slightest justify the actual Black response—the murder of Yankel Rosenbaum and the assault on Jewish homes for the next three days.

C.W.   But, to continue your hypothesis that the situation had been reversed, what if you were still up in the air as to whether the Jewish child had been killed accidentally? You would have called for an investigation to see whether this Black motorist actually ran into this Jewish child on purpose. Wouldn't you?

M.L.   Absolutely.

C.W.   You would be calling for a detailed investigation.

M.L.   A thorough investigation. But I would still make it very clear that we Jews are not in support of attacking random Blacks because some Black ran over a Jew. If there had been two hundred

Blacks putting that kind of principled demonstration together in Crown Heights, indicating their opposition to other Blacks who were rioting against Jews, the Jewish reaction would have been very different.

C.W.   I will grant you that point. The Black public condemnation of the anti-Semitic language and deeds of some of the younger Black folk in the community did not take the form of such a rally or demonstration. It took place in spaces where the press, for the most part, were absent.

M.L.   And the Jews were not hearing about it. Blacks and Jews in dialogue need to organize, take ads, and make public statements that would allow for this kind of public response to be heard.

C.W.   Where would be the places where both communities could hear about it?

M.L.   We could buy an ad together in the right-wing Jewish newspapers, in the *Jewish Week,* and in the *Long Island Jewish World.* In each place we say, "We're putting up our own money to send the message that we really condemn what has happened here. We want the Jews in Crown Heights to know that liberal Jews and liberal Blacks are standing up together saying, 'This is not acceptable behavior.' We are calling for an investigation of what happened. But in the meantime, we are saying absolutely that no matter what happens, there is no excuse for this kind of murder and beating up on random people." This is the kind of thing that we at *Tikkun* did after the massacre of Palestinians in Hebron in 1994, for example, so why shouldn't we be asking the same kind of response from progressive Blacks?

C.W.   I like that. Part of what you're saying to me that is very important is that we have to have arenas where progressive Black voices can be heard by Jewish audiences, and vice versa. My hunch is that various Black folk would not even know of those newspapers that you just mentioned. Just like large numbers of Jews wouldn't know that much about *Amsterdam News* or *The Oklahoma Eagle.*

M.L. Crown Heights was a moment in which a lot of Jews felt very betrayed because the Black voices didn't come forth.

C.W. If the Black voices were there but they just didn't hear them, then it's not a matter of betrayal. It's a matter of communication.

M.L. No, I think that the political obligation in this case was not just to speak out, but to take responsibility for making sure you were being heard.

C.W. But how do you do that if you don't have access to the organs? If you're speaking out in these Black forums but there's no press there.

M.L. It would not have been hard for ten Black leaders to get together and say, "We want to come to your synagogue, in Crown Heights, or in Manhattan, to express our concern over and opposition to what happened in Crown Heights." You'd have an audience. The Jewish press would be there and the Jews would hear about it.

C.W. I'll give you an example. When we had a huge meeting at Medgar Evers right in the center of Crown Heights, about five hundred people showed up—half Jewish, half Black. There was a rap group that was half Hasidic, half Black, accompanied by progressive Black and Jewish leaders like Richard Green and Dr. Laz. I gave the key-note address. Was there any report of that occasion? None whatsoever.

M.L. But that's not necessarily what I'm talking about. That wasn't a group of Blacks representing their Black community in order to condemn anti-Semitism.

C.W. The Black churches were represented with pastors. This was a community effort to bring together many people.

M.L. I know how this was billed. It was billed as a "bridge-building" kind of event. But building bridges is a step way ahead of the first step they needed to take. Namely, a Black saying, "This was wrong." You can't move from talking about some conflagration in the past to talking about reconciliation, without admitting you did something that was wrong in between.

C.W. It wasn't as if *we* did anything wrong. There were certain elements in the community that did things that were wrong and that we radically disagreed with.

M.L. You still need to say that: "In our community there are elements from whom we want publicly to dissociate. They did something wrong that we do not tolerate." I'll give you another example. After riots I hear people from all over the community coming together and saying, "We want to reestablish peace here." But they never say, "We want to establish peace based on recognizing the legitimacy of what these people were rioting about."

C.W. No, they aren't going to say that.

M.L. You have to deal with the grievance before you can expect to deal with the quieting of the grievance.

C.W. Part of the problem is that if a small group of Black folk behave in an anti-Semitic way, then that means that every Black person is now suspect of being a supporter of that *unless* they somehow publicly condemn it in such a way that everyone sees. To condemn it in a variety of ways that don't surface—partly given the way the media is structured these days—just reinforces distrust. People believe that all Black folk are anti-Semitic simply because they haven't heard sufficient condemnation from them. Can't they take for granted the fact that there is a moral core to the Black community, such that there will be these condemnations immediately? Especially given their interaction with this community?

M.L. The answer is no. The answer is that they cannot count on that. You have to recognize that you would not believe it either if it were the other way around.

C.W. I definitely would. If I had to ask Jewish leaders to condemn actions every time I saw any racist activity carried out by Jews, then I would be showing no trust in you at all. I recognize that there are certain individuals in the Jewish community who might engage in anti-Black actions. That doesn't mean Jewish leaders have to come out each time to condemn them.

M.L. Not when it's a case of one or two people. But if there were hundreds of Jews rioting in a Black community, you can't tell me that Blacks wouldn't expect Jews to say something publicly about this. I certainly would.

C.W. I would just take for granted that my progressive comrades would be unequivocally against it. It wouldn't so much be wanting to make sure you are on my side. The question would be: "What are we going to do about it?"

M.L. What if all of your progressive comrades had been telling you for the past eight years that their leader was some guy who was saying off the record, "Now I'm going to nigger town, baby"?

C.W. I'm sure that there are plenty of Jews who say that all the time. It's not a big problem.

M.L. I grew up in a Jewish community that was full of racial slurs. But those of us who became part of the movement *hated* that reality, felt embarrassed and ashamed of the racism that existed in sectors of the Jewish community. I wouldn't be surprised to hear those statements in some sectors of the Jewish community. But if I heard this kind of talk among progressive Jews, people who identified with the social change movements, I'd be totally astounded.

C.W. We know there are these residues of xenophobia in our community, including among our leaders.

M.L. I think you're letting people off too easily. The problem that I had with Jesse Jackson was that I went to him hoping to find connection and instead I found a level of insensitivity to Jewish issues that upset me. Here we have even the progressive brothers and sisters in the Black community identifying with somebody whom a lot of Jews —including progressive Jews—find problematic as a leader. A guy who has, on the side, had connections with somebody who calls Judaism "a gutter religion."

So when something like Crown Heights happens, we have a right to be asking for reassurance. I expect us to do the same for Blacks. I think Jewish leaders should be standing up and saying clearly, for example, "We oppose the racism of the way the L.A. riots were handled, and the way that the press described the whole situation." You absolutely have a right to ask us to do that, and we should do that. I don't want anything that isn't reciprocal. If you're asking, "Why are they immediately so paranoid and suspicious?" our history gives us many reasons to be paranoid.

C.W. I see what you're saying. But if a relationship is primarily grounded in forever testing because you are forever suspicious, then it's very difficult to get any genuine alliance off the ground. For instance, because Jesse Jackson as a Black leader has an insensitivity to Jews, then all Blacks must have some insensitivity to Jews. Therefore we have to test them each and every time we interact.

Jesse's insensitivity to Jews is his particular problem, and he has been trying to come to terms with it. However, assuming that his insensitivity is somehow transitive across the Black community is another sign of distrust.

I think it would have been a very good idea for the ten Black leaders that you talked about to call a news conference to condemn the riot. What I'm questioning is the notion that somehow those leaders are worthy of suspicion or distrust until they do it, because otherwise it looks as if the whole Black community is complicitous with these actions.

It's like when Farrakhan came to speak in New York a number of years ago. The supposition was that anyone who didn't come forward right away to condemn this man was de facto complicitous with him. From a Black perspective you'd say, "Wait a minute. We radically disagree with what he's talking about in terms of his anti-Semitic claims. But we're not in this just to be tested." Those who did come forward, like Dinkins, were viewed as reacting to whatever those outside the Black community said. They were viewed as selected and hand-picked.

So how do we create bonds of trust after that? This is one of the reasons why it's very important that interactions between Black and Jewish spokespersons take place on the ground. The Jews then know what these Black spokespeople are radically opposed to without having to wait and see when they have their press conference. Although the press conference is still important because you need public appearances.

Let's flip the situation and say that Jewish people are attacking and terrorizing Black folk the way Black folk were attacking and terrorizing Jews. If ten Jewish leaders were to come out, I would appreciate that. But it's not a matter of them having to meet our test. We're not testing them. We can't assume that the Jewish community as a whole is somehow complicitous with anti-Black activity just because they haven't given a press conference at ten o'clock on Monday morning. We have comrades over there whether they're at that press conference or not.

M.L. I agree with you. I'm not saying that progressive Jews should be suspicious. I'm saying that progressive Jews need this from their Black comrades in order to deal with those other Jews who *are* suspicious.

C.W. This is where public appearances make a difference. I'm all for public appearances. There should have been a Black public appearance. But once it reaches the point of testing to see whether Black people are trustworthy, it means that it's predicated on a deep distrust.

M.L. I understand what you're saying.

C.W. From the vantage point of the Black world as I understand it, no matter what an individual person does that is good, they're still distrusted by Jews and whites before they're trusted.

M.L. That seems to be true among Blacks as well. Aren't whites distrusted before they're trusted?

C.W. Yes, but we have a history of white supremacy and oppression. There is not a history of Black supremacy and oppression. Thus, distrust of whites does in fact become an element of survival.

M.L. But when that leads Blacks to open the gates to a Farrakhan, even the most progressive Jews become very distressed. Farrakhan said Hitler was a hero to his own people. What do you think the covert message is to an audience where he's bringing up Hitler as an embodiment of some great value? Why is he bringing up Hitler?

C.W. He brought up Hitler because he wanted to talk about somebody who created a people out of nothing. He could have brought up Napoleon, or Caesar.

M.L. You think it was a value-neutral choice to bring up Hitler? You think it had nothing to do with his anti-Semitism?

C.W. No, I think his anti-Semitism certainly tilted him in that direction. But that's different than casting him as a pro-Nazi figure, approving the murder of six million people. Farrakhan does not believe Hitler was a great man in the moral sense at all.

M.L. What do you think it means, to call Judaism a "gutter religion"? Where does that term come from?

C.W. Hegel! That comes out of anti-Semitic discourse! Out of a perception of a religion that is linked to a particularism, to the "one people" rather than openness to all in a universal way. He said it using it as a justification of the subjugation of Palestinian people. Although on historical grounds we know this to be wrong, yet versions of Judaism, as with all religions, *do* support subjugating other people.

M.L. Cornel, what I'm saying is that you are being narrowly legalistic. If I were saying similar things about Black Nationalism being "the ideology of the gutter"—

C.W. Much of it *is* patriarchal, homophobic, and xenophobic!

M.L. —You would understand the content of that to be racist. A content meant to stir up and play on a long history of anti-Black sentiment that was already there and could be re-evoked by using certain kinds of imagery.

C.W. Michael, I agree, but there are two considerations here. One is that you have to be fair to the person you're trashing. This is true for the Ku Klux Klan, for Kahane, and so forth. I think the evidence is there that this man is an anti-Semite and thereby warrants moral critique, but the claim that he's a Nazi spills over not simply on him but on the Black community as a whole. Farrakhan is then viewed as representing this strong or dominant tendency. If he's Nazi, maybe the whole Black community is Nazi.

M.L. My claim is not that he's a Nazi. There is a difference between a radical anti-Semite and a Nazi. However, the line becomes much more fuzzy when someone is so public in their anti-Semitism as to help create the conditions in which the Nazi can act feeling that he has cultural support, a community of people who understand and support his activities.

C.W. I had a little dialogue with Ed Koch about this. You know he's been on a lecture tour recently. He sent me his speech, and I was deeply upset about it. Why? Because again I see his equation of Farrakhan with Hitler as an attempt to demonize rather than to criticize, which doesn't help things because demonization sits at the center of white supremacist ideology.

We should be able to be rigorous and relentless in our moral criticism without demonizing folk. I don't believe that Farrakhan could be a Hitler even if he wanted to, which I don't believe he does, precisely because there's no way a Black person could play on hatred of Jews and aspire to the head of the nation state in a white supremacist civilization. So that the idea of Ed Koch saying that this is a new Hitler who has the capacity to aspire to the same level of power and privilege, let alone terror, that Hitler did, is so farfetched in terms of the historical context, that it becomes just another way of demonizing rather than really trying to get at what actually are the sources of Farrakhan's xenophobia.

That to me constitutes overreaction that has very negative consequences. Koch basically agreed with me; he said, "Yes, I see your point; maybe I'm going too far." "It's not about maybe going too far," I said. "This ups the ante to such a degree that it makes it even more difficult to bring moral critique to bear."

M.L. I think that every historical analogy has its difficulties. Certainly, trying to compare the United States in the nineties to Germany in the twenties is stretching. Yet there are some troubling analogues.

C.W. Contemporary America and Weimar Germany are both decadent places, but decadent in very different ways.

M.L. Nonetheless, there's a reason for wanting to draw these analogies, to highlight the possibility of new threats to American Jews or to Jews in the world as a whole that might have seemed implausible even five or ten years ago.

Not that we should tell lies. We shouldn't say Farrakhan is Hitler, we should say that Farrakhan is Farrakhan.

C.W. Exactly.

M.L. Racist dog that he is!

C.W. I wouldn't call the brother a racist dog, but a xenophobic spokesperson when it comes to dealing with Jewish humanity—but who, in his own way, loves Black folk deeply, and that love is what we see first. What you're seeing here are certain anti-Semitic residues that have been part of the Nation of Islam from the very beginning. You saw some of it in Elijah Muhammad, you saw some of it in Malcolm X. It isn't as if the Nation of Islam was somehow bereft of anti-Semitic elements until Farrakhan appeared. It's always been there in a subterranean way. It's become more visible under his leadership, no doubt, but at the same time he has emerged at a time in which this aggressive Jewish identity is being articulated, so that his anti-Semitism has a specificity now that it didn't have thirty years ago under Elijah Muhammad and Malcolm X. Therefore he is able to target the distinctive Jewish identity as well as particular Jewish elites and individuals who use power and privilege over against Black interests or progress as perceived by him and many Black folk. Then there's a vicious attack on him by the press, a vicious attack that he believes in many ways has to do with Jewish interests because it's disproportionately shaped by Jewish elites. In his counterattack, he ups the ante, by putting forward the strongest kinds of claims, like those regarding the number of Jewish slave holders, which increases the anti-Jewish sensibility and rhetoric. There's a more vicious attack on him, and by this time he ends up being called Hitler.

And so what do you end up with? You end up with a sensationalistic kind of battle royal between a xenophobe and a very powerful establishment that sees itself not simply defending principles but also keeping track of those who would be a threat to Jewish interests.

M.L. Quite appropriately so. I want to keep track of those who are a threat to Jewish interests.

C.W. The thing is, if that entails telling lies about him, describing him as Hitler—

M.L. No, we shouldn't tell lies: but when the guy says Hitler was a hero to his people and that Judaism is a gutter religion—

C.W. Farrakhan didn't say Hitler was a great man in any normative sense. He was comparing him to Alexander the Great, to Napoleon. Now, when we talk about Alexander the Great, we don't mean that we normatively approve of conquest and dispossession. He said Hitler was "wickedly great"—

M.L. Do Jewish leaders go around talking about how the founders of apartheid were "wickedly great"?

C.W. People have! The paradox of American democracy is that it was a breakthrough in freedom, but on the other hand it was based on the enslavement of Africans. George Washington and Thomas Jefferson are consistently viewed as great heroes in American history, despite their role as slaveowners.

M.L. The point is, that is not the aspect of their greatness that is salient to Americans when they praise Jefferson and Washington.

C.W. Farrakhan is saying that his anti-Semitism was not the aspect of Hitler that was salient to the German people, for them to vote him head of the nation state.

M.L. That's very much in contention. In other words, this guy was an out-and-out racist, he advocated racism. Jefferson and Washington did not go round the country campaigning on the retention of slavery by claiming that the problems facing America were those Black folk. Slavery was a background condition shared by everybody they were talking to. They didn't have to advocate for it, and people weren't choosing them on that basis. But when they chose Hitler,

Hitler was openly asserting that the reason they were unemployed is that the Jews had "stabbed them in the back" (because they were disproportionately anti-war and pro-socialist) after the First World War and had kept control of the economy ever since. "They have been on the side of our enemies screwing you and when I get into power we're going to screw them back." So I don't think the analogy with Jefferson and Washington is exactly right here.

C.W.   I agree: I'm not making a direct analogy between Washington and Jefferson as slave-holders versus Hitler as Nazi, let alone rampant anti-Semite, though anti-Semitism was a background condition in Germany. I think it's also important to note that Hitler's message was not solely anti-Semitic. He had a whole program of economic measures. They all were shot through with anti-Semitic elements, but it wasn't that his whole program was anti-Semitic right across the board and that the German people were so enthused by anti-Semitism that they chose him.

M.L.   A lot of people didn't buy his economic program as being very plausible and in fact he didn't really believe in it.

C.W.   A lot of people didn't buy his anti-Semitism either: they bought his ideas on the economy and ended up buying into the anti-Semitism.

M.L.   There's a difference between people who are drawn to anti-Semitic views and a core group, who put them at the center of their world view. They don't get drawn to them as a mechanism for expressing something else; they actually come to conceive of the world through the perspective of hatred of Blacks, or women, or Jews, or gays. So there's a difference between situational anti-Semites and pathological anti-Semites. Hitler was one of the latter. He had at the deepest core of his being this incredible hatred, and that element makes him very similar to Farrakhan.

C.W.   This is where we disagree. You believe that Louis Farrakhan is a radically evil person who has hatred at the core of his being. See, I don't think that's true. Anti-Semitism is one integral element in his attempt to account for Black social misery. But this hatred of Jews or even of white persons is not at the core of his being.

M.L. Alright, let's take someone who had anti-Black racism as a front condition. Take George Wallace. If Jews went around the country, to South Carolina and Louisiana, saying, "Who's a great American for us Jews? George Wallace! There's a great American. I'll tell you some other great people. The people who established apartheid in South Africa. Now, I'm not saying I'm for apartheid. I'm telling you these were great people, great leaders who energized their people." What do you think Black folks would be hearing? Do you think they'd be hearing my qualifications or do you think they'd be hearing my identification with a racist?

C.W. They'd be hearing your identification with a racist. The thing is, in some sense they would not be fully right. They could be wrong. In the same way, when Jews hear Farrakhan saying Hitler was wickedly great, and all they hear is that Hitler was the greatest man in the world, I can understand how that would happen, but they would be wrong. There's a possibility they could be actually wrong about that.

M.L. Using this kind of a discourse at this moment in American history isn't a neutral choice. Farrakhan is not a dummy. He chose it precisely because he knew that he was playing to an anti-Semitism in his own community and he plays with that. So he repudiates Khallid Abdul Mohammad, and then immediately says, "But I'm not repudiating the truths in what he says." Or he says, "These Jews owned 75 percent of all the slaves." So he repeats this wild falsehood that reinforces in mass consciousness a terrible anti-Semitic stereotype about who Jews are.

C.W. I think actually what he meant when he refused to repudiate the "truths" of Khallid Abdul Muhammad was that the most terrible reading of Black history would see it as a series of fundamental atrocities and barbarities vis-à-vis Black people. Khallid Abdul Mohammad talks about the devilish behavior of many white people vis-à-vis Black people. Now there are truths in that history, there's no doubt about it, and that's the most charitable reading. The uncharitable reading—and to some degree this uncharitable reading contains a number of truths—is that Farrakhan refused to call into question the way Khallid's ugly hatred mirrored the white hatred he criticized. That's where he's completely wrong. But the truths that Khallid Abdul Mohammad actually is putting forward have to do with devilish behavior of many white folk vis-à-vis Black folk. Any human being looking at that history would deeply resonate with it.

M.L. This is something that resonates in you, and in a different kind of way it resonates in me and yet we're committed again to our discourse here, not seeing each other as devils. You know that Baruch Goldstein—the guy who killed twenty-nine people in Hebron in 1994 and wounded I don't know how many others—could run the same rap about the non-Jew. They too were devilishly oppressive.

C.W. He would be right!

M.L. And probably he did. About the Arabs in particular and the Gentiles in general. He could run a story about the last two thousand years which would be absolutely right and decisive.

C.W. I can understand Baruch's rage, like I can understand Palestinian rage.

M.L. Exactly. But whereas we can understand the rage, ultimately what he does is so morally unacceptable and destructive to the interests of our and all people's liberation that I have to rage equally against him.

C.W. I agree.

M.L. You agree, but I don't hear you raging so much against Farrakhan and I've got some problems with that. I particulary objected when a mainstream civil-rights oriented organization, the NAACP, invited Farrakhan to to be part of their national Summit of Black Leadership in June of 1994. I organized a protest demonstration outside that meeting.

C.W. Your demonstration in Baltimore in June of 1994 protesting the Summit which had been convened by Ben Chavis, who was at the time the executive director of the NAACP, was a statement of opposition to anti-Semitism and homophobia, and I agreed with that end and hence came outside to explain to people why I supported your goals but still felt it appropriate to be inside. I believe in dialogue; but it's a question of being open to dialogue with a variety of different voices.

M.L. But isn't there a point at which it's reasonable for your friends to say that by engaging in a certain kind of dialogue with people who are out-and-out racists toward Jews, that you are legitimating that voice?

C.W. Not at all.

M.L. Let me just give you one argument for why I think it is. The NAACP said, "We have to invite this guy to our meeting because we want to have a dialogue between all the voices that exist in the Black world and he's one of them."

C.W. Not just a voice: he is an influential voice. Not the most influential, thank God, but he is an influential voice.

M.L. I'm saying that, just as we understand in general that social reality is constituted by people's beliefs in that social reality, so influential voices and their degree of influence is constituted by who is saying, "This is an influential and legitimate voice." When people say that about Farrakhan they bring him further into the center of Black consciousness.
Before this invitation by the NAACP, a lot of Black people said to me, "Don't give Farrakhan so much emphasis. It's you who are giving him the emphasis—you white people, selecting him out of the vast array of Blacks." Then all of a sudden I'm told, "We've got to have him at our leadership summit because he is one of the hundred main leaders in the country."

C.W. He is! Of influential voices, he certainly is. Do you think he's not influential in the Black community?

M.L. I'm not saying he's not influential. I'm saying he's a racist thug who should not be given legitimacy.

C.W.   I think we do have a fundamental disagreement here. One of the ironies of this situation is there's a significant degree to which Farrakhan himself has been a creation of the white press, and because the white press is hegemonic, it's no accident that Black people are going to be curious about who he is. In the same way that we know Khallid Abdul Muhammad is a thorough creation of the white media. You could go on 125th Street a year ago and ask ordinary Black folk who Khallid Abdul Muhammad was, and most of them have never heard of him. You ask them now, they know. And it's not because all of a sudden he's changed his views or got great insights into the nature of the universe, it's just that he's become the creation of the white media.

Farrakhan less so, but still he's been very much promoted by the white media in the last ten years or so. So people want to hear what he has to say. Now I happen to be a thoroughgoing Millian when it comes to dialogue: I think that people ought to have a right to hear a variety of views. I think that not only did Fresno NAACP have a right to invite Farrakhan but a duty to bring him in to ensure some kind of critical exchange. That way people can see the sense and/or the non-sense, the love and/or the hate, the insight and/or the bigotry that's being put forward.

I agree with you that the controversial nature of who he is means you're going to get a big crowd and make big money, but people need to hear what is being said. We have to believe that people have the capacity to criticize what they hear. I do not believe that Louis Farrakhan can ever be the leader of the vast majority of the Black community. That's the kind of confidence I have in the critical capacities of Black folk. So that I have no fear whatsoever that, even while they might be clapping at that moment, the vast majority of Black folk will ever join his organization. They have too much wisdom for that.

M.L.   Is this because they've been so smart in figuring out how to preserve their best interests in this society in the course of the past twenty years?

C.W.   The thing is, all of us are confused. All of our respective communities have levels of confusion.

M.L. Exactly! That's why demagogues like Farrakhan and Khallid Muhammad are so dangerous.

C.W. But at the same time, there are strong residues of moral wisdom in the Jewish community that make it difficult to transgress certain boundaries. Even while you've got anti-Black racism in the Jewish community, there are still certain boundaries across which the vast majority of Jews will not go. Similarly, we've got an anti-Jewish sensibility in the Black community, but there's boundaries beyond which the vast majority will not go. If Farrakhan goes beyond those boundaries, they're not going to go with him.

M.L. Since the NAACP summit took place I have had people say to me that they feel Black people are so pathological that until they get their shit together enough to purge this anti-Semite, they don't want to hear about Black pain.

C.W. These are typical racist statements that show precisely the arrogance and condescension we have talked about already. It's like Black people telling Jewish folk, "These people are so pathological in terms of what is going on in the West Bank that somehow they think that they can get support for their nation state when they are actually occupying another people." Nobody's saying the Jewish people are pathological, they just say they are making mistakes. So the use of that language among people *you* know, Michael, is itself reflective of just how deep the white supremacy still is, operating even among Jewish progressives.

M.L. Let me put it this way: I believe that only pathology could explain people's acceptance of racist, homophobic, and sexist leadership.

C.W. The Jewish establishment itself can be viewed as pathological in terms of its racism, if you consider the negative effect of mainstream Jewish leadership in organizations like the ADL and the American Jewish Committee. But that doesn't mean I would ever turn away from Jewish pain and suffering.

M.L. These organizations have done much to weaken the influence of the liberal, anti-racist, pro-peace and justice forces in the Jewish world. Still, they are not in any way comparable to the destructiveness of the Nation of Islam. There is no figure in the Jewish world comparable to a Farrakhan spewing out public hatred about Blacks. Blacks are putting out something about Jews that Jews are not putting out about Blacks.

However, I agree with you that Farrakhan should not be prevented from speaking. I am a free speech absolutist in saying that people should be able to say whatever they want. But that's different from arguing that every position, no matter how hateful or hurtful, should be *given a podium* by us or our allies. There's a very big difference between the right to speak, and providing the audience. We're always making choices about whom to help provide with audience, because there's a limited amount of time.

C.W. That's an important distinction.

M.L. Personally, I want the world to hear more of *you*, Cornel West, on television, and I hope they hear less of people who spew forth hatred and division among the oppressed. It's perfectly appropriate for us to try to convince other people that their time should be used toward achieving some goal and not some other goal, and in that sense, since my goal, and I believe your goal, is toward liberation and freedom and the development of humanity in a community of caring and love, it seems perfectly fine to say to people that if this is their goal they ought not to be wasting time on the Farrakhans and Khallid Muhammads (and whatever other haters are produced in the Black community).

C.W. One can achieve that goal by hearing voices that themselves can be impediments.

M.L. Absolutely one can. I'm merely saying the Millian argument, the free speech argument, doesn't do that. You'll have to make a different argument, namely that hearing this voice is useful toward that end.

C.W. But a strong argument can be made, because in the minds of some Black people might be the notion that somehow Farrakhan's messages may be the most emancipatory available. They may enter the auditorium thinking that's the case, though many will leave disabused of that notion.

M.L. I am not saying, "You are wrong to have a public debate with Farrakhan." I'm not against that, although I should say that in my own community I refused to debate Kahane, on the grounds that there were certain kinds of hatred that were so far out of the tradition that they no longer deserve to be considered part of the community's legitimate dialogue. Giving him that debate was in effect legitimating his voice within the community. I'm saying that when somebody fundamentally demeans Blacks or Palestinians, as he did, that they've gone beyond what is an appropriate level of discourse.

Of course there are many right-wing Jews who say the same about me, but so what? The issue is, are they right? You can't settle this issue on merely abstract formal grounds like "debate everyone," because sometimes the consequences of debating haters is to give them a legitimacy they don't deserve. But if some right-wing Jews decide that *I* am such because of my support for a demilitarized Palestinian state, then the way to counter that is *not* to insist on formal grounds that my views ought to be heard, but rather to argue on substantive grounds that they happen to be wrong, that I am not in fact spreading hateful views, and that respecting Palestinians, refusing to label an entire people "terrorists," and refusing to judge them by a different standard than the one I would have applied, say, to Jewish freedom fighters when they fought against British colonialism, is *not* an act of disrespect to the Jewish people, but rather an act of respect for our Jewish tradition, which says over and over again "One law shall there be for you and for the stranger who dwells within your midst." There's no way to avoid these kinds of detailed substantive assessments of reality. By contrast, I can show you a lot of reasons to believe that when you don't acknowledge the God within every other human being, as Baruch Goldstein and those who supported his massacre of Palestinians at Hebron seem not to do, and feel that it's appropriate to strike out against random Palestinian civilians, as some of the West Bank settlers have done, that you are in violation of major strands within the Jewish tradition. There's got to be a line drawn someplace to say there are certain kinds of views which are no longer part of the discourse.

C.W. It's not for me to draw those kinds of lines, for a number of different reasons. I think that if some good could possibly have come out of it, then a debate between you and Kahane would have been justified. I don't think that Kahane's virulent racism somehow precludes you, in the same way that I don't think that some of the virulent homophobia in people who are progressive on issues of class means that we don't talk to them, as wrong as they are. These different forms of hatred that people hold onto in no way precludes us from being in dialogue with them, even though we are quite clear and open about the hatred and we put a spotlight on it.

M.L. I want to distinguish between two different things here: providing a forum to debate, which might be legitimate under specific circumstances, as opposed to what you did when you participated in a conference of Black leadership with Farrakhan, and then had the major public statements coming from that conference be statements of "Black unity" without any public condemnation of anti-Semitism. This wasn't a context where you and others publicly said what's wrong with Farrakhan: You were in a room in which the supposition is, "We are all here honoring each other. We all share a common problem and we are all here as leaders trying to deal with this common problem."

Black leaders should have said, "This guy has gone beyond the pale and cannot be part of our meeting. He is kicking Jews in the balls. And those Jewish liberals who have stuck with us in greater proportions than every other sector of the non-Third World population are our major allies. These Jewish allies are asking us to publicly confront Farrakhan's racism and we Black progressives seem to be conveying back the message that we don't care what they feel. But we're in the same boat with these Jews, so we ought to be more careful about their feelings and concerns."

Legitimating Farrakhan is going to make it harder for Blacks to get what they want in the future. I guarantee that this meeting will prove to have been a setback for Black interests. It has already proven to be part of the causal chain that led to the ousting of Ben Chavis from NAACP leadership and to statements by some questioning whether there is even a need for an organization like the NAACP.

C.W. I think that people are making too much of it. You've got a number of voices in the Jewish world which have said ugly and racist things about Palestinians. Some of them—like Begin—have run nation states. But you had to be in dialogue with Begin, right? Now, are you saying you don't have any dialogue with anyone who has said such ugly things about other people?

M.L. Begin was elected by the Israeli public, so we had to deal with him. I would have a very different attitude if Ben Chavis had conducted a poll or an election, and then Farrakhan had been democratically selected to be one of the top leaders of the Black community. There were very few elected Black officials at this meeting, though hundreds have been elected to office as mayors, members of state legislatures, and members of Congress. Chavis made the designations as to who was the "national leadership" of the Black community. People like Henry Louis Gates and Julian Bond simply would not attend.

We're at a historical moment when Farrakhan doesn't have so much power in the Black world and I'm saying, "Don't accelerate his power."

C.W. I think that too much is made about Farrakhan. Farrakhan is another brother in a leadership position who has a highly truncated analysis and a very limited vision. There's hundreds of other voices out there. Imagine sitting around a table with, say, one hundred Black leaders. The cameras come in. Who's the first person they go to?

M.L. Farrakhan.

C.W. Exactly. Which says something right there about how white America thinks of Black leadership. Why do they go straight to Farrakhan? It's not because of his numbers. It's not because of his influence, relatively speaking. There are other people who are much more influential than he is. It's not because of his sway, his resources. Why do they go to Farrakhan?

M.L. I'm saying that one reason they could be going to Farrakhan is that they can see the potential power in his rhetoric of outrage that they know is partly true, because they know that they are in a racist society.

Farrakhan is a classic demagogue. Like every demagogue he articulates important truths mixed in with his distortions and lies. Farrakhan's anger at the ways that whites have hurt Blacks articulates a deeper truth about racism than a lot of those other Black leaders, some of whom are Stepin Fetchit men playing it so as not to catch the anger as much as he does. Not only does he articulate the anger, he articulates it in a racist and destructive direction that is likely to lead to overt struggle between the races. Either between Blacks and whites, or at least between Blacks and Jews.

Farrakhan misdirects people's anger toward a safe target, rather than at the ruling elites, who are the real source of our problems. Jews are safe because there are four to five times as many Blacks as Jews in America, and because Jews actually care about Blacks and hence are vulnerable to Black rage.

C.W. Yes, I know your view is widely accepted in the Jewish world. I can understand that, but I think it's wrongheaded. I think that what is at the core of Farrakhan's appeal in a large auditorium is not the demeaning of the Other. Just as I don't believe that fundamentalist Christians have anti-Semitism at the core of their message. Human beings are much more complex than that. Fascists are something else. Fascists are those who compress these components to such a degree that at the heart and core of their project is a primary, systemic degradation of others. The white press focuses on Farrakhan because he generates fear in the hearts of white people, and a press more concerned with white fear than Black suffering will always elevate a Farrakhan or a Khallid.

What is at the core of Farrakhan, though, is a manifestation of a Black rage articulated by a bold and fearless message vis-à-vis the white power structure. And it is articulated by a highly talented rhetorician. If you had someone of a universalist orientation who was as talented in terms of expressing that rage, you would get crowds, too.

M.L. You mean it's just an accident of birth that it's him that has this capacity but other Black people don't.

C.W. It's a matter of the combination of rhetorical skills that taps Black rage and takes the form of a bold and fearless critique. In terms of sheer rhetorical skill, there aren't a lot of universalists in the Black community who can compete at that level.

M.L. Why is that?

C.W. The universalist message is declining because of the polarization. At a moment of high racial polarization, a universalist message is going to be viewed as marginal. The results that Farrakhan has yielded so far have been symbolic and cathartic.

M.L. Why can't universalist Blacks produce that result?

C.W. Because the mood of the Black community is already one of closing ranks. So he can tap into that in a way that universalists would have difficulty doing.

M.L. I'd say the reason it is closing ranks is because of the larger context of American society's focus on selfishness. Black progressives are going to be as much defeated by this larger context as anybody, in their attempts to make an impact on the Black community. Which is why it's going to be in the interests of Black progressives to have a Politics of Meaning.

I must say that I have heard in my lifetime maybe a hundred Black preachers, each of whom was at least as mellifluous and powerful in their formulation as this Farrakhan guy.

C.W. But they don't tap into Black rage. They are not as bold or fearless vis-à-vis white power structure. That's been part of the problem. It's that combination of Farrakhan's ability to capture rage and this narrow form of expression that draws the attention.

If you asked people why they had come to see Farrakhan, they would say a number of things. One, he's so talented. He can actually perform. There's a histrionic entertainment dimension, which is true for churches and synagogues. Two, the content of his message. He focuses on Black suffering in a way that few people do. Three, his analysis of the cause of Black suffering is simplistic enough for you to grasp.

M.L.   You have to recognize his strength as well his craziness; and that's where there's a connection to Hitler. It's true that Hitler represented almost nobody in 1923; but it's also true that he was touching on the rage of people's powerlessness and was directing it in a crazily irrational way. That way would never put him into total opposition to the ruling class, and so the ruling class could figure out a way to use him if it became appropriate.

Farrakhan can play the role that now is being played in Italy by the neo-Nazis who are now a part of a reformist coalition government. Someday in the future, when ruling elites in this country have decided that the way to maintain power is to manipulate anti-Semitic sentiment amongst both Blacks and whites to deflect their anger against the system, this guy can play the role of being a representative of Black outrage at Jews. In that circumstance, Farrakhan would become, not the leader like Hitler, but an important element in an anti-Semitic, fascist front in American society. That is conceivable.

C.W.   It might be conceivable, but it's so improbable.

M.L.   How likely was it that some corporal thrown out of the army in 1923 was going to end up as Chancellor of Germany?

C.W.   But German history is very different. It doesn't have a history of Black-white divide. Farrakhan's message certainly has deep authoritarian content and character to it, but it is so virulently against white supremacy that it will continually force him up against the white powerful elite, who themselves would have to be the carriers of a fascist movement. That's why I don't accept the probability.

M.L.   Let me give you another scenario. Thirty years from now, America is economically dominated by Japanese and German interests. They are withdrawing money from America, turning us into more of a Third World country. They are concerned about a spreading nativist, anti-Japanese and anti-German sentiment that has the potential of becoming anti-capitalist as well. So they look for American representatives of their consciousness. As well as whites who are willing to articulate an anti-Semitic direction, they turn to Farrakhan as a way of deflecting the anger that is building against the ruling class. The way that resentment against that ruling elite is expressed is somewhat racist. They're looking for someone to deflect that racism onto, and they say, "The Jews are the ones to deflect onto and Farrakhan [or some Farrakhan-like figure] is our man."

C.W. I think we just can't downplay the role of white supremacy in the future of the country, unfortunately, though any form of xenophobia is simply inexcusable. That's what I think will continually force Farrakhan or a Farrakhan-like figure to swerve from the kind of coalition you're talking about, which is a precondition for a fascist regime.

M.L. He *serves* white supremacy. If I were a white supremacist, I'd invent Farrakhan. I'd say, "Nothing is going to help us better than this guy who's going to set up the major liberal non-Third World group in America, namely the Jews, as the enemy for Blacks who might otherwise be attacking us."

Time and time again in history we've seen alliances between groups which actually hold contradictory views with regard to ethnic hatred, but who have been able to suspend that.

C.W. You'll have to show how Farrakhan, whose fundamental commitment is against white supremacy, is going to join forces with white fascists whose fundamental commitment is the promotion of white supremacy.

M.L. A central part of Farrakhan's current policies are based on the notion that Blacks should build up their own capitalist institutions. He might be able to work out a deal with some section of the American ruling elite that says, "You join us in suppressing freedom of speech, and we'll give a cut to the Black capitalist institutions that you support, that you've been saying are the key to success for the Black world."

C.W. White fascists who are dedicated to white supremacy will give the money to Farrakhan?

M.L. Because he's not challenging white supremacy. That's the point.

C.W. You see, that's where we disagree. We're not talking about challenges, we're talking about what his fundamental commitment is.

M.L. I detect in much of your reaction to our fear of anti-Semitism a tone that suggests that Jews are overreacting. I think it is sometimes hard for Black progressives to take Jewish fears of Black anti-Semitism seriously. So let me paint another picture of how the impact of Black anti-Semitism might spread, a picture suggested by my son Akiba.

C.W. Akiba, he's a good brother, and he's sharp. How is he doing?

M.L. He's wonderful. He still talks about how wonderful it was to be with you a year and a half ago when you spent a week living with us in our house in Berkeley while we were working on the first draft of this dialogue, and how much he enjoyed the discussions with you about Jewish history and Black history. After graduating from college, he has made *aliyah* and is now living in Israel.

Akiba told me the following: one of the things that is going on in white culture, given the absence of any white protest organization, any major form for expression for white alienation, is that white kids in high school are more and more listening to rap music, including music with anti-Semitic themes. Just as in the late fifties it was Black music that entered the white mainstream and created a space for a certain amount of rebellion, that same phenomenon is happening today. White youth today are the major consumers of rap.

C.W. Well, that is not saying a whole lot because it is such a big group, but they are buying more than they were relative to before, that is true.

M.L. It is saying a whole lot when you think that rap music came out of a ghetto experience and seemed to be speaking to a particular experience of alienation, and now that alienation seems to speak to a growing number of white youths as well. Akiba says that white youth are adopting the language and categories of rebellion that have heretofore been characteristic of inner city Blacks, and that one of the elements being adopted is a certain legitimation of anti-Semitic themes, seeping from the anger of Black inner city youths inspired by the Farrakhans and the Khallid Muhammads and the culture of the Nation of Islam. If we project into the future five or ten years, one can imagine that more of Farrakhan's anti-Semitism, as well as his homophobia and sexism, will seem legitimate, and not only to Black youth, but to white youth looking for some way to express through culture their anger and alienation.

C.W. Many of these white kids are already hearing anti-Semitism and homophobia in their homes, in those white homes.

M.L. I'd argue that that's not been true in America for much of the past fifty years since the Holocaust. A large segment of white kids are hearing anti-Semitic messages with a sense of flagrancy and openness and extreme that they never heard and that hasn't been heard in this society for thirty, forty, fifty years.

C.W. In the public sphere yes. When I talk to Princeton students in terms of what their parents say about Jews, I hear funky stuff, brother. Real prejudice. Now these are Princeton, white, privileged elites to be, and *they* didn't need to learn anti-Semitism from Black culture.

M.L. Farrakhan didn't invent American anti-Semitism, to be sure. But there's a world of difference between privately held prejudices and the articulation of those prejudices in the public sphere. Meanwhile, while there has been in America a systematic campaign against racism, so that children in public schools often learn about the ways that prejudices against Blacks were developed and how distorted they are, there has been no similar attempt to expose and refute the common distortions about Jews.

C.W. No, no. Have you seen the textbooks out in suburbia? A little box about American slavery, that's it. It is not like you've got a whole lot on American racism and nothing on anti-Semitism. What you really have is no mention whatsoever of a Holocaust, let alone anything on the pogroms and so on, and a little box for Negroes, on slavery, and on Negro achievements later on.

M.L. But what I am saying is that this generation of American young people are learning a language to articulate the alienation that they would feel as young people in an oppressive, plastic society, and the language that it includes as a central element is anti-Semitism.

C.W. But you've got Guns 'n Roses and others who are quite xenophobic in their own way too, and they are not a part of rap music. I am granting you that there is a large role played by Black hip-hop culture and rap music on white students, but there are other sources too.

M.L. Rap isn't the only source of anti-Semitism. But first, let me explain why this could be so threatening in its impact over the course of the next thirty years. This anti-Semitism will play the same role in relationship to this generation because of its sexy character, and because of its ability to produce outrage amongst the older generation that marijuana played for a previous generation, for the generation of the sixties. Namely, as a symbol—

C.W. Become hip.

M.L. Become a hip symbol of the violation of the standards of the society. Not dangerous to the people who use it particularly, but nevertheless causes an extreme reaction amongst others, and hence will be remembered as kids grow older as a symbol of their youthful rebellion, of their strength, of their self-assertion. That this generation, that we are talking about, say between ten and twenty, who twenty years from now will be thirty- to forty-year-olds will be the ones suffering the brunt of further American economic decline and disproportionately facing unemployment. They will provide the potential white population for an American fascistic movement. American fascism, we fear, may become a viable entity within twenty to thirty years, in the face of that decline and the need of American ruling elites to promote xenophobic nationalism and repression of working-class struggles that the economic decline might generate. One of the targets of that xenophobia will be the Jews, and one reason that white working-class people will respond is that they will have absorbed from Black culture a cultural anti-Semitism as part of their rebellion against the norms of the society as they were growing up and were being influenced by increasingly hateful anti-Semitic themes that associate Jews with the white power structure and place the blame for capitalism's distortions on the Jews.

Remember that fascism in Europe was often part of a cultural rebellion from below that had explicitly anti-capitalist and anti-establishment elements to it, and there also anti-Semitism functioned as a displacement for anger against ruling elites. The "breaking taboos" aspect of anti-Semitism that makes it sexy to some Blacks is now in danger of spreading to white youth unless the Farrakhans and other legitimators of hate can be countered by other Blacks, equally angry at Black oppression, who help people understand why anti-Semitism is "the socialism of fools," a stupid and self-destructive way to express that anger.

I understand, of course, that your point is that there is so much pain in the Black community, based on economic oppression, that it seems a mistaken emphasis to focus on this issue. But my response is that if Blacks want to go beyond merely articulating the pain to the point of actually doing something political about ending it, and changing the economic system in ways that will alleviate Black suffering, you can't do that without having alliances with other groups, and the one group you have had the best alliance with has been Jews. Anti-Semitism is undermining that alliance, so it is self-destructive to not give the fight against anti-Semitism a higher priority. And in the long run, a culture of anti-Semitism will contribute, directly or indirectly, to the emergence of fascistic forces that will do far worse to the Black community than anything that has happened up until now.

C.W. In this scenario it is not Black people who are aligning with white fascists. That is the difference.

M.L. This is a different scenario from the others I proposed. It is one that may or may not include a Farrakhan as an ally, but rather focuses on the long-term cultural impact in the society of the legitimation of anti-Semitism that is now happening in some sectors of the Black community.

C.W. There is a real interesting way in which Farrakhan's obsession with Jewish power and linking it to Black social misery has a certain elective affinity to certain Jewish projections of Black power in the future, linked to potential Jewish social misery. I think both groups are less significant than we think. When I hear your fearful scenarios, what is interesting is the degree to which you ascribe such tremendous power to Black people in contributing to Jewish social misery further down the road. We must not overlook *present* social misery by highlighting possible social misery in the future.

M.L. But pay attention to the fact that this is being raised to you by people like me who not only demonstrated for civil rights in the sixties, but who continue in the 1990s to insist that American priorities must be reordered to end economic oppression of Blacks. People who fight for full employment, health care, and child care. People who oppose and expose the racism that continues in the police forces that patrol inner-city Black communities. People who continue to insist that America recognize that it has never rectified the long history of slavery and subsequent oppression of Blacks. It is *we* who are turning to you and saying that Farrakhan, Khallid Muhammad, the Nation of Islam, the Leonard Jeffries, and Afrocentrists, and other anti-Semitic elements are hurting us and undermining our ability to be effective advocates and allies.

So when I focus on Farrakhan—this is the guy who's wanting to hurt my people. And you're wanting to have an alliance with my people. So I'm saying you've got to pay attention to our upset. The message that we are hearing is, "Fuck you Jews; we don't really care what you think." Even when Chavis was removed from the NAACP leadership, people went out of their way to say that it wasn't because of his relationship to Farrakhan, but only because of his questionable settlement of a sexual harassment lawsuit against himself, using NAACP funds without adequate consultation. So this is where we feel like we are being told that we are not that important to you.

C.W. How can that follow from just sitting down and talking to Farrakhan? You see, that is overreaction! That's like saying that if you are in dialogue with Podhoretz you're saying, "Fuck you Palestinians." You're not saying that—you're just sitting down and talking with the man! Why not dialogue with Podhoretz? He deserves engagement, you know what I mean? I perceive deep anti-Palestinian elements in the pages of a magazine over which he has significant control, but that doesn't mean you'd be saying, "Fuck you Palestinians."

M.L. If this Podhoretz had gone around the country giving speeches saying, "I want to identify with this person who's in favor of the genocide of Palestinians," I'd have a very different feeling about talking to him.

C.W. Farrakhan has never ever come close to calling for genocide.

M.L. No—he's identified with Hitler. Didn't he talk about Judaism as a gutter religion? What the hell is that?

C.W. What he meant was that Judaism has been used to justify forms of domination. He was wrong in the monolithic use of it, but we know every religion has been used to justify domination. That's not in any way coming close to genocide: that's too exorbitant a claim. Not only that, but we have no evidence of the Nation of Islam engaging in violent action against Jews, or whites, for that matter.

M.L. Here again we suddenly are arguing around Farrakhan in a legalistic way that makes me very uncomfortable. This is the same argument I have in the Jewish world where I'm saying all the time, "West Bank settlers create a discourse of demeaning Palestinians that creates the context in which a Baruch Goldstein engages in murder." You don't have to say, "Pull the trigger!" in public: people are smart enough now not to say it in public. But your discourse of demeaning the Other helps create the extreme likelihood that something like that is going to happen.

Farrakhan did this in relation to Malcolm X. His discourse of violence and hatred created a context in which his followers would think he was authorizing murder, even if he didn't himself actually order the execution of Malcolm X. And I'm saying that, similarly, Farrakhan is creating a discourse of demeaning of the Other that will lead people, whether or not they've been explicitly so ordered, to hurt or kill Jews.

C.W. Yes, but at the same time, it's very important to note that anti-Semitism in the Black community was around before Farrakhan was born. And that it had its own life and logic before he came on the scene.

M.L.   But you yourself were saying it's rising now.

C.W.   Yes, and he has, I think, contributed to that. But you have to make some distinction between persons who physically attack Jews, and the Nation of Islam, that has a record of rarely doing so. It's not a compliment: it's a fact that one has to take into consideration when one begins to make claims about calls for genocide. If you do that, you have to look quite seriously at both the ugly rhetoric and the relatively complacent praxis, because genocide is a praxis that has to do with institutional mechanisms of attacks and so forth. Again, I think this lends Farrakhan too much attention.

M.L.   I don't think so. I think not just Farrakhan but the movement that he represents is dangerous to Jews and dangerous to the liberal project.

C.W.   Do you think he's more dangerous than Pat Buchanan?

M.L.   Definitely. Because Pat Buchanan or David Duke represent the forces on the Right that can provoke the reemergence of a progressive movement that might defeat them.

Farrakhan represents the possibility of dividing the progressive forces in such a way that we will be in no position to ever respond to a David Duke or a Buchanan. There will be so much hatred between Blacks and Jews that the core of these two communities—historically the center of the Democratic Party, itself the only force in America that provides a counterbalance to the ruling elite's ability to just trounce on everybody's interests without any restraints whatsoever—will be smashed. Farrakhan's forces represent the possibility of destroying the alliance between those two core groups. It's no longer a subjective alliance, but there's still an objective alliance (for example, between the Congressional Black Caucus and various liberal forces in the Jewish world), and he could destroy it. Not him alone, but the anti-Semitism in the Black world could undermine it to such an extent that Jews would no longer want to be part of it and Blacks wouldn't want them there.

C.W.   What responsibility would the Jewish community bear in terms of undermining this alliance? One could argue, based on the same logic, that the rise of Jewish conservatism is the most dangerous thing in the last twenty years because it contributes to the severing of ties between the two most progressive groups, and therefore Jewish conservatism is more dangerous than almost any other. I mean, I don't believe that, but the same logic could be used. I'm critical of Norman Podhoretz. I think he's wrong on so many issues, but he's still not that important: just as I'm telling you Farrakhan is not that important, even as we must combat both.

But from your logic, it looks as though Farrakhan is more danger-ous than Duke, more dangerous than Buchanan, more dangerous than the most powerful elites who are deeply conservative and xenophobic, precisely because your concern is with these two groups who have difficulty coming together. There's a whole host of different reasons why they have difficulty coming together. Farrakhan is one and Podhoretz and the forces and interests and thinking he represents is another.

M.L.   I don't underestimate the pernicious effect on Jewish con-sciousness of *Commentary* magazine and *The New Republic,* each of which has given a certain intellectual legitimacy to the racist tenden-cies in the Jewish world, most importantly the deep desire to imagine that Jews have no serious moral or political stake in ending the eco-nomic oppression of Blacks. But these are nevertheless *not* people who in any overt and conscious way say that Blacks are an evil force in the world.

I was distressed that you, Cornel, and Manning Marrable, and other Black leaders would participate in what seemed to me to be a quasi-legitimating ceremony for Farrakhan, particularly since its pub-lic theme was "Black unity," and in this context that meant unity *with* Farrakhan. At the time you told me that you imagined that being part of the Summit process would expose Farrakhan to a different way of thinking, and might pressure him to abandon his anti-Semitism.

So, it is particularly relevant to note that two weeks after that first Summit, on June 22, 1994, Farrakhan's national newspaper, *The Final*

Call, featured an article called "Hypocrisy and Conspiracy," by Minister Louis Farrakhan, totally dedicated to excoriating the Jews. Anyone who wonders whether Jews are dragging up ancient history when they cite Farrakhan's citations of the greatness of Hitler years ago can look at this reairing of the traditional anti-Semitic hate about Jews as the killers of Jesus!

Farrakhan outdoes many Christian haters in the way his "study guide" talks about the Jewish conspiracy to "kill the Apostle of God." Citing the Qur'an 3:53 "And the Jews planned and Allah also planned. And Allah is the best of planners," Farrakhan says the following: "The reader will note that in this verse an entire people is included. No distinction is made between the conspirators and the innocent. The plan written of is the plan to kill the Messiah. Such a plan is so wicked, so destructive to humanity, that it involves the totality of that people to whom the conspirators belong." In short, the blame for killing Jesus cannot be given only to those who participated —but falls on the entire Jewish people! And this message is what Farrakhan is emphasizing to all who will listen to him in 1994. He wants to instruct his listeners to not be angry just at some Jews, but at all Jews.

Farrakhan goes on: "The term 'Jew' is not exclusively limited to describe a people who call themselves 'Jews.' This term also describes a certain orientation of the mind and spirit. While a person may not be a 'Jew' in the religious sense, a person may be a 'Jew' by definition of his or her thinking and planned action(s) against the Apostle of God." This, then, is what it is to be a Jew—to be the person who tries to destroy God's Apostle.

Why did the Jews want to kill Jesus? "Jesus," Farrakhan tells us, "represented the ultimate threat to their exclusivity both in his condemnation of them by identifying them as the children of Satan and his declaration that God was *his* Father. . . . At the root of the lies and murder plots against Jesus, Paul, Peter, Muhammad was Envy . . . When one is an Envier, he or she always sees oneself as more worthy of the benefit or favour than the person or persons to whom the favour has been given . . . Since the Envier cannot climb up to heaven to the Grantor of gifts and benefits, his or her anger is focused on the recipient of Divine Favour. Though their efforts (lies, murder) are directed at the recipient, their actions are in fact a challenge against Allah (God) Himself to warfare."

This is the man to whom you and other Black progressives are offering "unity" and for whom these Black Leadership Summits provide a platform and a signal of public respectability. And then people wonder why Jews have distanced themselves from the Black community?

So, Cornel, can you tell what me what would motivate some guy to be resurrecting, on June 22nd, 1994, stories about the Jews as the people who are plotting against "the Apostle of God," resurrecting into popular consciousness the story that has been used for two thousand years to motivate Christians to pogroms and murder against the Jewish people? And to talk about the Jews as a kind of moral and spiritual sickness? The only person who would say this sort of thing is either a demented person, a fundamentally evil person, or a person who is so focused on getting power that he is willing to use some of the oldest lies and hate in the history of the human race to advance his own position.

C.W. No question that vintage anti-Semitic ideology is one element of Farrakhan's project. And what you are highlighting is precisely the conspiratorial theories, about Jews as killers of Christ, Jews as transgressors of apostles of God. You see the same thing in fundamentalist Christian literature; it just is not highlighted as much. It is one of the oldest lies about people. It is a pernicious lie nonetheless.

M.L. In this discourse, I believe that the word anti-Semitism is used by you in a way to avoid confronting anti-Semitism. You acknowledge that there's anti-Semitism, but it's as if you were saying Farrakhan had curly hair, or some morally irrelevant feature of a person, rather than as a reflection of the fundamental essence of what that person is. So I don't hear the moral outrage that might lead you to more fully reject and distance yourself from Farrakhan.

C.W. See that's the thing about it. In your view, to be an anti-Semite means to be a radically evil person. Or to be a racist, sexist, or homophobe is to be a radically evil person. All forms of bigotry are morally wrong—but to be radically evil cuts much deeper.

M.L. No. Again one of the fundamentals of the whole Politics of Meaning perspective has been to accept that many people get drawn to racist, anti-Semitic, sexist, homophobic views as a deflection of their fundamental anger and inability to direct that appropriately.

I don't believe that everyone who becomes part of an anti-Semitic movement is automatically evil. Sometimes the best way to win people away from these hate movements is to speak to legitimate needs that the haters are speaking to. In fact, I am hopeful that you and other Black progressives will do more to speak to the outrage and pain of Blacks that Farrakhan speaks to, and then to win Blacks to a much more progressive politics.

But there is a difference between most people who are drawn to these views as part of satisfying their meaning needs and the core group of people who put these views at the center of their world view and for whom the very meaning of their life is their hatred of the Other, whether that be Jews, gays, women, Blacks, Arabs, or whoever. In the deepest core of his being, Farrakhan appears to be a hater of Jews. This is his truth. He is a person who comes from this perspective on the world.

C.W. I don't think so, though. This is where we disagree. You believe that Louis Farrakhan is a radically evil person who has hatred at the core of his being. See, I don't think that's true. I mean I hate to use "anti-Semitic" now, I want to give weight to the term—but he does have anti-Semitic elements in his attempts to account for black social misery. But at the core of his being is not this hatred of Jews or even a hatred of white persons. I think it's much more at his core being to overcome Black suffering. And I think he's a very complex person like all of us. I just don't think that the dominant component of his being is hatred of Jews.

M.L. But by the way, I would not restrict it to a hatred of Jews because it is also a hatred of gays and lesbians and hatred of independent women.

C.W. In the section on homophobia in his book, he goes out of his way to talk about how the duty of Muslims and so forth is to love homosexuals and to acknowledge that they are human beings and so forth and so on, though he still condemns the orientation. It's one of the issues that we pushed him on when he sent the manuscript to us. Now whether he's just saying that to be manipulative? Open question. I don't think so.

M.L. Does he say that about Jews? To you? Muslims should love Jews?

C.W. He said it many, many times. Yes he has. Again. Is it empty rhetoric? Well, when you look at what he says in "Hypocrisy and Conspiracy," they clash. There's a fundamental clash.

M.L. Kahane said that he was worried about the best interests of Palestinians. That's why he wanted to ship them out of the State of Israel because they were not going to have their needs met in the State and Jews weren't going to have their needs met in the State. He didn't say that they should be killed.

C.W. Of course, Farrakhan has never said the Koran and the Bible commands me to hate Jews.

M.L. No. He just acts in this unbelievably evil way.

C.W. He brings back the classic anti-Semitic theological position in the Christian and Islamic traditions.

M.L. He says that Jews are a state of mind, a certain orientation of the mind and spirit.

C.W. But to cast this in a larger way, how do the Black and Jewish worlds deal with a Farrakhan? I mean, you have a majority of American Jews who believe as you do. That he is radically evil and at the core of his being is hate. You've got a majority of Black folk believing as I do. That he has anti-Semitic ideology as part of his struggle against black suffering. And that is not to be taken lightly. But at the core of his being is not this unredeemable and unreformable hatred.

M.L. OK. Since as a religious Jew I recognize that at the core of every human being is the way that they have been created in the image of God, I'll take back that formulation and not demonize the core of his being—but I still think it is reasonable for Jewish progressives to be imploring you, Cornel, and other Black progressives to be doing more in the public arena to delegitimate Farrakhan's ideas. Without restricting his right to say anything he wishes, I want you to say to others in your community, "We are not going to give him a platform from which to spew out his hatred. We are going to do everything we can not to go hear him. Not that he doesn't have the right to speak, but that we have to use our support to get people not to listen, but to use their time in more productive ways for the liberation of our people."

C.W. You see, I don't think that's a good strategy. I can agree with the impulse; I just don't agree with the strategy. When you tell people to entirely dismiss somebody, to make them entirely taboo, that's just makes them more interesting.

M.L. Perhaps you are right that tactically that is not the best way to approach the delegitimation. So fine, find a better tactic to delegitimate him. But strategically will you share that goal with me?

C.W. You are underestimating the critical capacity of Black people to make their own decisions when they hear a variety of different visions and arguments.

M.L. Well I'd be a lot more impressed with their critical capacity if they'd *already* rejected Farrakhan, after years of hearing this anti-Semitic and homophobic garbage. But, on the contrary, you've told me that his appeal has grown and that he is such a significant leader that he must be invited to a national summit of Black leaders.

C.W. The majority of black Americans do not follow Farrakhan. The majority of Black Americans sympathize with certain things he says about Black self-help. But they won't join his organization. That's already a certain kind of critical judgment being made.

M.L. Are more people joining it today or less people joining it today than in the past?

C.W. Slightly more, because there are more disillusioned young people. Because young people themselves tend to also have to develop their critical capacities and they tend to be much more attuned, not all the time but often, to certain kinds of excitement and charisma, boldness and fearlessness.

But if you want to exclude, dismiss, silence, and not allow Farrakhan to be part of the marketplace of ideas, then I say that frankly is unacceptable.

M.L. I have always been in favor of the marketplace of ideas in that way. But I want one of your strategic goals to be to get people to put less energy into the Farrakhans of the world. Do you share that with me?

C.W. Oh, sure. I come out of King's legacy, out of Fannie Lou Hamer's legacy. I want people to listen to those spokespersons who represent that legacy. Minister Louis Farrakhan does not come out of Martin Luther King, Jr., or Fannie Lou Hamer's legacy. That is part of the disagreement that I have with him. And it's deep disagreement, it's not just ornamental or decorative, but that's different from saying, well I wish people would listen more to my legacy, what I have to say, what so many others who are part of that legacy have to say, the same way you would want to say, well I wish people would take Heschel's legacy more seriously as opposed to some non-prophetic or some conservative figure. We are talking about a much larger context here than about how one goes about minimizing the worst aspects of Farrakhan's project in terms of the Black community in the larger society.

M.L. If we're agreed that people would be better off, and the Black community would be better served, if we could get people to spend less time listening to Farrakhan and more time listening to more progressive Black leaders, then what is your strategic idea of how we might accomplish that, or a tactical idea of how we might accomplish that goal?

C.W. One is you've got to institutionalize progressive voices that keep alive the vision of Martin Luther King, because there are a number of persons who right now sympathize and some follow the Minister Louis Farrakhan who in the early part of the twenty-first century will be progressives. You are going to have hundreds of persons who are fundamentally concerned about Black suffering, who go into Farrakhan's organization because they are concerned about Black suffering, and in the end feel that it doesn't provide enough vision and insight and analysis and end up progressives.

There is a real sense in which Black people are profoundly Jewish people, just as Jews are profoundly Black. I think that is one of the reasons why there is really a very unique relation between these two people. Not as if it is just a matter of these two groups coming together on self-interest or these two groups clashing because of a conflict of self-interest. I think part of the problem of the relation is on a more visceral level, these groups do have a very deep affinity with one another. That is part of the irony of Farrakhan.

One of the reasons why he is so obsessed with Jews is precisely because of the profoundly Jewish nature of modern African-American peoples as well as the profoundly Black nature of modern American Jewry. There is a kind of symbiotic relation owing not just to the focus around certain stories in the Biblical text that put an emphasis on justice, mercy, and righteousness, kindness to strangers, and about who sides with the oppressed and the tragic peoples who cry and bleed and are scarred and so forth. Those are real.

But there is also this sense of being a perennial people on the move, having to make and remake themselves as they are on the move, a people who fall back on the sense of the comic and the tragic in their art and life, especially as a means of preserving sanity against a world that seems to be over against them. Those are deep, very deep, elective affinities and they have an existential dimension that goes far beyond just the political similarities or historical similarities or the anti-Semitic barriers versus the racial caste system and so forth. It is hard to talk about them, but I think it is very real. But that is part of the problem because there is a sense in which Black and Jewish folk are almost stuck together, either at each other's throats or embracing one another, but that is still a kind of family fight.

M.L. This is one of the pathetic things also, from a Jewish standpoint, to hear the followers of Leonard Jeffries and other Afrocentrist Blacks telling us, "Oh you Jews aren't really Jews, you stole that identity from us Blacks." There are so many ways that the Black people could create an identity for themselves. Why in the world should they need to take our identity and claim that it was theirs or, as some do, that our Torah is really their Torah. Yet you hear this pathetic and hostile articulation from some of them who talk about "so-called Jews."

C.W. But I think it logically follows, because if initially Jews were those people who were suffering under an oppressive regime and who had a covenant with God in light of that suffering and who ascribe to a certain chosenness, then to the degree to which Black people perceive American Jews as more and more becoming typical white Americans: comfort, convenience, prosperity and so forth, to what degree do they actually meet that criterion of chosenness? This is not going back to Germany, not going back to Europe, this is actually in the new world context. It looks as if people of African descent more readily meet the criteria of what it means to be Jews, suffering, chosen, getting kicked in the behind, still keeping on, you see. They figure, "Wait a minute, we are the real Jews." To what degree do these people who call themselves Jews but who more and more in our eyes act like average Americans, bourgeois Americans living the good life and so forth, how can they call themselves Jews? We invest normative content in Jewry. To be a Jew means to be oppressed, to be struggling, to be a certain moral conscience of the nation and so forth. Certain elements of the Black world are saying, is it not the case that in the United States Black folk more readily meet these criteria than Jews of European descent?

M.L. Ironically, for the reasons that I just gave about who the Jews were in terms of their voting patterns, the Jews are the one group that is most Jewish in transcending its self-interest to go for a universal moral view whereas the Blacks are merely pushing for themselves and do not have a view that is expansive enough to even include Jews.

C.W. Not historically though, not historically.

M.L. Particularly to the extent that they get attracted to Farrakhan.

C.W.   Farrkhan's legacy is not the central legacy in the Black freedom struggle. The Black freedom struggle has always been predicated on something beyond Black self-interest—on moral grounds. Always.

M.L.   When forces like the liberals in the Jewish world and the Civil Rights movement converged, you had a transformation in the larger society that made even some ruling elites say to themselves, "Maybe we ought to go with a higher vision of who we could be." In other words, there were moments in the sixties where even ruling elites transcended their own narrow self-interest and went for a vision of the good that had been generated from below: a possibility of a different kind of logic in the world. That is infectious and spreads upwards throughout the whole society, opening up a space for everybody in every class to rethink their situation and their possibilities.

The objective economic structure of the situation stays constant: it rewards people for selfishness, not for construing their interests in terms of caring for others. But people's perceptions about whether they should follow the reward structure of the economy or whether they should allow themselves to be motivated by their own best image of who they could and ought to be depends very much on their assessment of what's possible at any given moment. Typically, the thing that is pointed out to me most immediately by both whites and Jews is, "Look at the most oppressed groups that used to believe in this idealism stuff. They don't believe in it any more. The Blacks are out for self-interest. The Jews are out for self-interest. All these groups that used to be for some higher vision, they've given up on it. Now if they've given up on it, why the hell should the rest of us think that it's possible?" To which you might reply, "Wait a minute. Why should the burden be on them?" It shouldn't be, but that's how it is in the real world. The burden is on the most oppressed groups to prove a possibility of transformation, because they have the most interest in it. And if even they are abandoning ship, you know you're in trouble—you know they know something.

C.W.   Oh yes, that's a widespread perception. That's a perception that has been deeply shaped by conservatives and neoconservatives. It's a perception that shows how out of tune and out of touch large numbers of white Americans are with Black America; it's a perception that reflects the levels of polarization and Balkanization in our society. All they see of Black America is what they see on television. They don't see grassroots leaders; they don't see the broad visionary leaders who are working day and night.

CHAPTER 10

Shared Crisis of Leadership

C.W.   We've talked a lot about the problems of some Black leaders. Yet progressive African-Americans often feel that the Jewish world confronts them with a Jewish leadership that seems insensitive to our concerns. In the past thirty years there has been a marked shift to the right in the kinds of statements and focus coming from the Jewish world, and that has played a role in the way that we in the Black community perceive who Jews are in America.

M.L.   Leadership is a very tricky issue in the Jewish world. On the one hand, there is a conservative leadership that has run many of the major Jewish organizations in the past thirty years, and which has sought to repress the voices of dissent. They are largely unrepresentative of younger Jews. On the other hand, the genuine progressives in the Jewish world have inherited the anti-leadership tendencies in Jewish culture and have become the vanguard of a knee-jerk, anti-leadership tendency that exists in the Left and has made it hard for anyone to exercise leadership.

Starting with Moses, who was constantly being rebelled against by the people he led out of Egypt, that tendency has always been present in the Jewish world. We have no compassion for our leaders, no willingness to accept their legitimate ego needs, and we subject them to considerable abuse. Most people feel this, and after a short while they decide they'll be "more modest" and not seek leadership.

The Right escapes these dynamics because it has less of a commitment to a democratic culture and because it has a more mature understanding of the need to compensate leadership materially. So it has been able to create institutions that function effectively to represent the needs of the most wealthy or powerful sectors of American Jewry. The American Jewish Committee is a perfect example. Created by a handful of wealthy German Jewish families, it represented itself as *the* Jewish establishment by being able to raise funds from its core of wealthy Jews, to hire a large staff of professionals who would represent and advance its political positions in the world, and a network of powerful friends in the *New York Times,* other media, in the federal judiciary, and in other key positions in government and the economy. Today it has a core of a few hundred well-to-do people in the country who provide the finances, and maybe a few thousand more who, at the most, may occasionally come to some activity or other. Yet, it projects itself as *the* organization of the Jewish world. The American Jewish Congress is the same way—a very small active membership, a slightly larger group of people who sign up as members in response to a direct mail campaign, but who are not involved in any other way, and a staff and fancy building that can make a good impression on visitors. The vast majority of organizations that belong to the Conference of Presidents of Major Jewish Organizations have a fundamentally similar story—a small membership base but enough finances to maintain a staff and an office and a newsletter.

The ADL has a slight variant: its staff is successful in direct mail campaigns focused on fear of anti-Semitism, so it gets several hundred thousand people to send in money as membership dues, though this membership has zero capacity to democratically and critically review the work of the leadership, which is a paid staff. Few of those who send in their money have any idea of what the ADL is up to politically —they are sending in their money because they want to support an organization that historically has challenged anti-Semitism. I think many would be very surprised to learn of the ways that the ADL has treated Jews who critiqued Israeli policy toward Palestinians.

Similarly, the largest fund-raising operation in the Jewish world, the UJA/Federations, raises money for local causes like homes for the elderly and for Israel as well. Yet I think that, given the poll data that show that most American Jews were critical of the Shamir government's policies of building settlements in the West Bank and were closer to the position of *Tikkun* and others who supported the Israeli peace movement in the 1980s, they would probably have been quite shocked to learn that monies they were donating to Israel were actually freeing up other monies to be used to strengthen the occupation of the West Bank, or that within the Federation world itself there was a culture of blind support for the Israeli government that was used by then Israeli Prime Minister Yitzhak Shamir to strengthen his hand in dealing with dissenters in Israel. Indeed, many liberals used to tell me that they felt scared to say publicly in the world of the Federations what they were feeling privately about Israeli policy on the West Bank because doing so would lose them all chance to have influence. Yet this reflected the sentiments of those with wealth and power in the Jewish world—not of the majority of American Jews. But these institutions themselves developed a culture that was oriented toward the wealthy fund-raisers, a culture that played to money and power which could sustain the powerful staffs that snubbed any serious democratic process. No wonder, then, that many young people, growing up in the Jewish world, got the impression that only the wealthy really counted in this world, and that the world was about celebrating those who had money or those who knew how to raise it from those who had it. These younger Jews have been walking away from this kind of Jewish world.

C.W. So why didn't these younger Jews create alternative organizations?

M.L. Some did. There was New Jewish Agenda, the New Israel Fund, Project Nishma, and *Tikkun*'s Committee for Judaism & Social Justice. Yet these younger Jews had far less financial resources available, and their own ambivalence about their experience of Jewishness as a materialistic and spiritually deadening experience made them far less likely to want to give their resources to challenging the established Jewish leadership. Instead, many simply walked away.

As a result, those who share their insights about the materialism and spiritual poverty of Jewish institutions—but who understand that Judaism and Jewish history and culture are far too valuable to be ceded to the conformists and conservatives who have heretofore dominated many of the established Jewish institutions—find themselves without financial support to try to change the Jewish world. Jewish progressives who provide leadership have no staff, no money, do most of the clerical work themselves, and then get attacked for being too egotistical. If they act decisively in a crisis, for example when the Intifada started or when the Hebron massacre took place, they are assailed by their own constituency as being undemocratic.

Then, there is an obsessive "political correctness" that tends to emerge among Jewish leftists, and this too undermines the potential success of progressive organizations. Well, eventually the most talented people become sick and tired of trying to provide leadership in this kind of a context.

C.W. But if people are leaving the Jewish world, why don't the established Jewish institutions recognize that they too will be in trouble in a few generations?

M.L. They do, and they've launched a variety of "Jewish continuity" campaigns. But these are all beside the point, because they are under the control of the very people who have caused the problem in the first place. So they seek public relations efforts to strengthen Jewish ties—a better way to package the same old material. Or they seek to turn Jewish youth on to Israel by having them spend a year there—without any answer to the question of how to build in the U.S. a Jewish life that would feel spiritually meaningful and politically and ethically congruent with the liberal and progressive sensibilities of these younger Jews.

C.W. The picture sounds bleak. Is there any hope for a different kind of progressive leadership emerging in the Jewish world?

M.L. Absolutely. From my standpoint, the most important development has been the emergence of a Jewish renewal consciousness that is attempting to reconnect Jewish spirituality with a progressive Jewish politics. One of the central ideas of Judaism was that there could be no division between the spiritual and the ethical, that to be spiritually attuned meant to fight against injustice and for a world based on love, love not only of neighbor but also of the stranger (there is a specific Torah commandment, often ignored by the Jewish right: Thou shalt love the stranger. Not just be generous and caring, but love is commanded!). Jewish renewal is based on a reintegration of politics and spirituality, a sense that the fight for social justice, for a world based on caring and love and mutuality, is central to the spiritual reality of Judaism.

In a variety of ways, this consciousness is growing in the Jewish world—and it constitutes a significant Jewish renewal. But it is in its baby stage today, without adequate resources or organizational framework. There are important components of this consciousness in every denomination of Judaism, and in many organizations (including the Reform movement's Religious Action Center, the New Israel Fund, Americans for Peace Now, Lilith, Agada, the Jewish Fund for Justice, the American Jewish World Service, and, most importantly, Aleph—Alliance for Jewish Renewal). *Tikkun* magazine provides the place where the ideas and strategic thinking for this development take place. But we have been hampered by lack of funding from *any* Jewish organization or from many Jewish liberals who agree with the politics but are so reactive against our positive view of Judaism and the potential of Jewish spirituality that they prefer to give their financial support to non-Jewish liberal causes. So we end up being too liberal for the Jews and too Jewish for the liberals, particularly Jewish liberals who still haven't fully worked out their (often justified) anger at Jewish institutions that offended them for their racism or indifference to the pain and suffering of anyone outside the Jewish world. Without adequate funding for staff, is it any wonder Jewish progressives and liberals are ill-equipped to get our views known—and this intensifies the alienation of younger Jews who, not knowing of the growing Jewish renewal consciousness, leave the Jewish world in disgust at its materialism, conservatism, and insensitivity on Israel-related issues.

C.W.   What can your non-Jewish allies do to help you?

M.L.   One thing that would help is if non-Jewish progressives were to validate Jewish leadership in larger progressive arenas. One of the things that has traditionally been the case on the Left, and in any kind of progressive social movement, is that people look around the room and say, "Do we have enough Blacks here? Do we have people representing the Chicano community? Or gays? Or Native Americans?" But you never, ever hear somebody say, "Do we have somebody speaking as a Jew here? Somebody representing our Jewish sisters and brothers in a coalition?"

C.W.   There already are a lot of Jews in the room and in the leadership.

M.L.   But that's not the same thing. I'm saying, "Do we have Jews speaking *as Jews?* Do we have Jewish leaders speaking as Jewish leaders?" In other words—imagine if we had a Black person who completely rejected the notion that Blacks were subject to racism; we wouldn't say that we have solved our problems dealing with the Black world just because there happens to be a Black person in the room. No: we want somebody who is speaking from the perspective of the consciousness of a positive identification with the progressive tendencies within the Black world. Similarly, if someone said that privately they were gay, but that they actually had no relationship to the gay movement or its struggles, no progressive group would think that they had accomplished representation of gays by including such a person in the leadership.

There could be a tremendous value in any larger coalition if progressive Blacks insisted that they wanted progressive Jewish leadership in that room speaking specifically *as* progressive Jews, people who identified and were proud of Jewish history and culture and who really cared about Jews as Jews. This is a whole different consciousness.

C.W.   That would require us looking for voices that, in the U.S. context of the mid-nineties, are not necessarily voices associated with the oppressed. When most people look around and say, "We want an indigenous person's voice, we want a Chicano voice," usually that is predicated on the notion that we're looking for people trying to speak for a community that is subordinated, oppressed, and exploited. In today's social configuration, there isn't really a particularly poor Jewish community that's highly visible and associated with being oppressed and exploited.

M.L. We're getting down to a hidden gripe here.

C.W. I'm thinking that in the eyes of many people in that room, asking for a progressive Jewish voice as Jew as opposed to asking for a progressive indigenous person's voice as Indian, represents a very different kind of calculus.

That might be something we need to radically call into question. We could say, "We're looking for progressive voices as spokespeople for various communities. Even when those communities are not currently associated with low income, nor do they have immense difficulty in getting access to resources. They can still play a very important role as progressives and as particular members of their community." That's a shift. We're calling for a shift.

M.L. Exactly. We're talking about transcending a narrow, economistic definition of what oppression is. The alienation and the decline in solidarity and trust that undermines long-term relationships and families and friendships is based on the frustration of the psychological, emotional, and spiritual component of our being that I call our "meaning needs." This deprivation of meaning is also *real* oppression, and leads people to despair, to violence, and to living lives of pain every bit as experientially real as pain generated by poverty.

I believe that much of the violence and self-destructive, drug-oriented behavior in the Black community, like that in white American suburbs, is a reflection of the crisis of meaning that pervades the entire society, though it manifests in different ways in different economic, ethnic, and social circumstances.

Progressives have had a great deal of trouble recognizing the deprivation of meaning, since their political heritage alerts them only to economic deprivation and deprivation of individual rights.

One place where progressives have moved toward a broader understanding is in their recognition of the oppression of gays. In San Francisco many gays are living on an economic level far superior to that of white working-class people from WASP backgrounds who are raising kids. And there are no legal barriers in San Francisco to gay rights. There is hatred in the society and sometimes there are acts of violence against gays, just as there remains hatred in the society toward Jews and occasional acts of violence, particularly directed against synagogues and Jewish institutions. Progressives have no hesitation in saying that gay people are oppressed, and hence in recognizing non-economistic forms of oppression, but they refuse to do this with Jews.

C.W.   Although you still have explicit discrimination against gays in terms of citizen's rights. If they remain in the closet, then there's no problem with regard to gaining access. If they don't remain in the closet, then the homophobic discrimination does become quite continuous. That's true for anti-Catholic discrimination, anti-Semitic discrimination, and race discrimination. Gay discrimination is quite continuous with those earlier forms.

M.L.   The specific form of Jewish oppression is one which the Left has never absolutely dealt with. This is why a Black-Jewish coalition has got to deal with the reality of Jewish oppression if it is going to be real.

The first element of this reality is that Jews have been put into an intermediate position, in between the ruling elite who own the major economic institutions and the American majority, which has little real economic power. Jews become the middlemen—the lawyers, doctors, government bureaucrats, social workers, school teachers, and college professors. They appear to the vast majority of the population to be the public face of the ruling elite, who can be taken out and subjected to popular rage when the economic system is collapsing. This pattern started in Eastern Europe, where Jews were forbidden by law from owning land, but were allowed to be the small shopkeepers, tax-collectors, and foremen for the wealthy Polish landowners. And this pattern continued in twentieth-century Western Europe, where Jews did not own the means of production, yet appeared to many working people to be the embodiments of power because Jews were the public face of the system.

Every argument that can be made about Jews not being oppressed —and hence not being a legitimate group to call upon when we're asking, "Where are the Jews in the room?"—could have been made at least as effectively in Weimar Germany in 1920. "What do you care about the Jews? They are economically secure. The Jews are the doctors, the lawyers, the professors; some of them are in the ruling elites and own big corporations."

C.W. You're saying that the recurrent power of a thousand-year-old anti-Semitic ideology and practice means that, whilst it may look from the vantage point of non-Jewish fellow citizens *as if* Jews are secure, that security is always one of relative illusion.

M.L. Here's the reality. In my lifetime one out of every three Jews alive has been murdered. The Left not only didn't recognize that, but in some ways in Europe was complicit with that same process. In the Soviet Union it was permeated with anti-Semitism. Nowhere has the Left acknowledged and purged itself of this covert anti-Semitism.

C.W. You can't say that it was complicit with the killing of one out of three Jews. You can say the Left has a history of anti-Semitism. That's very different from Nazi attacks or from trying to exterminate Jews. You're going to have to make a distinction between being complicit with an anti-Semitic sensibility, and complicit with genocidal attacks on Jews.

M.L. It didn't favor those genocidal attacks, but it didn't do very much to stop them either.

C.W. But you had a resistance movement all over Europe that was Left and that was against the Nazis.

M.L. Tragically, even in the resistance movements there was considerable Jew-hating, and as a result resistance movements did little when various Jewish ghettoes attempted rebellions against the Nazis, and little to block the trains taking millions to the death camps. Let's take an analogy. Let's say that you had a struggle going on against the Confederacy whilst there was slavery. It's composed of all kinds of Left people who want to overthrow the Confederacy. *But* when slaves run away from their masters and say, "We want to join with you," that group says, "You can't side with us. We're not going to give you arms. We won't have anything to do with you."

C.W.   A lot of these well-to-do Jews who had gone moderate and conservative during Weimar Germany were the same folk who were anti-Communist and anti-Leftist. They hated the Left, and scapegoated it.

M.L.   Yes, but very few of those were the people who were asking for help in a struggle. Many of them had already succeeded in leaving and going to Palestine. I'm talking about 1943–44 when there were anti-Fascist rebellions that were primarily being led by Leftist Jews.

C.W.   I'm trying to resist the notion that somehow the Left was just like any other group when it came to Nazism. On the contrary, the Left disproportionately resisted Nazism.

M.L.   I don't want to make my argument dependent on this point. My fundamental thrust—and I've dealt with it in detail in *The Socialism of Fools*—is that this Left has never seriously dealt with anti-Semitism. There's no reason to believe that when somebody comes into the Left they are going to learn about the history of anti-Semitism, or about how it has not been dealt with in the past. Or about the way that the Soviet Union, and other groups that were the primary public representations of the Left to mass consciousness, actually supported anti-Semitic practices and were not criticized by the majority of people who identified themselves with the Left.

C.W.   So what is necessary for people in that room to recognize is the validity of looking for Jewish voices speaking as Jews?

M.L.   It is necessary for them to recognize that Jews have been another oppressed group. It is absolutely inconceivable that there could be any other group in American society which could say, "One out of every three of us has been murdered in the past fifty years," which would still have to argue its right to be considered as an oppressed group.

C.W.   I don't think so. If in fact we were meeting in that room in 1910, Jews would have no problem pointing to their ghettos and saying, "We represent an oppressed people. We are struggling against anti-Semitic barriers." In 1994, even given that one out of three were killed, people look at Jews' particular position within the society.

M.L. Once again, that position is the same one we had in the 1920s in Weimar Germany. In other words, you have an inadequate understanding. The fact that the Left didn't have a category to understand the vulnerability of Jews in the 1920s is proof that these categories are inadequate to describe who deserves to be considered an oppressed group, whose self-interests ought to be at the table.

C.W. That's an important point. You're saying that if we cannot acknowledge the cyclical recurrence of vicious anti-Semitic practices and we only look at social structure, then we're missing something. Let me ask you a question. If, for example, the Nazis had never arisen, would you still argue that Jews in Weimar Germany in 1920 were oppressed? Without the killing of one out of three subsequently?

M.L. If it didn't occur for the next one hundred years, or anyplace else, then I'd say anti-Semitism was no longer such a significant factor. Then Jews would have less of a right to claim to be disabled. *But* . . .

C.W. . . . Nazism did occur.

M.L. Right. It's like saying, "If after slavery they hadn't continued legislation against Blacks . . ."

C.W. That's a different thing. You can't compare those two cases because it wasn't just cyclical recurrences of anti-Semitic practices after a group had achieved a certain prominent social and economic position. During the Reconstruction, Blacks never, ever had any significant power or prominence in the United States. You can never compare the position of Black folk in terms of the American social structure to the position of Jews in Weimar Germany or in America in 1994. There's no comparison.

M.L. Up until now we've talked as though all I'm basing my argument on is the possibility of a recurrence of anti-Semitism. On this possibility alone, I'd say there are sufficient grounds to bring it to the table. Let's actually look at the world and see what is happening. In this country there are right-wing forces which continue to talk about Blacks and Jews as the enemy. David Duke, a Nazi, got about 40 percent of the vote running for the Democratic nomination for Senate in one state.

Then you have a whole movement of thought in Europe that is denying the existence of the Holocaust. In Poland's last election candidates were trying to prove that they didn't have Jewish origins. In Hungary you've got a resurgence of explicitly anti-Semitic groups. In Slovakia you've got forces which identify with the Nazis. In Croatia you've got the president saying, "The Holocaust has been greatly exaggerated." In what used to be the Soviet Union you've got forces using anti-Semitism to attack the opposite side in the current debate. Each side says, "No, the *other* guy is Jewish." That is so scary that people are running away to live in tents in the deserts of Israel because they are afraid of being killed in Russia.

We're talking about anti-Semitism as a current reality of this world. It hasn't gotten to a totally scary place in the United States, but it is not just a paranoid fantasy projected from the past. Yet I hear few progressives talking about this startling revival of anti-Semitism, though I believe it is a serious and dangerous phenomenon.

C.W.   You've got a strong point there. We're not just talking about cyclical, recurring anti-Semitic practices from a U.S. point of view, where they look less likely to happen than has been the case elsewhere. Globally speaking, anti-Semitism remains a very potent force.

M.L.   Exactly. I didn't even mention Japan, where anti-Semitic books are best-sellers.

C.W.   Your point is that we need to educate progressive people to recognize that when we decide who is oppressed and exploited, we should not depend solely on where that particular group is in the social structure. We need also to consider their particular vulnerability. Given the cyclical recurrence of vicious global anti-Semitic practices, and the degree to which anti-Semitism remains a potent force in the world, Jews—no matter where they are socially and economically —are vulnerable, and the possible objects of anti-Semitic abuse from above or below. This warrants their voice being heard alongside any other oppressed group's. Is that a fair representation of your argument?

M.L. I have been trying to argue that there is a level of spiritual and psychological oppression that is as real and as fundamental as any other form of oppression. This Politics of Meaning is very difficult for people on the Left. That's not to say that this form of oppression requires that it be dealt with quicker, or that it is more important— just that it is as real. It's the oppression and pain that comes from denying our human capacity; it's the frustration of our "meeting needs."

C.W. But this is true for human beings as a whole.

M.L. It's not just a Jewish case.

C.W. What happens is that you end up with the head of IBM who is having a spiritual crisis at the table alongside his workers whose wages he has just slashed. There has to be a point in which your analysis of oppression recognizes that there are in fact struggles going on. No one would deny that the head of IBM might be in a spiritual crisis. But he is wielding real economic power.

M.L. That's right. But I think that you have to distinguish between a Left that constitutes itself around who is most oppressed and who has more power or less, and a Left that constitutes itself around a positive vision of what it wants to see in society.

C.W. It's not either/or. It could be both.

M.L. It could be both and it should be both.

C.W. But those who are spiritually oppressed can move away. Those who are getting kicked in the behind in terms of their health care have material limits.

M.L. You don't have to change the situation. Those who are getting kicked in the behind because there's no health care have not managed to get together a Left that can change the society.
If this were 1960, I'd have nothing on my side but an abstract, theoretical argument. But this is 1994, when we've had movement

after movement of the oppressed coming forward, putting forward claims, and getting kicked in the ass.

C.W.   But you can't *blame* the oppressed people for the conservatism at work. That's like blaming those Jews in the 1920s who were called alarmist for saying that anti-Semitism was right around the corner. It's like saying they brought Nazism upon themselves by calling it into question.

M.L.   The Jews in the 1920s screwed it up. The Jews and the progressives should have beaten the Nazis. I fault the Left and I fault all of the forces that should have devised a plan. Instead of demonizing the fascists (yes, they were demons, but saying so didn't win any support among those who didn't already share that perception), they should have been asking, "What psychological, emotional, and spiritual needs are these people speaking to that gets such a powerful response, and how do we speak to those same needs without reverting to anti-Semitism or xenophobic nationalism?"

The same thing is happening again. The triumph of the Right in the 1970s in this country was absolutely connected to the failure of the Left. Also to the way that the New Left in the late sixties made it seem as though everybody who wasn't on our side was our enemy. To the point where Nixon could run for reelection in 1972 claiming that the Left were the elitists. What was that about? It was about the feeling that so many Americans had, correctly, that a lot of the people on the Left felt contempt for them because they hadn't yet come to the positions that the Left held. We had a moral arrogance that turned people off. That wasn't just morally wrong, it was self-destructive. It helped create the victory of the Right.

C.W.   That's one element.

M.L.   Here's a second element. The alienation produced by a competitive market society creates growing powerlessness at work coupled with growing self-blame, and this leads people away from political struggle and toward growing inner frustration, rage, or depression. These feelings are brought home into family and personal lives, making it increasingly difficult to sustain loving relationships. Moreover, the narcissistic personality styles encouraged by the marketplace and its "look out for no. 1" mentality further weakens our ability to sustain loving relationships. So even when white working people are able to get adequate employment to make ends meet, they still find their lives filled with pain, a pain which they interpret to themselves as self-inflicted because they have little understanding of the larger social context. The Right spoke to that—and the Left has almost always missed these issues.

Part of what we need to do is frame a vision of a good society that can talk to people about where they are in pain and help them think. Help them understand that their pain is connected to the pain of the most oppressed. The Left keeps on emphasizing what is so different about our pain from everybody else's. I recognize this pathology, because I hear a similar kind of discourse among some Jews: "Our Holocaust has nothing to do with anybody else's suffering. It's totally unique." It is totally unique, but emphasizing that all the time separates us from everybody rather than leading us to identify with other people's suffering.

Those who are most oppressed in this society need to identify with the pain and suffering of those who are *less* oppressed, so that they can figure out a way to let other groups identify with their pain. That is what I want out of Blacks and out of the Left in general. I want the Left to get off of its moral high horse about how much worse our suffering is from other people's, and instead try to get other people to see how their suffering is connected to our suffering. Then they can feel that they absolutely want a place at our table. The kind of mentality that says, "My suffering is worse than your suffering" guarantees the isolation of the most oppressed. I know that emotionally this is going to be very hard for liberals and progressives, and it's going to be hard for the Black community. I'm now going to make a controversial claim. What I'm advocating is that these groups move beyond an exclusive focus on the suffering of the *most* oppressed and begin to validate the suffering of those who are *less* oppressed on material grounds or grounds of "rights-denial," but who are nevertheless oppressed by the frustration of their meaning needs.

I know how hard it is for Jews to recognize that non-Jews have also had suffering, and harder still, perhaps the hardest, to imagine that some of the Germans (not all, but some) who were attracted to the fascists in the twenties and early thirties were *not* evil people, but people whose lives were in so much pain that they were willing to grab on to anything that seemed to address that pain. Yet in my view the only way to ever have stopped the rise of fascism would have been for Jews and the Left to have recognized that pain, addressed it, and offered alternative solutions to it besides those offered by the fascists.

And this is precisely the only strategy that will ever significantly help African-Americans in this country. They have to be able to forge, either alone or with liberal and progressive whites, a politics that speaks to the pain of those who have *not* responded to the politics of "liberal guilt" and "help the oppressed." They have to find a way to make those who have been indifferent to the fate of Blacks hear that Blacks care about the pain of the white majority, realize that that pain is rooted in a system of selfishness that really does not serve the best interests of most whites either, and hence is offering a Politics of Meaning that challenges the ethos of selfishness and the economic institutions that generate that ethos, a politics that is as much concerned about alleviating the pain of whites as it is to alleviate the pain of Blacks, and that recognizes that in a fundamental way both pains are rooted in the system of organized selfishness.

It's not relevant to respond here that "it's not the job of Blacks to fight white racism" or "It's not the job of Jews to heal the pain of anti-Semites." Of course, in some abstract moral sense, we don't have the moral responsibility to heal the pain of our oppressors. But from a strategic self-interest perspective, this is precisely what we need to do.

It's important to help working people—whites, including white men, Blacks, Chicanos, Asians, Jews—see that their suffering is linked to the suffering of others. It says, "Yes, we want you to tell your story of how you're suffering. We want to know about what is bothering you at the work place. We want to know about why you're feeling miserable, pained and depressed about your life." And that can only work if we understand pain not in a narrowly economistic framework, but in terms of the fundamental alienation and lack of recognition generated by a competitive, materialist, selfishness-oriented market society.

The Left has to structure itself in a way that encourages people to see their pain as part of other peoples'. Why doesn't that happen? It doesn't happen because the people who are the most oppressed are hurting so much that they can't think about this other guy's pain because it looks less real and hurtful than their pain. So the people who are hurting feel the need to say, "Only my pain is real, and your pain is less." In a way, it becomes people's only claim to dignity—that they can claim the uniqueness of their oppression. Yet it's a terribly self-destructive strategy, because it actually perpetuates the victim position—*not* in the way conservatives say when they claim that this becomes a substitute for people trying to work their way out of poverty, but rather in a different way, namely by people not taking the political steps necessary to build an American majority capable of ending the economic oppression, steps that would involve recognizing as real and important the non-economic forms of pain that are rooted in the deprivation of meaning. Even though it's understandable, and I don't blame anybody for being in that position, it is a problem because it's self-destructive. You need to feel that person's pain in order to then help yourself deal with your pain. In terms of American politics, it's a whole different strategy.

C.W. How is the Politics of Meaning different from the politics of compassion?

M.L. They could be very closely connected. It's a question of understanding what you are compassionate about. It's recognizing that human beings have a complex set of needs that involve not just economic security, but are also psychological and spiritual. We need love, we need meaningful work, and to be embedded in a community of meaning and purpose which has a moral goal. The deprivation of these needs can often lead people to shoot each other on the street, just as much as the deprivation of economic needs can lead to family violence, alcoholism, and drug abuse.

C.W. Your argument is that a Politics of Meaning is predicated on a particular kind of philosophical anthropology in which love, care, and concern have as much status as material resources. A philosophical anthropology that resists accepting the nitty-gritty struggles over resources as the sole arena wherein a political conflict takes place, and pays attention to the structure of meaning. If empathy and compassion were understood in such a way that they would filter through your philosophical anthropology, you would really have a Politics of Meaning.

M.L. Exactly. That's why it's not sufficient to call it a politics of empathy or compassion because those words have been narrowly appropriated to mean just the material needs of the poor. The use of the term "Politics of Meaning" is useful because it reminds us that deprivation can be psychological, ethical, and spiritual—and not only material.

C.W. When it comes to Black-Jewish relations, how does that Politics of Meaning flesh out? When Black people talk about Jews, should they look not simply at their level of prosperity but at the level of meaning?

M.L. Ideally, Black progressives should recognize that other Americans, even those who are financially more successful than the Black community, are nevertheless victims of a society that systematically denies and frustrates the possibility of meaning. Those who experience the crisis of meaning are potential allies for Blacks—or potential enemies if that crisis of meaning is interpreted in a right-wing framework instead of in a progressive framework. Instead of thinking of Jews only as a potential or an actual oppressor, Black progressives should see Jews, and other groups, as people who are probably suffering from a level of oppression that is cutting out their spiritual and ethical guts.

I believe that there are Politics of Meaning strands that have been happening throughout *all* the social movements. Martin Luther King was a definite example of that. If only Black people could look at Jews that way instead of thinking, "Why are these fat cats coming down here and wanting to be part of our movement—is it because they want to dominate or control us?" they might be thinking, "It's logical that these Jews would want to be part of our movement because they're also getting screwed over by society. Their oppression is harder for them to recognize than ours is, so those who recognize it first are probably the most sensitive of that group, so they need to be given lots of encouragement to help spread their perceptions to others of their group who don't yet understand the meaning needs or who don't understand the connection between that form of oppression and the economic and political oppression that we Blacks are experiencing. So since these people *do* make those connections, they are important allies. So, welcome to you, let's work together."

C.W.   I personally agree with what you said. But to Black perceptions, the question becomes: how do you reconcile the sense, on the one hand, that large numbers of Jews are being screwed because of the lack of meaning, and on the other hand, the perception that some Jews are contributing to the screwing of others by wielding power or voting for Reagan? How do you reconcile this kind of discrepancy? On the one hand, they're potential allies because there is no doubt that their quest for meaning has frustrated their levels of relations, and their need for love and concern. But on the other hand, a slice of the Jewish community is wielding power that is over and against working people and poor people.

M.L.   How do you do this? By having the same kind of complex account of the world that Jews are going to need to have, in order to realize that they can have an alliance. At some point Jews are also going to have to have a more complex analysis of who Blacks are, beyond what the surface presentation of the facts would allow. And the same for Blacks vis-à-vis Jews. Instead of just seeing Blacks as the people who are taking some of their jobs, requiring higher levels of taxation to take care of their needs, scaring them on the streets, and being the ones most likely to stab or rob them.

There are two choices. We can go with the way things appear to be constituted, in which the primary dynamic is going to be one of conflict between these two communities and in which Jews can align more and more with the conservative interest in this society. Then we're back to a picture of American society in which the hope for a Black-Jewish alliance as a primary means of transformation goes down the tubes. Or else we can try to go with a picture of reality that emphasizes the potential elements that would bring these two communities together. That picture is one in which Jews will have to look at Blacks not just as potential muggers, but also as potentially sharing a common set of interests. Blacks are going to have to look at Jews not just as potential exploiters, but also as people who have a common set of oppressions.

C.W. I wonder whether there are actually more options than that. There are conservative elements in the Jewish community that, even given their frustration and quest for meaning, will remain conservative. There are moderate elements in the Jewish community which can go either way. There are progressive elements in the Jewish community which traditionally have been the majority but now see their numbers are dwindling.

M.L. They can be the majority again.

C.W. We pray to God that they will be. One of the functions of our dialogue is to ensure that will happen. There are going to be progressive Jews in the community who have a hunger for the kind of dialogue that we're talking about, no matter what. Our aim is to try to expand that base.

We're talking about some sectors of each community having much stronger proclivities toward engaging in this than others. When you look at the Black community, there are conservative elements that will most likely try to distance themselves from any such dialogue. The moderates are open. The progressive Blacks are going to be engaged in this no matter what. The question then becomes not so much the either/or that you cast, but, "What are the various ways in which we can get beyond just the progressives talking to one another—as difficult as that is?" We must bring in the moderates, and hope that further down the road the more conservative elements in both communities will at least be open to dialogue. But we're not beginning there. If we began there it would be all sheer despair. Try to get Norman Podhoretz to talk to a member of the Nation of Islam. You're not going to get off the ground.

M.L. Let me make some suggestions here about what could happen. My guess is that it would make a difference in the Black world if, for example, Jewish institutions gave some part of their resources to dealing with the issues of poverty, oppression, and joblessness.

C.W.   I would say the particular issues that Jews as Jews in America focus on are anti-Semitism and Israel. What are the issues that Black people as Black people focus on? These three: police brutality, discrimination, and stereotypes.

So how do Black people concerned with Jewish relations keep track of anti-Semitism and speak boldly about it, wherever it is, in any community? How do Blacks attempt to talk about Israel in the United States in such a way that we are in tune with the issues of security, survival, and protection for Jews in Israel, in the same way that we are involved in principled critiques of any other nation? And then, on the other hand, deal with police brutality, discrimination, and degrading stereotypes.

M.L.   Right, Jews have to talk to those issues.

C.W.   They have to talk *and* they actually have to be part of an organized and mobilized group. We're not going to talk about Blacks talking about anti-Semitism. You have to be out there . . .

M.L.   . . . showing that you care.

C.W.   . . . in Black churches and community centers saying, "We're not putting up with anti-Semitic garbage. The Black Freedom Movement at its best has never put up with this. Why should we put up with it now?"

M.L.   I think this kind of discussion can be translated into a reality if each side agreed it was going to struggle with these issues. Through trying to get such agreement in the Jewish community I know that the Jews are up against the feeling that these Blacks don't give a damn about them. "They will screw us, just as other non-Jews have screwed us in the past. Our problems, pains, and insecurities are not relevant to Blacks because they think we're really the oppressors."

C.W.   What's so complicated is what Blacks are hearing and what Jews are hearing.

M.L.   We both know why it's complicated. Because the conservative case is based on something real. Jews really do face crime. They really do face higher taxes in order to take care of others and they have to make sacrifices.

Blacks really do face situations in which Jews have power over them. We know that in both cases there are realities that have to be acknowledged as present but not as the whole picture. Those realities have to be understood differently.

C.W. That's the challenge.

M.L. You're right. That's what could be done.

C.W. We get right to it. Then we have to say that the history and so forth are embellishments of the core issues that seem to separate, or at least create tensions between, these two communities.

M.L. I've already told you about what was wrong with Crown Heights. I heard Dinkins' response on TV after the guy who had killed Yankel Rosenbaum had been acquitted. He said, "I didn't really know what was going on, but I called out the troops as soon as I knew about it." In other words, he gave a speech that was totally self-justificatory. The problem was not that he was wrong—although reports a year later showed that he really didn't do everything that a competent mayor should have done. But that's not why he deeply disappointed the Jewish people.

The problem was that he didn't even begin to understand what it was that Jews were concerned about. Jews weren't concerned that he take the rap over Crown Heights. Jews were concerned that he recognize that when there are Blacks going into the streets and throwing stuff at Jews, breaking windows, beating up Jews, and in this case, killing a Jew, that that is the most overt expression of a deep problem of anti-Semitism in the Black community that hasn't been adequately dealt with.

Jews know there is a real problem with anti-Semitism in the Black community. All that Dinkins had to do was admit that, and address it.

C.W. I think what you just said is absolutely right. Dinkins would in fact agree with you; he just didn't do that himself. Some New York Jews think Dinkins is anti-Semitic and that's why he didn't do it. That's a very important difference, and a very sad state of affairs.

M.L. De facto, the difference doesn't add up to that much.

C.W. Yes it does. It adds up to a lot when a group in New York says a Black mayor who has been supportive of Jewish interest is really anti-Semitic. Then the Black community looks at a Dinkins, who is perceived as being supportive of Jewish interest, and says, "See how Jews did him in? He was out there supporting Jewish interest for forty-five years and in one day, he's Hitler. In one day he's demonized like Farrakhan." That's very important in terms of perceptions from the Black world.

M.L. I would say that there is a perception amongst liberal Jews that we don't have that many Black allies that we can count on, talk to, and have this kind of conversation with.

C.W. There are two reasons for this. One is that in the Black world, there's a sense that liberal Jews want to handpick the Blacks they talk to. You screen them and make sure they condemn the right people before you have a dialogue.

Two, there's a lack of possible spaces where Blacks and Jews actually come together. Jews don't know of a number of the progressive Black voices, like these preachers who are very much in the Black world but who don't interact that much. We don't have long histories of interaction between progressive rabbis and progressive preachers. We have to go back to Heschel and King for that. Although it is happening these days, too. The late Marshall Meyer and Gary Simpson—the Brooklyn pastor of the largest Black Baptist church in America—came together.

You can see some kind of movement in this regard. It can't be a matter of each side selectively handpicking these folk so that other people feel as if it's just the exceptional, good folk who are being chosen. Then we'll have a nice little warm dialogue rather than serious engagement. On the other hand, we have to facilitate means by which these voices that are respectful—we don't want disrespectful voices in either community because that reinforces the worst—might disagree. They're in the process of trying to understand what the Jewish world is like from a Black vantage point, and what the Black world is like from the Jewish vantage point. That's something to which we hope our own dialogue here will contribute.

CHAPTER 11

Strategies for Reconciliation and Healing

M.L. Do African-American progressives have a strategy for how to overcome the anti-Semitism that does exist and how to confront the problems being faced by inner-city Blacks?

C.W. As to anti-Semitism, the first step is to get our community to acknowledge that there is a problem. You have to convince people that it is a problem. Black people are facing so many difficult issues today—Blacks don't have enough resources, and food and housing and health care and so forth—that it's not always obvious to African-Americans that alongside of these there's also the problem of anti-Semitism. You can't go into the Black community and say their major problem is Black anti-Semitism because you will be talking to people who have kids who can't get food or education, you see.

But on the other hand, you can't allow the fact that young kids aren't getting enough health care and food to obscure the fact that Black Anti-semitism is a problem.

You've got to acknowledge anti-Semitism, but not make it seem that you think that this is the major moral problem facing our community—which is often the way it is represented in the mainstream media.

M.L.   I entirely agree. The major problem facing the Black community, like the major problem facing the rest of the population, is the dominant ethos of selfishness and reckless disregard for others, an ethos that then allows so many Americans to turn their backs on the poor, a majority of whom are white, but also turn their backs on the concentrated suffering of the Black community. Though I believe that fighting anti-Semitism and every form of racism, sexism, and homophobia is justified in its own terms, and is the morally right thing to do, it's also the prudential thing for Blacks to do. Publicly and systematically fighting anti-Semitism could help Blacks restore the kind of political coalition that would confront the ethos of selfishness that has been growing in America. And that is the only way Blacks will ever succeed in ending the hunger and poverty you rightly cite as being at the top of Black people's agenda.

C.W.   Yes, that struggle is important. And part of the way we need to proceed is to indicate that this is not some new opportunistic concern, but that the struggle against anti-Semitism itself has a rich history. You have to accent the ways in which great Black, heroic freedom fighters have been strong critics of anti-Semitism. Du Bois, Frederick Douglass, Martin King, Ella Baker, Malcolm after Mecca, and many other leaders throughout our history have a legacy that needs to be built upon—people who were critical of anti-Semitism. The major weight of the Black Freedom Movement has been against anti-Semitism—so it's not just West or Henry Louis Gates or Bell Hooks who are critical of anti-Semitism—no. We're just echoing a richer tradition that came before us. When this history is made more explicit, more Blacks will understand that to engage in anti-Semitic rhetoric or actions runs counter to one of the important trends within our own history.

M.L.   I also think it needs to be pointed out that one can't successfully fight against racism in the U.S. while simultaneously participating in anti-Semitic racism. In my view, the fight against racism requires an assault on the ways that people split off from their consciousness the needs and concerns of others, legitimating that splitting by finding some aspect of the others that is supposed to be the "basis" for not thinking of these others as equally made in the image of God and hence not equally deserving of one's own immediate attention and caring. That's why I've placed so much emphasis on fighting the ethos of selfishness, because I see this as another way to get into the underlying economic and political framework of American society that encourages this kind of racist or xenophobic nationalist splitting, and hence creates the conditions for people to turn their backs on others and explain to themselves that they have "a right" to take care of themselves without regard to what's happening to others. Yet that turning away from others, shutting one's ears to their cries, runs against what most people really want—it is a depressive reaction, based on having given up their hope that people would be emotionally and spiritually and morally there for us. Such despair is based in part on having become convinced that the underlying message of the competitive marketplace is true, namely the message that tells us that "no one is going to be there for you, nobody is going to take care of you, so you'd better watch out for yourself and do everything you can to advance your own interests at the expense of others, because otherwise others will do that to you and you will be screwed." It is the undermining of that message that is, in my mind, the prerequisite for defeating racism.

But what's your strategy for fighting against racism in the U.S.?

C.W. Well again to me it's a multi-level strategy. One, I don't think we can talk seriously about fighting racism in America without beginning with economics. That we really have to talk quite seriously of significant Black economic power. And that takes the form, on the one hand, of within the private sphere more access to capital and credit. And on the other hand, in the public sphere of more investment in working poor and very poor communities, which is part of a larger redistributive strategy overall. I don't think we can start thinking about fighting racism in America unless we ultimately talk about Black people gaining access to decent-paying jobs and resources. Which means we've got to talk about redistribution in some significant way. But that's only at the economic level.

At the cultural level, we have to talk about rebuilding and reinvigorating institutions—like family and communities—that promote Black self-respect and Black self-affirmation and Black self-love, because we cannot talk about fighting racism unless we also talk about the way in which racist perceptions of Black people have been internalized. And so it's not just a matter of those institutions in the economic sphere, but it's also a matter of the perceptions, self-perceptions of Black people themselves. And so, how do you do that? You do it by building institutions. Stronger families, stronger civil associations, stronger churches and synagogues and mosques within the Black community. That's the second level.

The third level is the political level. We must talk about more effective modes of organizing and mobilizing Black people as well as other progressives to provide means by which people are empowered to fight for the redistribution of wealth in the economic sphere, as well as the institutional means of promoting Black self-respect in the social sphere. And that's a matter of political agency and political action.

It's hard to imagine at this moment actually uprooting white supremacist sensibilities. But for me it's always a matter of degrees and gradations. I never believe that any form of institutional evil can be completely eliminated in the world. Patriarchy, homophobia, racism, it's always a matter of pushing it back. Betterment, amelioration, relative progress, we certainly can make relative progress. So it's hard to give a timeline. But it's a multi-level strategy that I have in mind.

If America continues down the road that we've already traveled for the last fifteen, eighteen years, there's no doubt in my mind that we're headed toward a slow disintegration of American civilization. Which means that twenty, thirty years from now, most of the country will be if not uninhabitable, will have such a low quality of life that it would be simply deplorable. Most, not just portions, will be overrun by crime, violence, assaults, and so forth.

We have seen a subtle war being carried out against Black communities in the past two decades. Disinvestment across the board in working class and poor communities. And the shift from permanent jobs to temporary jobs, and the shift from a job to no job, and the shift from social services at level ten to level four, and the shift from a bad educational system to a thoroughly decrepit educational system, right across the board. That's thorough disinvestment, the withdrawing of resources from these communities.

The conservatives have gained political power partly because they have been able to speak to various issues of meaning and value. Manipulated issues of race and gender. By manipulate, I mean convince persons that somehow it is in their interests to side with a more powerful elite as opposed to siding with their fellow working-class people, and working middlers (middle-class people in the workforce) in this society. The conservatives have been able to shape the society in the image of a very, very unfair model. You're absolutely right. But that's been true in this country for a very long time.

M.L. One way that many Jews and many white people in the U.S. use to distance themselves from the suffering in the Black community is to tell themselves that "so much has been done for Blacks already, and now it's time to move on to other issues." Yet this is far from the situation you are describing.

C.W. Not since the 1920s have so many Black folk been so deeply disillusioned and disappointed with America. There were rising expectations for about a month and a half after Clinton's inauguration. He claimed to be concerned about race, at least behind a broader rubric: job training and job creation. He knows that increasing minimum wage would mean one quarter of a million people would be lifted from poverty. What does he do? He backpedals.

It's fairly clear that those rising expectations have been dashed and therefore the disillusionment sets in even deeper. With Reagan and Bush you had no expectations at all, and rightly so.

More than that, it's the sense that the Black working poor are undergoing such devastating levels of disintegration. The sense of hopelessness is so deep, and the sense of futurelessness so pervasive, that there is a widespread gangsterization of much of urban Black America. That gangsterization is currently so deeply saturated in some Black communities that it's taken on a life and logic of its own, with the cold-hearted, mean-spirited disposition, the paranoia, and the distrust each of the other. You expect to see this among young people, who have tremendous difficulty ever pulling off a sustained act of solidarity. I'm talking about the Black community, although much of it spills over into the larger community—and mirrors the larger society and culture.

That's the level of devastation and disintegration that we're talking about. It usually takes a generation or two, if ever, to turn something like that around. We're talking about a kind of last chance for this country to deal with issues of race. If it continues to fester, you'll have a third generation of gangster mentality. I can't see this country surviving that intact.

The Black communities are centered right at the urban cores of this decadent civilization. The most likely response is more prisons and more police, but they can't continue to do that. No way.

M.L. Why can't they continue?

C.W. There are not enough policemen. When I was in a little town in Texas, I saw gangs chasing police down the road. There were only 45 policemen and the Crips and the Bloods had 175 people in each gang. That's a small town, but there they've got the police completely overwhelmed. In L.A. it's the same thing. Or New York and Detroit. If there was an actual, serious confrontation between the Black gangs and the police, they would have to bring the National Guard in.

This gangsterization has taken on a life and logic of its own, owing to the deep, festering problem of the invisibility of Black misery. Substantial numbers of young people now are really reaching the point where they have no significant connection with the public life of the country at all. That's what I mean by "apocalypse now."

M.L. You're talking about riots or urban insurrection. But Americans basically should be able to handle these. When Black discontent takes the form of military conflict, we know what the United States does.

C.W. They bring in the National Guard. They've got the largest military force in the world.

M.L. Exactly. It's apocalyptic from the standpoint of the needs of the Black community, but the social system that it leads to is more repression.

C.W. "Dealing with it" only means clearing it out of the way for the moment. It's just containing that particular expression at that moment.

M.L. Society feels more and more that it needs to use instruments of overt oppression.

C.W. And under a Democrat just as much as under a Republican. Look at Johnson's or Robert Kennedy's F.B.I. dossier on King. There is not a history of Democrats being less prone to using repression when they saw fit.

M.L. If repression is on the agenda, then most people feel that the right-wingers are better at it than the Democrats. Because of that the country may move further and further toward right-wing forces and coalitions that are likely to be a cover for, or closely aligned with, explicitly anti-Semitic elements.

C.W. You have to consolidate your networks within your respective communities. Primarily in order to expand the business class, expand the communal bonds of support, expand the political clout for the various kinds of programs to be put forth. Not just programs of social services: we're talking about regulating banks so that redlining becomes less pervasive; we're talking about checks on government procurement so as to give access to the billions of dollars that the federal government provides in terms of contracts. All these are attempts within the system to enhance the quality of life of Black folk. If we don't come up with a multiracial, progressive strategy, then we are simply headed toward Armageddon.

M.L. Armageddon? What do you mean?

C.W. I mean race war. And it won't be like Muhammad Ali versus Joe Frazier. We're talking about Mike Tyson versus Cornel West, in the ring. We're talking about 11 percent of the population against 65 to 70 percent. For the Black folk who are already perishing, that rate would increase.

M.L. How do you envision it? Each side gets guns and starts shooting each other?

C.W. That's part of it. Sure. Very much so. Quarantining Black communities, arresting progressive Black spokespersons like myself and others. That's quite imaginable in this society.

M.L. But surely this is not the only alternative. This kind of dissolution of society is the logical extension of the current dynamics: everyone pursuing his or her own interests without regard to the impact on others. But in the research I conducted for the National Institute for Mental Health, and in my own work as a psychotherapist, I've found that most people, while caught in the dynamics of selfishness, would actually appreciate and yearn for a different kind of society—one based on caring. There are millions of Americans who show this in small ways—they volunteer in public and private agencies, they pitch in when their communities offer them opportunities to do so, and they happily engage in generous acts toward friends and family. But they also have come to believe that it would be crazily self-defeating for them to act on this caring ethos in the larger society, in their economic or political life. They've been taught that the world is governed by materialism and narrow self-interest, and that they would be irrationally self-destructive if they were to act on a different set of assumptions. So what you see happening in this society is that people are pulled between a part of them that really wants to act according to their own highest moral vision and another voice inside that tells them that they would be stupid to do that.

Most people, while responding to the reality of a society in which everyone else can be expected to act on narrow self-interest, and in which they must themselves act that way for self-protection, nevertheless hate this way of being and desperately seek an alternative. They seek communities of meaning and purpose which transcend the selfishness of the competitive market society. Sometimes they find those kinds of communities in religious or nationalist forms that are benign, but all too often they find those communities inextricably linked to racist, anti-Semitic, homophobic, or xenophobic programs. Our task as liberals and progressives is to develop a Politics of Meaning that can address these same needs for a community that is committed to caring for each other, but which does not link that caring to a denigration or assault on "the evil Other" (be they African-Americans, Jews, gays and lesbians, or anyone else).

C.W. I hear what you're saying.

M.L. My approach is very different from saying, as liberals are often perceived as saying to the white majority in the United States, "You guys already got what you need and you should be paying attention to Blacks or poor people on justice and fairness grounds alone." That form of political injunction to "liberal compassion" doesn't work in a society which is increasingly committed to selfishness.

A Politics of Meaning involves exposing the ways that the dominant cynicism and materialism all contribute to people believing that the only rational thing they can do is to continually narrow their arena of caring and to shut their eyes and ears to the pain of others.

C.W. But the problem is whether this Politics of Meaning would ever be strong enough to deal with the entrenched xenophobia. It can't just be a moral appeal.

M.L. No, it can't just be a moral appeal.

C.W. That leads to the issue of systemic change. In other words, the moral appeal is linked to a call for systemic change. If there's no possibility of this, then people are going to fall back on the short-term —that is, more conservative—way of looking at it.

In my view, the major issue facing American civilization right now is the erosion of the nurturing and caring systems. Especially for children. I think that a focus on the state of America's children is probably one of the most important springboards for the next wave of social momentum. That's not to say that other issues aren't important: the trade unions are, I hope, coming alive, the ecological movement's still going, the womanist and feminist movements are still very important. But I think in terms of something new, that can produce something innovative, we need to focus on the state of America's children. I think it's a way of fusing what you would call a Politics of Meaning with various forms of compassion. I think the majority of American people still have very deep compassion about the state of America's children. One could argue that it's less so for Black children, but nevertheless more so than they ever had in the history of this country. Racism is still around, which means Black pain has less status than other people's pain, but racism has been hit more head-on in the last thirty years than it ever has. So that means you've got large numbers of white and Jewish and other non-Black peoples sensitive about Black children's pain, and that's important.

The question of children can't be viewed simply as a breakdown in families. The breakdown in families is but one instance of a larger erosion of the systems of nurturing and caring, and that's why your talk about shifts from selfishness to caring is very consonant with what I'm talking about.

M.L. I think so too. The only thing I'm always on guard against is the formulation of this caring in economistic and "objective" terms. Because what you have with the welfare system is objective caring, but meanwhile the people who are getting cared for don't feel, subjectively, like they are being cared for, and the people who are giving them money don't feel like they are doing anything in a caring way. You can argue that all of these social support systems are objective caring: but the liberal welfare state was set up in such a way that it separated objective caring from subjective feelings and didn't worry about whether the objective caring was being done in a caring way. That leads to the strange resultant that people once again get the message that caring itself is something inappropriate in the public arena, that it should be kept in private life or in religious life, but has no public function. And the more people believe that, the less likely they are to support even the "objective" kind of caring.

C.W. At first glimpse, it's difficult to be be hopeful. The evidence of the decline and decay around us is so overwhelming. No one is going to listen to glib hope because they see too much against it. Yet such pessimism feeds the conservative efforts to defend the status quo.

But one of the reasons that I feel Blacks and Jews are important is precisely because these two particular groups are indispensable elements in sustaining progressive possibilities. There's no guarantee that we can pull it off. But if these two groups began to internally erode in relation to each other, with high levels of tension and friction, then the possibility of progressive politics in America also erodes; and then we open the door to the apocalypse that I'm talking about.

M.L. Exactly, I agree with you. All the more so now that Clinton has so deeply disappointed so many of the people who originally supported him because of his failure to articulate and fight for a unifying principle.

C.W. Mrs. Clinton did identify publicly with the Politics of Meaning position that had been developed in *Tikkun,* but then found it difficult to stay publicly identified after the press assaulted that principle.

M.L. Precisely. The Clintons had excited people because both explicitly and implicitly adopted the Politics of Meaning, with its insistence that human needs are not only material but also ethical, psychological, and spiritual. By ignoring this dimension of experience, by imagining that the only thing that is being denied to most Americans is a certain material level of being, the liberal and progressive forces had managed to isolate themselves for the past twenty years, while the Right was able to speak to these other needs.

The devastation wrought on the American psyche and family by the deepening impact of the materialism and selfishness of the competitive market could never be recognized as a "political issue" by liberals and progressives, because those kinds of non-material consequences failed to show up on their radar, which had been exclusively focused on economic well-being and individual rights.

The pain of the majority of Americans became increasingly a psychological and spiritual pain, manifested in the breakdown of families, the decrease in loyalty in friendships, the difficulties in imparting values to their children, and the growing sense that they were living in a world in which they could count on nobody and were deeply isolated and alone, a world in which everyone seemed to be out for their own narrowest self-interest and in which it seemed increasingly irrational for them to act on any other principle because, if everyone is out for self-interest, then if they don't watch out for themselves, they will get screwed.

Living in such a world has caused deepening individual and collective pain, and the Right has been able to articulate that pain and then direct it in a distorted way—by blaming the psychological and spiritual consequences of the competitive market society on some "Other" that is seen as the disruptive force. In the twentieth century, the primary "Other" have been Jews, African-Americans, and now, in the last twenty years, homosexuals, "uppity" feminist women, and in the nineties even liberals. Yet liberals have totally misunderstood this attraction of people to the Right, assumed that people were drawn to it solely because they were already racist, sexist, homophobic, etc. Meanwhile, since the liberals have a conception of what it is to be human that is itself narrowly materialist and individualist, the only pain that could be registered was that of people being denied rights or economic entitlements. So the liberals have directed their energies toward the groups that have been excluded economically or have been denied rights, and this is all to the good (I fully support those struggles). But they've been unable to *win* those struggles because they have made the majority of Americans feel that *their* suffering (the spiritual and psychological consequences of the competitive market) were merely personal problems that have nothing to do with the political or economic order, and should be dealt with "in the private realm" by going to therapy or going to church or synagogue.

The implicit liberal message has been, "You, the American majority, have had your chance to have a good life. We have created a fair and equitable society and a free marketplace in which you could have shaped your fate in any way that you chose. So if you are in pain, it's only because you screwed up your lives. Don't complain to us about that—because you have no one to blame but yourselves. On the other hand, these African-Americans, gays and women who have been left out, they *do* have a right to complain and we will take care of them." With that kind of message, no wonder the majority feel that the liberals and progressives have little understanding or sympathy for them, that these liberals and progressives are really elitists who disdain ordinary people.

For a time it looked like Clinton was going to forge a new kind of politics, and that's why his embrace of a Politics of Meaning was so hopeful, because it promised a recognition of these other levels of pain facing most Americans. But the hopeful and optimistic part, the part of us that wants to go for our highest moral vision and for a society based on caring, received a substantial setback during the first two years of the Clinton administration. There was a moment after Clinton was elected in which for a few months many Americans allowed themselves to be very hopeful that the selfishness and me-first-ism of the Reagan/Bush years could be changed. Though Clinton always insisted that he was a New Democrat who really advocated quite conservative policies, he also adopted much of the language of the Politics of Meaning that he had, according to what he personally told me, encountered in *Tikkun* magazine. While his advisors proclaimed that "it's the economy, stupid," many Americans responded to something quite different: Clinton's often explicit promise to change the dominant framework of thinking in America from the dominant ethos of selfishness to an ethos of community, shared responsibility, and caring for others.

The excitement Clinton had unleashed, however, had a flip side, because the hopefulness produced a tremendous anxiety in the very people who allowed themselves to be hopeful. Most Americans had had numerous experiences of being snookered or taken in, either in personal relations where they found their partner more interested in exploitation than in mutuality, or in public life where they had found preachers and politicians who had betrayed their trust before.

Had Clinton stuck to the Politics of Meaning or, for that matter, to any other coherent moral vision about how to move the society from selfishness to caring, and made the central goal of his first two years the forging of a broad public understanding of what these ideals really might mean in practice, he would have won the hearts and minds of tens of millions of Americans. Instead, after his wife Hillary found herself under ruthless attack and ridicule by the media for making the Politics of Meaning the center of her first health care speech (in Texas, in April of 1993), Clinton quickly backed away from articulating a coherent vision and made his central goal that of appearing "presidential" and having the kind of "savvy" that would win the respect of Washington insiders and the corporate world. So his presidency focused on a series of legislative goals that more closely fit the conservative agenda and that had little in common with his promise of substantive change in the dominant ethos.

His first year in office was given over to the struggle for deficit reduction (a traditional conservative concern) and NAFTA (in a version that generated opposition from most liberals and enthusiastic support from most Republicans in Congress). In his second year, he fought vigorously for a crime bill whose underlying philosophical premises were derived from conservative analyses of crime, and which was more dedicated to increasing the number of prisons than to experimenting with methods for crime prevention. Even his health care plan, while admirably committed to universality of care, was critically flawed by his decision to reject single-payer ideas in favor of preserving the profit-orientation of the health care system (from insurance companies to health maintenance profiteers to individual health care practitioners)—which led to the development of a bureaucratic monstrosity that played into the big-government fears that many Americans have developed (often for good reasons, given the insensitivity and unresponsiveness of the way government has frequently been).

Meanwhile, for most of the first two years Clinton seemed to be backing away from promises he had made on Bosnia, on gays in the military, on Haiti (he finally reversed himself the month before Congressional elections, and then in a way that seemed ambiguous), on human rights in China, on environmental sanity, and in dozens of other ways.

No wonder, then, that people quickly despaired about Clinton, and his popularity fell dramatically. Rather than defending their own Politics of Meaning, the Clintons backed away from their own coherent framework, and rather than insisting that their Administration present programs that manifested a central value and vision, the Clintons began to appear to be driven by the need to be popular, even at the expense of moral consistency.

"What else could he do?" the pragmatists wonder. "After all, a President must try to stay popular or he will be powerless to get his legislation through!" But it was the pragmatists who were to be proved wrong. The hunger for meaning and purpose in this society cannot be answered by an opportunistic pragmatism. "Politics is the art of the possible," these pragmatists insist—but what they miss is that what is possible can be greatly expanded when people fight for what appears to be beyond the framework of opportunistic possibility.

What the Clintons seemed to be doing was to be worrying more about their own political survival than about any transcendent vision of the good. But this, of course, was precisely the kind of selfishness that governs most people's lives, which they both wish to transcend and doubt that it is possible. They had elected Clinton to one of the most powerful elected positions in the world—and then they had watched in horror as this supposed champion of change toward a social good had instead demonstrated himself to be more worried about his own self-interest than about articulating and fighting for a vision of the good.

No wonder, then, that people felt betrayed by Clinton, and at the same time began to revert to the side of themselves that is skeptical about collective social action and believes instead that everyone is motivated solely by self-interest and that they had better act in the same way. If even the President couldn't feel secure to fight for his ideals, then, many reasoned, they too ought to be worried about their own self-interest. The part of them that might have responded to calls for a new way of thinking and doing things together was undercut by Clinton, so they reverted to the part that wanted self-interest, and for many that would involve lower taxes, less responsibility to others (sometimes expressed in the form of "less government"), and less willingness to pay higher health care premiums in order to ensure that others would receive care. In short, Clinton's own opportunism modeled a conservatism that led people to abandon Clinton and his programs, which were subsequently described as "too liberal."

By July of 1994 Clinton was advocating for the health care plan before Congress by claiming that it was "the truly conservative" plan and that its vitality would be guaranteed by the free market. Indeed, throughout the Fall campaign, as in much of the past two years, Clinton tried to show how truly centrist, mainstream, and conservative he really was. But when most Americans want conservative politics, they feel more certain that they can find it it in the real conservatives of the Republic party, and that is precisely what they did in the 1994 Congressional elections. Yet in so doing, they were not choosing conservatism versus some other view, like the Politics of Meaning, which was being argued for and which just didn't win enough public support. Rather, they were choosing between variants of conservatism and between people on the Right who had the integrity to stick with their positions even when they were seemingly unpopular, and people in the Democratic Party who seemed to seek popularity by trying to recast themselves as conservatives. Meanwhile, most people feel that liberals are wimpy precisely because of this behavior—their inability to fight for what they believe in. No one feels safe with this kind of a political leader—because they don't feel that they can count on them to stay strong when things get rough. Contempt for liberals is directly related to this sense of lack of integrity and unwillingness to stick with one's position at the moments in history when it isn't immediately popular.

Clinton could have failed to pass any legislation and still been a very popular President had he tried to fight for a coherent worldview. But it was only the Right that was smart enough to know that what really counts in the long run in politics is your ability to provide a morally coherent worldview and get people to think in terms of that framework. So while the Democrats eschewed ideology in favor of being practical, they actually were very impractical.

The New York Times wondered aloud in the week before the 1994 elections about the "paradox" that Clinton had delivered economic improvement, and yet people seemed even more unhappy than they had two years earlier. For those who believe that human beings are only motivated by economic concerns, or the need for individual freedom, this would indeed be a paradox. But the whole point of the Politics of Meaning was to insist that people have psychological, ethical, and spiritual needs that are not being met by a competitive market society, and cannot be addressed without challenging the me-firstism and selfishness that have become "common sense" in the marketplace and in personal lives.

I do not mean to suggest that the core economic and social justice concerns of the liberal and progressive agenda should be abandoned. Indeed, an ethos of caring leads us immediately to confront our obligation to the less privileged. A progressive Politics of Meaning, as opposed to the conservative or reactionary versions of a Politics of Meaning that are currently being advocated, would strengthen the ability of the traditional progressive social change movements to make their case, precisely because that case would no longer be framed in terms of the self-interest of the most oppressed, but in terms of the moral well-being of all of us. And this is very important, because as long as the majority feel that the social justice agenda of the progressives only benefits a small part of the population, they are unlikely to be moved. Feeling themselves to be victims and relatively powerless, they are often enraged by liberal formulations of politics that seem to ignore their pain and insist that the only real pain is that of "the most [economically] oppressed."

The progressive movements need to make a revolutionary transformation in their own way of thinking, so that they can see that spiritual and ethical needs are just as central as economic needs. By focusing on what all people have in common, a Politics of Meaning actually begins to build the political infrastructure for a resurgence of progressive politics. And this leads to the most biblically based of all these insights: that it is precisely by overcoming our focus on our own needs that our own needs are most likely to be met. For too long liberals and progressives in America have appeared to function as a special interest group, getting governmental benefits for their special needs without regard to the effect on everyone else. And in the end this leads to their losing precisely the benefits they sought. They are too effective in achieving their own self-interest for people to correctly perceive these groups as genuinely concerned about the welfare of others, including the psychological, spiritual, and ethical welfare of the American majority. If the Politics of Meaning can allow for this reconstitution of liberal and progressive politics, it has a chance of remaking the contours of mainstream politics as well.

C.W. Once you cast the Politics of Meaning like that, then it becomes a way of accenting the prophetic elements of various religious groups—including the prophetic element within the democratic tradition, namely those that would accent common humanity, and those that would accent the various critiques of class, race, and gender-based hierarchies.

M.L. And that would accent our critique of selfishness and our need for care.

C.W. To me, that is the core of what prophetic means. I think this is where our positions really coincide. Both of our traditions place a fundamental stress on what I call non-market values. A central question for us is, "How does one keep up a prophetic element within the Black and Jewish community, so that they come together in recognizing that they oftentimes go against the grain?" For the most part in America there is a white Jewry and a separate Black community. The answer: overcome that racial divide by accenting prophetic common ground.

Although we're calling for much more than that. I'm calling for a dialogue about the relative failure or success of the U.S. experiment in democracy. That is, something bigger than both communities. We don't want to limit our dialogue just to prophetic Black folk and prophetic Jews, although these may be the ones who really lead the way and open up the possibilities for dialogue.

M.L. What's the actual form in which a Black-Jewish alliance could take place? What are the ways in which the prophetic elements in both of these communities could connect with each other? In our own cases it's amazingly fortuitous that we ran into each other and developed a connection. I must say that the only time I see a Black-Jewish dialogue taking place in some organized structural way is through Jewish mainstream institutions, which are very much out of touch with this kind of prophetic consciousness.

As far as I can see, there aren't any serious organizational links between Jewish progressives and Black progressives. Right now there aren't even any mass Jewish or Black progressive organizations. I don't see any institutional structure for an ongoing connection, dialoguing, or strategizing between progressives in these two communities. I wonder if you have any ideas about how we could or should do that?

C.W. I think that we need to call an emergency meeting of major progressive leaders and progressive intellectuals of our two communities. Not to form just an exchange between talking heads, but to launch a strategy for serious cooperation.

One dimension would be to create links between the grassroot members of neighborhood organizations, and get them involved in dialogue. Dialogue is a form of struggle: it's not just chitchat. Create a dialogue that focuses not just on the vulnerability of both groups, but on these larger issues of justice, democracy, and the crisis in our own communities. Then try to hammer out some programs that relate to the everyday lives of these groups. It could be tutoring, it could be struggling against tenant abuse—it could be a whole host of things. We have to put this on the agenda because we're concerned not solely about the self-interest of the respective groups but about the future of this country. That would serve as one source of the revitalization of public life in the country as a whole.

In the last two years I must have met with thirty to thirty-five Black-Jewish groups in synagogues and churches around this country and you really do have large numbers doing the right thing. These were primarily liberal and progressive Blacks and Jews who engaged in serious, candid dialogue about where the tensions are. These folk realize that we are sliding down a slippery slope, and are willing to do something about it on a personal and a collective level. To that degree I've been inspired. It's a difficult dialogue, but it's still going on, among everyday folk. They know they are cutting against the grain, and there's a lot of tension. But I see people willing to say, "Let's engage in conversation that provides an understanding of why we're at an impasse." Opening the forms of communication, and understanding this opening as a prelude to a more substantive struggle. In a large number of these different places where I've met, what's emerged has been living-room dialogues with Blacks and Jews. This is the kind of thing that I think can be one of the spin-offs of what we're calling for. It won't be just at the national level, but at the neighborhood level. The major institutions and community organizations reflect on the possibilities, and from there begin to program the most important needs in light of each neighborhood. I've seen some communities move from under tremendous obstacles. That's the more hopeful side. The less hopeful side is that, once one gets above ground, the conversation becomes more shrill, more sensationalist and polarized, so that the possibilities of bridging the chasm become more difficult.

M.L. In terms of the transformative voices in the Black world, let me ask you what it is that makes you optimistic or not optimistic? What is your strategy for how a progressive Black force is going to reemerge? Because if there were a progressive Black force that had something of the quality of a Martin Luther King tradition, then it would be a lot easier for us in the Jewish world to connect with.

Whereas if the only people who are articulating Black rage are also articulating anti-Semitic rage, it's extremely difficult. What ought to happen?

C.W.   There are a whole host of persons who are part of the same legacy of King's still at work in the Black churches. For example, the United Theological Seminary at Dayton, Ohio, under President Darryl Ward, my Black brother, has the largest program of training for Black preachers. Hundreds of them are part of the legacy of King. They are rarely sought out. Very few people in the white or Jewish world even know them.

Or take Gary Simpson, the pastor of the largest Black Baptist church in America, Concord Baptist Church in Brooklyn. He's a young man; he's the one who preached the sermon against anti-Semitism after brother Yankel Rosenbaum was murdered, and wrote the letter to the *New York Times*. The council of rabbis had never heard of him. The first thing they did was invite him in, and they found they had one of the most visionary, articulate, humane persons they ever knew. There are many thousands of men and women like Gary Simpson in Black America.

Do you think large numbers of people in the white world or in the Jewish world would seek these people out? Not yet. Gary Simpson's got a whole network of people who are building on the legacy of King and Fanny Lou Hamer. There are many many King-like figures on the grassroots level in the Black community, but with the chasm in place we hardly ever hear about them. And so one has to go out to do the kind of thing I was talking about before to bring these folk together.

For example, Brother Rabbi Jacobs, who's up in Westchester county, brought brother Reverend Mark Taylor to speak at his synagogue. They had a fascinating exchange, and now they've hooked up. And these small hookups can take place around the country. Why? Because there are many more progressive Jews than the Black world recognizes, both in and outside of the synagogues: there's many more progressive and prophetic Black folk in and out of the church who are interested in this kind of thing, even though they know that at a higher level, in newspapers and on television, you've got this battle going on. When I'm really down and out I tend to want to go to this grassroots level and see this kind of interaction taking place. And I say, "Even though we don't have any grounds for thoroughgoing optimism, we don't have any grounds for despair. We can at least have some hope." Because this kind of thing is taking place. It's not a movement. I don't think we're at a point now when we can talk about a movement amongst progressives at any level. But we've got some momentum created, and we hope down the road to produce a movement. My work with The New Party—Joel Rogers, Josh Cohen and others—as well as Democratic Socialists of America—is part of this effort.

M.L.   Let's go back to what our two communities can do together. Building on your idea of a national gathering, I propose a conference aimed at launching a campaign of healing and repair in both communities, aimed at undermining the anti-Semitism in the Black community and the anti-Black racism in the Jewish community.

But then we need to launch an ongoing campaign and an ongoing organization committed to shaping a climate of opposition to racism and anti-Semitism, so that those who wish to reject or combat racism or anti-Semitism in their own communities will find a community of people ready to give them support and to validate their perceptions.

The mechanism for generating a change in consciousness on these issues would involve a balance between a large-scale public assault and smaller efforts individually tailored to the needs of specific communities or subcommunities. On the one hand, we could create a widespread public awareness of the problems, and a climate that supports public repudiation of racist and anti-Semitic ideas and practices.

The focus of the campaign cannot be exclusively against racism or anti-Semitism. We would have to show people how these kinds of sickness are expressions of the dominant selfishness of American society, and we do not believe they can be fully defeated without addressing the need to shift the dominant discourse from an ethos of selfishness to an ethos of caring. This Politics of Meaning goal will be an ingredient in the way that we formulate the discourse in our campaign in both the African-American and the Jewish communities. Demeaning of others is often associated with reactionary forms of meaning-oriented communities, so our task is to provide alternative frameworks of meaning that do not associate to anti-Semitism or racism. In general, our goal is to revalidate a commitment to democratic ideals and to the Jewish notion of *tikkun,* as healing, repair, and transformation of the world. Meanings derived from these commitments can provide an alternative to racist ideologies and world views.

I envision us mobilizing every major culture hero, musician, sports hero, intellectual, artist, television or movie star, disc jockey, talk-show host, preacher or minister or rabbi, teacher, social worker, health care worker, and many more to use their positions to become publicly identified with this campaign and to use their influence to bring these issues into public scrutiny and to fight for a different way of thinking and being together. And I envision the careful fostering of dialogue groups, support activites, and joint education.

Equally important, I envision mobilizing a significant section of the Jewish world to consider using financial resources on a community-to-community aid program designed to provide immediate and substantial assistance to those in the Black community who are seeking to develop their community's resources. But that must be done in a way that does not foster paternalism or resentments. It can't be done as "charity," but it can be done as part of a campaign for a Politics of Meaning, because in that framework people begin to understand that doing acts of caring for others is not a self-denigrating or self-undermining action, but rather a self-fulfillment and self-affirmation of their own most fundamental needs. And that way of thinking has deep roots in the Torah, and in the religious traditions of the Black community.

Ultimately, however, there is no way to defeat the ethos of selfishness in each of our communities without taking on the larger selfishness of the entire society. Black culture and Jewish culture today are both massively shaped by the dominant media and by the assumptions built into the world of work. Those who are most "successful" in material terms in both communities are those who have best mastered the ethos of selfishness of the competitive market, learned to think in those terms, and then become experts. But the corrosive effect of the culture is so powerful that even those who have not been successful blame themselves for not adequately mastering the ethos of selfishness, and so they work at "improving themselves" by learning the latest techniques. Being "cool" is knowing how to "take care of yourself" in these self-interested, materialistic, and manipulative terms, and it is often counterposed to being a shlep or a geek or a fool, namely those who don't know how to maneuver for themselves.

It's utopian to imagine that as long as the larger society rewards this way of being that we are going to be totally successful in undermining these dynamics in our own communities. But if we don't, racism and anti-Semitism will persist.

It becomes a central part of any strategy against racism and anti-Semitism to also be fighting against the dominant ethos of the capitalist market, and hence, whether we call it Politics of Meaning or something else, to be creating a political movement that recognizes the psychological, ethical, and spiritual dimensions of human need. Jews and Blacks could become the vanguard in American society of a struggle for this kind of Politics of Meaning, a whole new conception of what politics should be about, and we would do that not just to save the soul of America, but because it is in the long-term best interests of our communities as well. In fact, that's really an important part of the lesson: that if anyone really considers their long-term best interests, it is to live in a society that is not governed by everyone pursuing their own short-term interests without regard to the consequences for others.

I could envision, as part of this, a yearly national Summit on Ethics and Meaning, sponsored by our two respective communities, and aimed at assessing the Ethical State of the Union. It is through this kind of direction, in which both Blacks and Jews unite to critique the selfishness and materialism of the larger society and to reaffirm a commitment to ethical and spiritual values that are under attack in the daily operations of this society, that we can highlight what our two communities potentially have in common: a vision that could heal America. So when we say, "Let the healing begin," we are not just talking about healing the anti-Semitism and racism in our respective communities, but also about healing the larger American society which has for so long been distorted by racism, anti-Semitism, sexism, homophobia, and an ethos of selfishness and materialism. If we can combine the struggle within our community with a campaign in the larger society, we have something powerful to offer.

It may seem particularly difficult to move in this direction now that the the Republicans dominate Congress and have launched a full-scale assault on social programs. And as their attack disadvantages Blacks all the more, there will be an inevitable tendency for liberals to go back to the defensive strategies that they attempted in the 1980s, focusing all their attention on the specific material impact of cutting social programs and screaming about the damage being done to the poor. Framing politics in this same old way, of course, only ensures the continued domination of the Right, which has convinced the American public that the erosion of values in American society is caused by these expansive social programs which encourage permissive social values.

Yet this is a perfect moment for an alliance of Blacks and Jews to advocate a Politics of Meaning that explicitly takes seriously the most fundamental "traditional value": Love your neighbor as yourself. A progressive Politics of Meaning would reclaim the biblical value of caring for others that was central both to the Torah and to Jesus. In fact, these biblical ethics stand in sharp contrast to the ethos of selfishness, enshrined in the politics of Newt Gingrich, Rush Limbaugh, and the very *un-Christian* Christian Right. A Black-Jewish alliance aimed solely at combatting cutbacks of social services won't succeed in either community, because Jews are not going to put themselves in the position of being called "patronizing" or being told that they are really doing this whole thing for their own selfish interests, and Blacks are not likely to want to have Jews in an alliance that is aimed just at improving the material conditions of Blacks. But if the alliance is about this larger social transformative goal, and if the struggle against anti-Semitism in the Black community and against racism in the Jewish community is framed as part of that larger struggle, then a real alliance might be possible. And both groups would rightly feel proud to be bringing to the larger American society a Politics of Meaning perspective that is so badly needed. So a national campaign and national conferences that were focused in this way might be an important new direction for the coming years.

It is precisely because both our communities already have a foundation for this alternative way of thinking, in the Torah, in the New Testament, and in some of the more humanistic trends of Islam, that it becomes possible to imagine a real working together that is neither patronizing nor self-negating. If we can get foundations, corporations, and individual donors to support it, this campaign against racism and anti-Semitism in both communities could be an important direction for healing activity.

C.W. This is a hell of an idea. Let's see if we can bring other people and some serious resources into such a campaign.

CONCLUSION

Grounds for Hope

The problems of racism and anti-Semitism are closely linked to the ethos of selfishness and materialism and to the abiding crisis of meaning and values that pervades the Western world.

It would be naive to believe that these problems admit of easy solutions.

The enduring reality of Black poverty and social misery or the history of the hatred of Blacks cannot be willed out of existence by a dialogue between Blacks and Jews. Nor can we expect the legacy of Western societies' long history of hatred toward Jews to disappear without trace from American society.

But there is nothing inevitable or structurally necessary about Black antagonism toward Jews or Jewish antagonism toward Blacks.

In this dialogue, we've explored some of the reasons for the tensions. We have not arrived at a unified position on all major questions. Even between us, tensions persist, disagreements are sometimes intense, and, as in any important relationship, there are moments when we feel closer to each other and moments when we feel more distant.

Yet in the years that we've participated in this dialogue we've come to understand each other's perspectives and the experiences on which it is based. And we've moved from caution, to mutual respect, and finally to deep caring for each other. And we think that that same process is possible for our respective communities.

We think that the kind of dialogue we've been having can be replicated in thousands of homes and communities throughout Black and Jewish America. But it must be replicated inside the context of a larger struggle for democracy and social justice.

In the course of our dialogue we've come to understand the ways that the specific problems facing our respective communities are linked to the larger problems in American society. But as we've discussed those problems, we've come to believe that Blacks and Jews can be important agents of healing and transformation for the larger society as well.

We've come to feel that the role that Blacks and Jews could play in the larger society may be impeded by the tensions between our two communities. So we are all the more committed to healing some of the hurts that have occurred, acknowledging the pain, and trying to move beyond it.

We have no illusions that any of this will be easy or that the tensions will be resolved in the next few years. It's often easier to inflict psychic pain than to heal it. Inflicting pain takes hardly any time at all; healing it may take decades.

Nor do we have any illusion that psychic pain can be healed fully as long as Black poverty and social misery continue. For that reason, we reject any strategy for healing that separates the ethical, psychological, and spiritual dimensions from the economic and political. It is only in the context of a reinvigorated struggle for social justice and the reconstitution of democratic community that a progressive Politics of Meaning can flourish.

Yet, in the course of this dialogue we've become more encouraged and energized about the possibilities in each community. The more we've come to understand, the more we've realized that behavior in each other's communities that seemed irrational and intractable really does make sense, can be understood, and that in itself it gives us a first handle on what we might do to change things.

Our hopefulness is not, however, a product merely of empirical research or a reasoned conclusion from "the evidence." Rather, it is a statement of faith, a commitment to finding the ways in which we can build on the positive possibilities and not just focus on the problems and difficulties. We refuse to shut our eyes to the problems and difficulties that persist. But we also refuse to allow those problems and difficulties to define the range of possibilities.

Given our faith, our commitment to hope, we are able to see reality better, because we are able to highlight those positive possibilities that exist in our communities which might be built upon. In that sense, though we rely on faith and a commitment to hope, that faith and commitment is not without rational foundation or empirical support.

Ultimately, however, it was the actual experience of caring that we developed between the two of us, far more than the words and ideas, that provided us with the basis for our hope. Because we believe that that kind of caring and warmth can develop much more widely between our two communities, we are hopeful that this dialogue is the first of many more to come, and that you, our readers, will replicate and go beyond what we have done here.

A Post-O.J., Post–Million Man March Update

M. L.   Where are we in race relations after the O.J. Simpson acquital and the Farrakhan-led Million Man March?

C.W.   It's fairly clear that the gulf is quite deep between the Black and white worlds and the Black and Jewish worlds. Blacks and whites, Blacks and Jews, live in such different worlds and look at the world through such different lenses. This poses a huge challenge. We have to cultivate a much deeper understanding of the various perceptions from the different worlds.

M. L.   Why is the perception so different about O.J.?

C.W.   In the Black world there is a deep belief that O.J. didn't do it. The lack of scars or bruises—how can someone kill somebody so brutally and mercilessly without some scars or bruises? When they took pictures of O.J.'s body, there were no bruises or scars. Just a little nick on his finger. One would think there would be some fighting back or injury to the assailant.

And then there is the profound distrust of the police department, the criminal justice system, in the Black world. Nearly every Black man one knows has been abused by this criminal justice system in some way, whereas large numbers of whites tend to live in a world of denial when it comes to the abuse of Blacks by this system. It is outside their world and their experience, and that makes it hard to believe.

M. L.   Leaving aside for a moment the question of guilt, I do find it surprising that many people have difficulty understanding the way that police act to frame those whom they oppose. We had years of this during the anti-war movement, all well documented in the Congressional hearings about the F.B.I.'s COINTELPRO program. Of course, I found all that material much more believable since I personally was framed and sent to prison because of my role as a leader in organizing anti-war demonstrations. So for me it is much easier to understand how a whole group of police people could get together to plant evidence or frame someone for their own reasons.

C.W.   But many people thought at the time, "Lerner probably really did something illegal," because they find it so hard to believe that the police could treat people this way.

M. L.   Yes, I remember my own shock the first time I saw police throwing nonviolent demonstrators against walls and beating them up, while the demonstrators assumed a Gandhian nonviolent passive and unprovocative pose. Anybody who had those kinds of experiences could believe that the police would do such a thing.

But even so, in this case we have a classic wife abuser and a woman who had been so terrorized that she came to believe that her death was imminent from him. So isn't there denial going on in the Black world about the reality of male abuse of women?

C.W.   You have to distinguish between a wife beater and a wife killer. So we have something going on that is wrong and immoral; some wife beaters become wife killers, but thank God they don't all become wife killers.

M. L.   "But he's never denied killing her," some people say.

C.W.   He said he was innocent from the first.

M. L.   What is your theory of what happened?

C.W.   I don't have a theory but I can speculate, as long as you understand that this is nothing but speculation.

This killing has many of the features of a typical merciless killing in the drug culture, so one just ponders what reasons one might have for killing her in this way. I've heard a rumor that O.J. and Nicole were both linked in some way to some kind of drug activity. No one knows what the actual motivation of a drug-related killing might be, what kinds of intrigues or jealousies or gangsterism lead to this kind of action, so again, let me emphasize that this is pure speculation.

But on this speculation, who knows? It may be that the district attorney's office didn't pursue this line of inquiry and hence never traced any of the potential leads that might have taken an investigation in this direction.

So the Simpsons might have both been in trouble with the drug culture. They could have owed money; they could have gotten into a fight with a drug dealer. Ron Goldman was just an innocent bystander, but who knows what relationship Nicole or O.J. might have had to the drug situation.

So someone in that drug culture sets out to kill Nicole, and Goldman is there, so he is killed. And then O.J. may have showed up because he had a sense that something was coming down, and then realized he couldn't save her or couldn't help and that perhaps his life was in danger, so he split the scene and may have even run for his life.

M. L.   So why didn't he call the police?

C.W.   I don't know. On his account, he just found out that she was killed when he got to Chicago, so there is a discrepancy in this story too—that's why it is just speculation.

M. L.   But, as opposed to this speculation, why not go with what many say is a more plausible account—namely, that he killed her? What about O.J. or the situation makes you reluctant to imagine that he killed her?

C.W.   No scars, no bruises, no nicks. That strikes me as very odd. It would be interesting to know whether people who do such brutal stabbings have scars. Moreover, there is no weapon, no eye witnesses.

M. L.   *Somebody* did it. . . .

C.W. And somebody ought to pay. But I don't think it is O.J.

M.L. Some jurors said, "I think he did it, but I also had to obey the rules of reasonable doubt, and there was reasonable doubt." I can understand how they might have come to this position. The disgusting racism revealed by Officer Fuhrman isn't an isolated incident any more than the brutal beating of Rodney King by three L.A. policemen three years ago—nor is this a problem confined to L.A. We have a surplus population in America, a population that can't find jobs because the jobs aren't there. If every one of them had the latest technological skills, there still wouldn't be jobs for most of them. And without jobs, they present a problem. They want food; they want clothing; they want shelter; they want a way to support those whom they love. And the society is unwilling or unable to provide that, so out of its own guilt it responds with anger, racism, repression, prisons, and, most pervasively, a police force that seeks to repress and intimidate.

Given the reality of racism as a pervasive aspect of American society and the way it has been permitted to flourish among the police, the discovery of specific racist intent on the part of Mark Fuhrman would reasonably raise questions about the integrity of the evidence in this case. I do not purport to know what this racist cop did or did not do, but I do think that it is not unreasonable, given the explicit statements he made about the way police plant evidence to frame Black clients, to believe that he would have planted evidence in this case.

Nor is it hard to imagine a motive for doing so. Fuming over the racist reputation that the police department had won through the national exposure of police brutality against Rodney King, L.A. police officers could easily be imagined to have been waiting for some opportunity to "vindicate" themselves. "Here we are, being scorned by the world for our alleged racism," some group of L.A. police might be imagined to have been thinking, "and meanwhile *we* know what it's really like out there on the streets of the inner cities. Every day we face danger and violence, and it often comes at us from unexpected sources because, no matter how well behaving some of those people seem to be on the surface, you never know when one of them will turn out to be a violent type. If only there were a way to get people to understand that when we beat up these suspects, we do it because we know that all they understand is toughness. Just look at how these people treat each other and the violence they use toward each other. If only we could find some way to show the public how even the best of these Blacks is really untrustworthy and quick to violence." By showing the world that some Black that everyone in the world perceived to be a "Mr. Nice-Guy" was really a violent creep, these police could have imagined that they were actually serving the best interests of society. Some subsection of those thinking this way might have been those who knew O.J. Simpson. On the other hand, they knew that O.J. was a person whose public persona was wildly at odds with his reality as a wife batterer. Some might have hoped for a day when this contradiction could be exposed and O.J. shown to be "just another violent Black man" who would fit their racist vision of the world.

But that desire to frame a Black person could still have been totally consistent with Simpson actually being a murderer. We might have been facing a case in which evidence was planted to strengthen a case against someone who was in fact guilty but who might have been positioned to get away with it. Realizing that, police might have been all the more infuriated and all the more ready to plant evidence. But when the jury was faced with the general condition of racism, the specific condition of a major handler of evidence being an overt racist, and the record of evidence mishandling by many others in the force (whether or not they were consciously conspiring with Fuhrman to frame Simpson), I can understand why some might have concluded that there was reasonable doubt. If one is confined to this kind of narrow construal, the jury's behavior might be understandable. But so too would be the outrage of so many Americans who believe—along with some jury members apparently—that here we have a murderer going free.

But you and other Blacks seem to have a stronger position than that there was a reasonable doubt: you think that he didn't do it. That's the part that I don't get fully—why you feel that way.

If you believe that the police planted evidence, why not still allow that he probably killed her, even though there was evidence being planted or tampered with?

C.W. That's a possibility. But I don't believe it. The D.A. overloaded things, perhaps, to be sure that they got someone.

M. L.   Acknowledging different perceptions, what do you think the likely impact of the trial is going to be on Black-white relations?

C.W.   An exponential escalation of white anger and white rage. This might take the form of greater permission to hate. It might take the form of great support for right-wing politics. It might take the form of contained contempt for Blacks.

M. L.   So this is a disaster.

C.W.   It's bad news. What it does is allow negative feelings that were there already to emerge in public. I listened to talk radio the day of the verdict, and the hate that spewed out was remarkable. To give one instance: I listened to a woman who had recently adopted a little girl who is half Black. She described her outrage at the verdict, then said that she and her husband had talked things over and decided that they should tell their daughter, who would be home from school in a few minutes, that one half of her is evil and one half is good so that she should be aware to fight against her Black half. And the talk show host says, "You are absolutely right."

There is a continuum of white anger and white rage—this crosses ideological lines in the white community, so one might find white progressives feeling this kind of thing.

M. L.   Is it so hard to understand the rage of feminists who have been dedicating their energies to opposing male violence against women if now they feel that this verdict might encourage more violence?

C.W.   I can definitely understand this. If you think he's really guilty, you've got a wife beater and a wife killer. But if you think he is a wife beater, not a wife killer (and this is atrocious enough), you still have to make that distinction.

There is a real challenge for white feminists on two fronts. First, the relative silence about the life of Eunice Simpson, O.J.'s mother— in terms of the domestice violence she has been through. She has been through some deep trials and tribulations, but there is no talk about her life. You have to talk about her experience of domestic violence. But feminists have not revealed much concern about this.

Second, we do have reports of Nicole hitting her maids, abusing them. But there is not a word about this from feminists. Male on female violence is much worse, but why don't people note this other form of violence and include that in our conception of domestic violence? Domestic violence cuts also across class, race, and gender lines.

M. L.   Yes, but the danger that many women face from male violence is still the major problem, and the Simpson case understandably makes many women feel all the more vulnerable. If there is rage, it is partly in response to that.

I also believe that there is a whole other dimension of rage that the Right has tapped into. There is a way in which this murder is a visible symbol of the denial of respect and sanctity of Nicole Simpson and Ron Goldman, and this hurts everyone, not only because it is deeply wrong but also because so many people in this society feel that they too are daily disrespected and their sanctity denied. They live in a world of work, which gives them no recognition except to the extent that they can accumulate wealth and power, and they live in a society so fixated on "taking care of no. 1" that they often become the objects of other people's manipulation.

I believe that the escalation of interest in crime, and the identification with the police, is not totally reducible to a covert expression of racism. There is also this other dimension, the dimension of people feeling that they are being emotionally and spiritually brutalized, that a crime of nonrecognition is being daily perpetrated against them, and though they can't quite identify where that crime is coming from, they know that they feel ripped off and diminished and not recognized for the holy and good part within them. It is this that leads them to identify with the victims of crime so intensely, to be outraged that the victims' needs are never addressed, and to see the police as their potential saviors who will redress the wrong that has been done to them.

If the Left had a Politics of Meaning perspective, it would understand this dynamic and address it because it would be able to understand more fully this level of human need, the need for recognition, the need to have one's life make sense and feel part of some framework of meaning and purpose, the need to have one's holiness recognized. If it did, it could then help people understand the ways that the competitive market and its ethos of selfishness is really a central culprit in how they are being ripped off. But since the Left and liberals and progressives don't understand the Meaning issues, they can't understand why people identify with the police and love to see them nabbing the criminals. Many people attribute this identification to a covert racism, but then they have no way of understanding why so many Blacks like these same television shows and also identify with the police in the shows. From my perspective, some of the rage at the Simpson verdict is rage about the way people feel unprotected and vulnerable in this society, not just to narrowly defined crime but also to the daily ways in which they are not being recognized and in which their humanity and sanctity are being denied and ripped off.

But from your perspective, Cornel, what should Blacks or their progressive supporters be doing or saying today in light of the reaction of whites?

C.W.   We have to get in touch with our own anger and rage about the response of whites to the response of Blacks.

M. L.   But is there anything besides racism that you can imagine as a legitimate basis for white upset at the verdict?

C.W.   Sure. There is rational disagreement about the verdict, and then people feel that justice was not done. That's perfectly plausible. A majority of whites really believe O.J. was guilty and therefore justice wasn't done. That's not just racism.

M. L.   So wouldn't it make sense to validate their reaction, even while disagreeing about the basis of it?

C.W.   They fundamentally believe injustice was done, though I disagree with their interpretation of the evidence.

M. L.   But if that is the belief underlying their reaction, then why would we be justified in feeling rage at their reaction?

C.W.   Because it was more than just reaction to the verdict. In the days immediately following the verdict, the media frequently aired claims that Black jurors emote but don't think. Second, the media suggested that Black people's jubilation at the verdict had to do with their barbaric disposition and insensitivity or indifference to the fate of two white people. Both of those claims are profoundly racist claims.

M. L. Is the second a racist claim? Wouldn't it be possible for a white person to imagine that Blacks were insensitive or indifferent to the fate of white people and yet to see that as a plausible response to a history of racism against Blacks. No Jew would be surprised to hear that Jews were not shedding lots of tears at the death of some wealthy German family at the hand of a German Jew.

C.W. But these are innocent people. They are white, but they can't be linked to any specific contribution to Black oppression.

M. L. But if you get that, then isn't there some level of insensitivity in cheering the freeing of O.J. without a corresponding sense of hurt and horror that this murder has taken place?

C.W. People had a year and three months to respond to the death itself with hurt and horror—and many Black people did respond that way in June 1994.
The jubilation had to do with the perception of some Blacks that another innocent Black man was about to be railroaded by a criminal justice system with which they have very bad experience, and then suddenly he had been saved from that.

M. L. Is there any strategy for how to counter this anger in both communities?

C.W. The only alternative is to do more of the kind of dialogue that we are doing now—besides the alternative of lack of communication, and that won't work. But communication may not have much of a resultant—and that's part of our predicament.

M. L. Well, Jews may have some skepticism about the efficacy of communication, particularly in light of our experience with Farrakhan. As you'll recall, a year ago, when you went to the NAACP Black Leadership Summit, you argued that you needed to be in that context to help broaden Farrakhan's perspective in a more universalistic and humanistic way and specifically to challenge his anti-Semitism. But now, a year later, after all that dialogue, a week before his march he talks of Jewish "bloodsuckers," just as the week after his summit he had his newspaper reissue a statement about Jews killing Jesus. So isn't this one case where we can learn about the limits of rational dialogue?

C.W.   Not all the fault falls on one side. Let's look at Farrakhan's language on two occasions.

Farrakhan says bloodsuckers are all those who extract money from but don't contribute to the community. That includes Italians, Arabs, Jews, and on other occasions he has talked about Black businessmen bloodsuckers too.

M. L.   But this is a wild distortion because Jews *do* give back to the community. For example, as you and I have noted, Jews were the one group that voted for Democrats almost at the same level as Blacks in 1994, and that means they were rejecting Republican appeals to people in their economic bracket to reduce their tax burden by cutting social programs that are disproportionately aimed at the Black community. This is a solid way of sending financial support to the Black community through taxes.

C.W.   Voting activity is different from economic activity. Farrakhan was talking about the way businessmen take money out of the community without contributing to it.

M. L.   Jews remained in the Black community as teachers, social workers, health care professionals . . . and in those ways very directly gave back to the community.

C.W.   True, and that is important. But in talking solely about the economic activity per se, we are talking about the way the capitalist system is structured so that there are entrepreneurial slots in which money is made and very little is seen to be given back to the community that supports those businesses. If he had not said Jews, but had said Koreans, Italians, Arabs, etc., there wouldn't be any big flap. Is it all right when he talks about these other groups, but when he talks about Jews the red light goes off? Wouldn't you think that when he includes these other groups, as he did in his recent statement, he is moving toward a systemic analysis of entrepreneurs in the Black community, no matter what color?

M. L.   The red light goes off because he has a history of attacking Jews. If his organization were putting out material talking about the Black role in slavery, or the Italian role in killing Jesus, or the role of Arabs in slavery—

C. W.   There has been public acknowledgment of that role. True, though there has been a highlighting of the role of Jews, and I've been critical of that.

But you should also give attention to the quality of his extraordinary speech at the Million Man March. This was his one chance to show off what he really thinks about the world, and in that speech there was no anti-Semitism. The speech represented a real advance. Instead of a blanket condemnation of whites, he distinguishes between whiteness and white supremacy; that frees white brothers and white sisters in such a way that they can fight against white supremacy. And he says "Black supremacy is repulsive to God." I see this as an attempt to move in a more universalistic and humanistic way, and that move should be publicly embraced.

M. L.   It seemed to me to be a tragic and telling reality that while calling for atonement on the part of other Black men, he was unable to publicly atone for his own anti-Semitism. This would have been the perfect moment to do that, and had he publicly repudiated anti-Semitism and urged his followers to do so also, he would have dramatically escalated his political credibility.

It was quite impressive for many of us to see Black men being willing to embrace the theme of atonement, just a few days after the Jewish day of atonement, Yom Kippur. Farrakhan was brilliant in connecting to that theme because only a person with self-respect can publicly atone; so many Black men doing so was a powerful sign of their own dignity and sense of self-worth. And that broke a lot of public stereotypes. I congratulate the Black community and the Black men who participated in that act, and it certainly raised my hopefulness about the possibilities ahead.

Yet there is one aspect of the Jewish conception of atonement that was missing. In the Temple in ancient days, the high priest would lead the atonement by publicly confessing his sins. It is this recognition that even the most elevated amongst us is still deeply flawed that is central to the Jewish conception of atonement. Yet when Farrakhan calls for a national day of atonement, he is unable to atone for his most publicly recognizable sins. Had be been able to do so, he would have been teaching other Black men that one could really be self-critical without losing respect. From my perspective, the reason he couldn't do that was he is so deeply anti-Semitic that this seems impossible to him.

But from your perspective, why didn't he do that?

C.W. Hard to say. Remember in the early part of his speech where he says that all prophets have a defect in their character, and so do I? I think that part of the speech was a very abstract acknowledgment of the degree to which he has sinned. When he talked about Jewish pain and Black pain and the fact that both communities have great pain—it would have been good if he could have said, "I used language that contributed to Jewish pain and Jews have used language that contributed to my pain." What he did say was that we've got to transcend the pain.

M.L. But there's a fundamental inequality here. Jews didn't start out attacking Farrakhan; he searched us out and targeted us, and then Jews responded.

C.W. Well, from his perspective much of the antagonism started when Jews attacked Jesse Jackson for his Hymietown remark, as though they themselves didn't engage in similar demeaning language about Blacks. But whatever the history, there has been escalation on both sides that has contributed to the proliferation of misunderstanding and misperception on both sides. On Farrakhan's side you have the references of "the Jews" and monolithic characterizations of the Jewish community, associating Jews with Black pain inaccurately. On the Jewish side, you have direct analogies of Farrakhan with Hitler, also inaccurately.

M.L. I don't see this as analogous, because attacking a particular leader is very different from attacking an entire people. It's only Farrakhan's megalomania that allows him to see these two as equivalent, because he thinks he is the embodiment of the Black people and anyone who attacks him attacks all Blacks.

Meanwhile, don't you see the way that Farrakhan provides whites with a reason to distance themselves from the Black movement? Are you saying that you don't see the dangers in Farrakhan?

C.W. I said in my *New York Times* piece explaining why I was participating in the Million Man March that I understood that for many whites Farrakhan was their worst nightmare.

M. L. But then I'm told that you physically embraced him.

C.W. I physically embrace people whom I've spent quality time with across the board. No matter what color or gender or sexual orientation.

M. L. This was in public and was seen as a public symbolic act.

C.W. Anyone I physically embrace in private I embrace in public too. And especially after a speech that showed such movement away from earlier xenophobic formulations. In that sense, my dialogues with Farrakhan were not in vain, at least as measured by that one speech, which was a very important speech actually.

M. L. Doesn't it trouble you that this is someone who is perceived by many Jews as an anti-Semite, many women as a sexist, many gays as a homophobe, and that this is the man who now you and other progressive Blacks are associated with?

C.W. In *dialogue* with—to push, to challenge.

M. L. But if the goal is to champion the needs of Blacks, particularly economically oppressed Blacks, and this man is seen by potential allies in this struggle as an overwhelming obstacle to their commitment to the cause, and you yourself acknowledge that these others are responding not totally irrationally but in response to concrete things that Farrakhan has said and not publicly repudiated, why don't you view him as an obstacle to your goals rather than as an ally?

C.W. When you are working on both fronts at the same time— Black operational unity is one front, and the other front is a progressive multiracial front that talks about white supremacy, male supremacy, corporate power, homophobia, and ecological abuse—you will sometimes find yourself between a rock and a hard place because some in the Black united front will hit white supremacy but have other views with which you disagree, and those in the multiracial progressive movement may have conscious or unconscious racist sensibilities with which you disagree. But you must work in both to push them beyond where they are.

M. L.   Jewish progressives could have used that line of argument to build solidarity with Kahane or Shamir. But we didn't.

C.W.   But if all Jews felt that their backs were against the wall and all Jews were going down together, then Kahane would have been part of that united front. You and Kahane would be together and might both end up in the same concentration camp.

M. L.   So you believe that the situation of oppression against Blacks is comparable and makes alliances with racists and anti-Semites plausible?

C.W.   But there's no purity in any side. Even in the multiracial progressive movement you also have leftists who are racist and homophobic, even as they fight against it.

M. L.   But if they fight against it, that's very different than if they espouse it. If Farrakhan were merely unconsciously anti-Semitic, then he would open himself to Jews who could help him deal with these issues.

C.W.   That's what he called for in the speech. He has got to be able to sit down and understand how his language contributed to that.

M. L.   Jews have met with him in the past and nothing changed.

C.W.   As I understand that meeting, it ended up being a very defensive meeting. Something more is possible now. I've never given up on those in the progressive, liberal, or even the conservative movement—pushing them beyond their white supremacist sensibilities—so I refuse to give up on Minister Louis Farrakhan or any other Black person because of their xenophobic sensibility. That is my way of being in the world.

M. L.   But what if the Black movement by aligning itself with Farrakhan actually has the consequence of weakening the white support that might have been there for reducing poverty and oppression?

C.W.   Your question assumes that there was a strong multiracial movement focusing on overcoming Black suffering and that white withdrawal renders it nearly impotent, whereas the fact is that we are all relatively feeble at this point, so a stronger Black operational unity and a stronger multiracial movement, despite its deep tensions and frictions, is both necessary and utopian at the moment.

We have Black politicians who are willing to sit down with Jesse Helms or Strom Thurmond but won't sit down with Farrakhan. So Black unity is very difficult to forge. In addition, we have progressives who are friendly with those of Negrophobic sensibilities at *The New Republic* while trashing efforts to build bridges. Hence, progressive movements are difficult to forge. Therefore, we must be willing to push, criticize, and not give up on any one of us.

M. L.   What do you think would emerge from a meeting between Jews and Farrakhan at this moment?

C.W.   I would like to see on Farrakhan's part both a clarification of what he has said and an apology for any pain that he might have caused to the Jewish community.

M. L.   If he did that apology first, people would certainly be willing to meet with him.

C.W.   But it has to be a two-way street, and whoever is speaking for the Jewish community would have to acknowledge demonization and escalation of targeting. The results of such a dialogue would be lowering of the temperature and focusing on the issue of Black social misery and suffering and Jewish anxiety and sense of vulnerability. If we could reach that point, I think some of the air would be cleared and we would be forced to deal with the most formidable task, which is fighting the powerful right wing in the country, especially the big-business and banking elite.

M. L.   There's a big question about whether such a meeting should be with Abe Foxman, chair of the Anti-Defamation League, and other members of the Jewish establishment, in which case the meeting would focus attention exclusively on anti-Semitism, or with Jewish progressives, who would want to communicate a clear sense of commitment to ending Black suffering, even as we insisted on Farrakhan publicly campaigning against Black anti-Semitism.

C.W. The dialogue should happen, either in two separate meetings or in one full meeting. I'd be open to both meetings.

M. L. When I broached this in shul on Tuesday, I was suddenly surrounded by angry liberal Jews who were saying to me, "How would you possibly doubt what Farrakhan stands for now that he has repeated this bloodsucking remark?" And my sister in L.A., when I mentioned being in discussions with other Jewish liberals and progressives on this topic this past week, said, "Go to the yellow pages and look up under 'Get a backbone.'" In other words, such a move is perceived as an ultimate proof that one would not be willing to stand up for Jewish interests even when the other side is kicking us in the face. Yet your interpretation of recent events is very different.

C.W. I don't see you as sacrificing Jewish interests because you want to be in dialogue with someone who is causing Jewish pain. Black folk have been talking with white supremacists from the very beginning. King said, "I love Bull Connor." Why would being in dialogue be reneging on Jewish interests? That strikes me as shortsighted.

M. L. Well, I would have strongly disagreed with you last year, when I thought that meeting with Farrakhan would give him public credibility that he should not have had. I think your participation in that meeting, and the participation of the NAACP, helped escalate Farrakhan to the point where he could be in a position to call for the Million Man March. I'm less sure now only because he already has the public credibility after this march, so it's harder to say that meeting with him would give him much. But others say that his goal is simply to appear to have tried to meet with Jews while being unwilling to stop his organization from continuing to promote anti-Semitic ideas. And this then plays into his game plan, which is to convince everyone that he is the key man in the Black world and that everyone who wishes to work with Blacks must go through him. In that case, meeting with him would achieve nothing for mutual reconciliation.

C.W. That assumes that he has no interest whatsoever in trying to move in a humane direction or be humane. That is your basic assumption. And that is the assumption I disagree with. If people believe that he is the embodiment of evil, then every move will be seen as a capitulation to evil. But if you believe that there is a possibility of movement, then you engage. Some people will perceive me as being used, manipulated, naive, and so forth. But that is the way I proceed with anybody. Many Black folk have used this kind of reasoning against me in relationship to my connections with white folks and Jews, but I do what I think is right.

M. L. If I saw a shred of evidence that this guy was willing to move away from anti-Semitism, I think I'd be very much more inclined to try to initiate some kind of meeting. The problem is, when a guy makes this bloodsucking remark a week before his major march, it's got to be because he wants to be known as an anti-Semite in certain Black circles where that has resonance. Farrakhan is not stupid and would certainly know that his remark would cause a furor. He wanted that.

C.W. In his mind, he wants to tell the truth as he sees it in relationship to entrepreneurial activity in the Black community. What we need to challenge is the language in which his truth telling takes place so that it is not anti-Semitic.

M. L. But if I began to give public talks about the long history of Black murderers, and this became a central part of my dialogue, don't you think Black progressives would shun public association with me?

C.W. No, they would sit down with you and counsel you on how to speak the truth about Black criminal behavior without being xenophobic.

M. L. I see Farrakhan as a tremendous threat to Blacks because he espouses a pro-capitalist ideology and urges Blacks towards a politics that separates them from whites and because he has been willing to use the kind of demeaning-of-others rhetoric that will deeply alienate Blacks' potential allies. So even though I agree that the allies haven't been that strong recently, I think the reason for that has been the general failure of the Left to be able to articulate a vision of politics that speaks to the American majority, and that Farrakhan and what he represents will accelerate that inability to find common ground. So precisely because I care so much about the fate of African-Americans, I'm deeply distressed when he emerges as a leading figure for the Black world.

C.W.   I want to affirm your deep empathy for Black suffering. I've witnessed that throughout the years we've been dialoguing together.

But what you've given is the worst possible scenario. There is another scenario: Farrakhan's high visibility could reinvigorate the King legacy and the democratic wing of the Black freedom movement precisely because of the tremendous sense of urgency that more people feel now. Precisely because Farrakhan generates such fear and anxiety among whites, the white hunger for multiracial progressive leadership and movements can become more pronounced.

M.L.   But from my perspective, instead of going this route, the Black world would have been far better served had Cornel West and Henry Louis Gates, Jr., and Manning Marable and Michael Dyson and Bell Hooks and Pat Williams and other Black leaders gotten together and formed an alternative leadership and been the ones to be calling for a Black march. And now, it's still not too late for you to organize an organization that would have a more progressive bent than that which is represented by Farrakhan and the National Black Leadership Summit.

C.W.   I give Farrakahn credit for calling the march. He sensed the degree of urgency. The challenge now is the degree to which others will provide alternative leadership to Farrakhan, by building on the King legacy and King's vision of the direction for the Black community.

M.L.   I strongly disagree with your assessment of Farrakhan, but I do respect your thinking and agree with you that this kind of dialogue that we have been conducting is an important part of the process of healing to which we are both committed. From my perspective, it would be naive to believe that Farrakhan could be influenced or changed in a meeting with Jewish leaders. The only reason I could see for such a meeting would be if it could signal to many Blacks that there is a significant grouping of Jews who remain firmly committed to ending Black suffering. There is such a grouping—and it is a very large and significant section of the Jewish world. And I believe that now, when Blacks are facing escalating attack, it is our obligation to stand in solidarity and to do so publicly. Yet I would be reluctant to do anything in the process to strengthen the public credibility of someone like Farrakhan, whom I regard as destructive both to the best interests of the Black community and to the best interests of Jews, women, gays and lesbians, and many others. So this is tricky water to navigate because, at the same time, I deeply respect you, Cornel, even though at times I continue to disagree with your stance.

I am encouraged by the way you speak about the issues. It makes me think that healing remains possible, though the events of the past few weeks have made things more difficult. But we are going to have to do lots more talking and encourage lots more dialoguing between our communities. I still hope that we can find some foundation support for a national gathering of Jews and Blacks to explore these issues. And I'm hopeful that at our National Summit on Ethics and Meaning, in Washington, April 14–16, 1997, at which you and I and Reverend James Forbes and Anna Deveare Smith will be speaking, will be an occasion to continue some of this discussion as well.